A Better World, Inc.

Alice Korngold

A Better World, Inc.

Corporate Governance for an Inclusive, Sustainable, and Prosperous Future

Second Edition

Alice Korngold
New York, NY, USA

ISBN 978-3-031-31552-7   ISBN 978-3-031-31553-4   (eBook)
https://doi.org/10.1007/978-3-031-31553-4

Photo credit: © Matthew Mo

This Palgrave Macmillan imprint is published by the registered company Springer Nature Switzerland AG
The registered company address is: Gewerbestrasse 11, 6330 Cham, Switzerland

For my beloved family
Ethan, Ellie, Gabe, and Ben
David, Madeline, and Eli
Margaret, Matt, Charlotte, and Eloise
and,
especially, Gerry

Preface

The timing of being invited to write this book was serendipitous. The moment my book agent and editor suggested that I write a new edition of "*A Better World, Inc.*," I knew what I wanted to write about. While I have written all three of my books with enthusiasm and belief in the topic, this one is truly a passion.

Like my other books, this one makes the case for companies to collaborate with nonprofits to find solutions to challenges facing our communities and our world. And while each book, and all of my work, has addressed justice, equity, and inclusion, this book gave me the chance to pull it all together into one cohesive, compelling vision: a vision of an inclusive, sustainable, and prosperous future.

There are three factors related to this vision: Companies and their boards, an inclusive world, and a sustainable world.

First, the appeal in each my books is to companies—to show them the way they can grow their value by finding solutions to social, economic, and environmental challenges. Because only companies have the vast resources and global footprint to make a better world possible, and it is in fact in their self-interest. Some companies have started down this path, others need to follow.

Second, a sustainable world is fundamental to success. Climate change is an existential threat to people and the planet.

Third—the one about which I am especially passionate—is that *only* a truly inclusive society can achieve peace and prosperity. A world in which each and every person is valued. Where each person can achieve their potential. Where each person is welcomed to participate in society. This is a matter of humanity. But it's also incumbent from an economic perspective that instead of marginalizing large swaths of people, we appreciate and include them in the global marketplace. This is the only path to peace and prosperity.

The boards of directors of the world's companies hold the power to either make or obstruct a vision of an inclusive and sustainable future. Corporate boards have authority that affects the creation of wealth and its access, the employment and earnings prospects of the world's citizens, the fortunes of suppliers, and the portfolios of retirees. Boards determine business policies and influence public policy, regarding education, training, healthcare, and human rights. They decide which countries to invest in, and which to neglect. So, we can only achieve a better world if companies and their boards understand that inclusion and sustainability are not only good for the world, but good for business.

Fifteen or twenty years ago, it might have seemed laughable to appeal to companies and their boards to advance solutions to social, economic, and environmental challenges as central to their business missions. Today, however, as you will read in this book, investors and regulators are driving ESG (environmental, social, and governance), a model that puts the onus on companies to give an accounting of their environmental and social impacts, as well as their financial impacts.

The intention of this book is to show companies the way to help build an inclusive and sustainable and prosperous future for all.

I have the good fortune to engage every day with people who are dedicated to important causes—people from all sectors. Even when the world around us has seemed so toxic—politically and ideologically—I get to immerse myself in work with people whose energy, passion, and enthusiasm is contagious and inspiring. I am grateful to them.

My children and grandchildren inspire me to consider the world we will leave to them. This is about their futures.

I hope this book helps shine a little light on a way forward to a better world.

New York, NY, USA   Alice Korngold

Acknowledgements

I feel fortunate to live a life that's infused with love, joy, curiosity, learning, and humor. Grateful for my family, friends, and colleagues who inspire me every day to explore, seek to understand, and yes, make a difference.

My friend and colleague Funmi Arewa talks about "the journey of awareness" as we grow by opening our minds and hearts to the lives and experiences of people from different backgrounds. My friend and colleague Gabby Burian inspires me by always making a difference in the lives of people around her and across the world. My "journey of awareness" and commitment to service have been important parts of my life since childhood, but feel more charged than ever by the times we live in, my ongoing life experience, and conversations that are more candid and open than ever.

I have the great privilege of working every day with people from a variety of life experiences, with a range of points of view, who work in many sectors, from nonprofits, to businesses, to academia, and in parts of the world that are near and far. In spite of some deeply distressing circumstances and issues that surround us—politically and ideologically—my days are spent with people who are actively engaged in meaningful work to improve their communities and the human condition. That is energizing and inspiring, and a blessing.

This book would not have happened if my book agent, John Willig, and my editor, Marcus Ballenger, hadn't contacted me out of the blue last spring and asked if I'd like to write a new edition of *A Better World, Inc*. The time was right, they suggested. I was elated! Not a moment of hesitation. Whenever people have asked me if I'd ever write a third book, I always responded that I might if I had something to add to the conversation. When John and Marcus got in touch, I knew exactly what I wanted to talk about—the fundamental connection between inclusion, sustainability, and a better world. A better world cannot happen until both inclusion and sustainability are at the center. And having always been struck by the might of corporations, and especially boards of directors, I believe that they must embrace this vision if it is ever to be so. Fortunately, there are forces at work that give us hope, as discussions about the role of business in society are increasing and evolving.

Thank you to friends and colleagues who spent much time and effort contributing ideas, information, and insights to this book—and also making valuable introductions to helpful sources. You have enriched this effort.

I have an abundance of gratitude for Melanie Meyer, my friend and collaborator of nearly three decades. She has been part of my work process and product for all this time. There is lots of warmth and humor sprinkled about our work days. Much appreciation to Denise O'Brien, with whom I began my journey building social enterprises, and whose love and support continue to inspire me.

My deepest love and gratitude is for my family. My amazing children, each of whom contributes to building a better world, from healthcare, to sustainability, education, mentoring next generation immigrant girls, to renewable energy. And my grandchildren, who are ages two to eighteen, from whom I learn the most, and with whom I laugh the most. It's especially fun to see how each one manifests their gifts and curiosity in their own unique ways. And Gerry, my high school sweetheart, and husband of fifty years (yes, fifty!), with whom life is one long conversation about ideas, with lots of love and humor.

My work is motivated and inspired by my children and grandchildren and by a passion to help make for them A Better World.

Praise for *A Better World, Inc.*

"*A Better World, Inc.* (2023) provides vital insights for companies seeking to increase their value through innovative environmental, social and governance changes. Bolstered by years of experience, compelling research and case studies, Alice Korngold demonstrates that inclusion and sustainability are essential elements for companies to advance their interests while building a better and more prosperous world. These are issues near and dear to my heart."

—April Miller Boise, *Executive Vice President and Chief Legal Officer, Intel*

"*A Better World, Inc.* (2023) is essential reading for corporate executives and board directors. With compelling research and case studies, Alice Korngold shows that inclusion and sustainability are fundamental for companies to grow value and advance prosperity – for business and society."

—Michael Cherkasky, *Co-Founder and Board Director, Exiger*

"Alice Korngold's new edition of *A Better World, Inc.* provides a fresh and compelling vision for business executives and boards seeking to grow value for their companies. Drawing on robust research and case studies, as well as her vast experience, the author shows that advancing inclusion and sustainability are integral in building a more prosperous world that benefits business and society."

—George Majoros, Jr., *Co-Managing Director, EagleTree Capital*

"Alice Korngold's board governance and strategic vision gives me hope for a prosperous and equitable future. She emphasizes the need for collaboration among business leaders, governments, and NGOs to tackle global challenges and create value that will be reflected across our top and bottom lines and, most importantly, in our communities."

—Kennedy Odede, *Founder and CEO, SHOFCO*

"Drawing on three decades of experience as a thoughtful and thought-provoking broker of meaningful engagement between the corporate and the NGO sectors on diversity, equity, inclusion, and belonging, and board governance, Alice Korngold shows that inclusion and sustainability are foundational to advance prosperity."

—Sarah Degnan Kambou, *Vice Chair, Global Impact, and Immediate Past President and CEO, International Center for Research on Women*

"As demands and expectations for corporate boards continue to grow, how boards execute their obligations increasingly matters. Korngold's key insight in *A Better World, Inc.* (2023), is that corporate boards' commitment to inclusion and sustainability issues is not only a good idea but, as well, critical to greater board efficacy."

—Michael Heise, *Professor, Cornell Law School*

"The theme of Korngold's new book that resonates is that solving challenging problems is good for business. Moreover, today a few leading companies are poised to solve a dual challenge: providing what society needs in terms of food security and quality of life, while solving the climate-related imperative of reducing emissions. This is an exciting period."

—W. Scott Tew, *Vice President, Sustainability, and Managing Director, Center for Energy Efficiency and Sustainability, Trane Technologies*

"Alice Korngold's *A Better World, Inc.* (2023) establishes that inclusion and sustainability are requisite conditions to advance prosperity. She also demonstrates the importance of diverse boards to effectively fulfill their obligations to grow the company's value in the face of the most pressing issues. Each chapter provides insightful research and case studies showing the imperative to embrace, engage, and promote all communities."

—Deepak Bhargava, *Distinguished Lecturer, CUNY School of Labor and Urban Studies*

"Alice Korngold continues to be an important voice drawing attention to the role business can play in making our world a better place. Her insights are noteworthy and inspirational."

—Olufunmilayo (Funmi) Arewa, *Author and Law Professor*

"Based on her thirty years as an advisor, author, and thought leader in sustainability, corporate governance, and diversity, equity, and inclusion (DEI), Alice Korngold has integrated these three themes to make a compelling case for corporate leaders: that inclusion and sustainability are fundamental to achieving prosperity, and that stakeholder partnerships have the power to help solve our global challenges on food security and climate change."

—Rodrigo Santos, *President, Bayer, Crop Science Division*

Contents

About the Author

Alice Korngold leads a global firm that provides advisory services to company executives and the boards and leaders of NGOs. Korngold authored *A Better World, Inc.: How Companies Profit by Solving Global Problems...Where Governments Cannot* (Palgrave Macmillan, 2014) and *Leveraging Good Will: Strengthening Nonprofits by Engaging Businesses* (Jossey-Bass, a Wiley Imprint, 2005). She has published numerous chapters and articles on board governance, ESG, sustainability, diversity, equity, and inclusion, and measurements and ratings. She taught a course on "Sustainability and Corporate Governance" for the Master of Financial Accountability, York University in Toronto, Canada. She guest lectures at universities worldwide and speaks at corporate and nonprofit forums. She holds bachelor's and master's degrees from the University of Pennsylvania.

1

Introduction: An Inclusive, Sustainable, and Prosperous Future

What people can positively achieve is influenced by economic opportunities, political liberties, social powers, and the enabling conditions of good health, basic education, and the encouragement and cultivation of initiatives.
—Amartya Sen (1999)

"THE WORLD FACES SOCIAL, ECONOMIC, AND ENVIRONMENTAL CHALLENGES that are projected to increase exponentially over the coming decades." That was the opening sentence in the original edition of this book, researched and written one decade ago. Back then, dire warnings predicted the consequences of failing to take sufficient action to address climate change, environmental degradation, poverty and weak economic development, inadequate access to health and education, and the abuse of human rights. Unfortunately, there have been insufficient efforts to halt or reverse the negative trajectories. As a result, the world is worse off today. Additionally, the COVID pandemic has exacerbated global conditions, as has Russia's invasion of Ukraine and other regional conflicts.

Before providing details on the mounting challenges facing the world, let me state up front the reasons to be hopeful. First, the severe consequences of inaction are impossible to ignore; climate change is wreaking havoc; and the pandemic, now in its fourth year, continues to afflict people far and wide. Second, not only are some companies recognizing opportunities to grow value by finding innovative solutions to world problems, but many companies are reconstituting their boards of directors to include people with more relevant

© The Author(s), under exclusive license to Springer Nature Switzerland AG 2023
A. Korngold, *A Better World, Inc.*,
https://doi.org/10.1007/978-3-031-31553-4_1

and diverse experience and expertise than ever before. Finally, we are learning valuable lessons, as discussed in this Introduction and in each of the following chapters. Some of the cultural and structural changes might help to bring some solutions.

Now, for the challenges. In spite of activity to address our problems, progress is insufficient. There have been many meetings of the world's most powerful people and bridges built. During the past ten years, leaders from every country in the world have convened again and again at Conferences of the Parties (COP), described further in the Climate and Environment chapter; as well as annual meetings during the United Nations General Assembly (UNGA), every fall in New York City; and the World Economic Forum (WEF), every winter in Davos, Switzerland (Some meetings were suspended during 2020 and 2021 due to COVID).

Additionally, in 2015, all 193 United Nations (UN) Member States adopted a set of global goals, referred to as the Sustainable Development Goals (SDGs), to succeed the Millennium Development Goals (MDGs). Described as a "shared blueprint for peace and prosperity for people and the planet, now and into the future," the 17 SDGs were designed to be achieved by 2030. The new 2030 Agenda aimed to end poverty, improve access to health and education, reduce inequality, end human rights abuses, and stimulate economic growth, while also tackling climate change and working to conserve our oceans and forests (United Nations "SDGs").

Despite this important work, we are far from accomplishing what is needed. Instead, evidence shows that the world's social, economic, and environmental problems have worsened. Furthermore, by failing to make adequate progress, other challenges have been exacerbated, including conflicts and violence, mass migration, food insecurity, and wealth inequality. According to the 2022 SDG progress report:

> Cascading and interlinked crises are putting the 2030 Agenda for Sustainable Development [the SDGs] in grave danger, along with humanity's very own survival. The Report highlights the severity and magnitude of the challenges before us. The confluence of crises, dominated by COVID-19, climate change, and conflicts, are creating spin-off impacts on food and nutrition, health, education, the environment, and peace and security, and affecting all the Sustainable Development Goals (SDGs). The Report details the reversal of years of progress in eradicating poverty and hunger, improving health and education, providing basic services, and much more. It also points out areas that need urgent action in order to rescue the SDGs and deliver meaningful progress for people and the planet by 2030. (United Nations, 2022)

"We are entering a new age of heightened economic fragility," warned Kristalina Georgieva, the managing director of the International Monetary Fund (IMF). This will mean "greater uncertainty, higher economic volatility, geopolitical confrontations, and more frequent and devastating natural disasters—a world in which any country can be thrown off course more easily and more often" (Partington, 2022). Furthermore, Georgieva cautioned that the world faces a "fundamental shift away from relative stability to an age of breakdown in international relations and more frequent natural disasters."

Many of the most pressing issues, such as environmental degradation, climate change, poverty, and human rights, are cross-border issues. National governments acting alone lack the authority and resources to provide adequate responses. The international community has too often failed to achieve measurable progress in meeting commitments to deal with these global problems. Conflicting interests between developed and developing nations, rich and poor countries, North and South, East and West, and various political ideologies interfere with agreements on many world issues.

Collaboration between countries and across sectors is a major challenge, according to Fatih Birol, executive director of the International Energy Agency. Unfortunately, Birol predicts that without collaboration, progress in addressing climate change will be highly challenging and "could be delayed by decades" (Horner, 2022).

The NGO sector has made strides in advancing the human condition but lacks resources and scalability sufficient to make transformational progress. Working alone, however, without adequate support and engagement from governments and businesses, NGOs cannot affect the scope of change that is required.

In the face of these difficult challenges, some creative responses are emerging from the business sector. Unlike governments, businesses in the twenty-first century cross national borders, spanning oceans and continents. Modern corporations respond to customers, employees, and investors across the globe to profit and thrive. Moreover, companies are learning that they must be attuned to the needs of the world's population to maximize profits. This book tells the story of global corporations that have aligned their profit-making missions with efforts to build a better world. These companies have come to understand that they can enhance their bottom lines while improving global conditions, often by collaborating with NGOs and governments.

Based on the research and case studies for this new edition, the conclusions made in the original edition are affirmed here: that *only* companies have the vast resources, global footprint, and market incentives to create and scale innovative solutions to the world's most daunting challenges. As shown in the original edition, and affirmed here as well, businesses that make progress have three things in common: the board of directors understands the value proposition of addressing social, economic, and environmental challenges; the company is effective in engaging stakeholders; and the company collaborates with nonprofit organizations, governments, and sometimes other companies.

Racial equity and justice, and gender equity, were major themes in the original edition of this book. It has become clear, however, that these are not simply aspirational goals. Instead, it is evident the lack of racial equity and justice, and gender equity, are fundamental and systemic problems that need to be addressed in order for companies to grow value and for society to thrive. This is apparent in the United States and worldwide. This book stipulates that companies, as well as governments and NGOs, must put their full attention into understanding how the failure to achieve racial equity and justice, and gender equity, has hindered society and business, and actively remove the obstacles to progress. This is the only path to sustainability and prosperity.

A Vision of a Better World

In the opening of each chapter in both the original and new editions of this book, there is a vision of a better world as it relates to the chapter topic. For the human rights chapter, for example, it is the ethic of reciprocity, often understood as The Golden Rule: Do unto others as you would have them do unto you.

An overarching vision for a better world would expand on that guidance by imagining a world where every person has an opportunity to achieve their fullest potential, live in peace and safety, and enjoy community with others. This is a vision that is good for business as well as society.

Racial Equity and Justice are Fundamental to Build a Better World

It is tragic that the degradation and marginalization of groups of people based on ignorance and bias not only denies fundamental rights to targeted people, but also holds all of us back from achieving the vision of a better world. Hatred and discrimination inflict suffering, infect society, foment violence, and hinder peace and prosperity. Another result of these toxic conditions is the utter waste of valuable human talents and contributions: people from diverse racial and ethnic backgrounds, women, migrants, refugees, and asylum seekers, LGBTQ+ individuals, people with disabilities, and people who were formerly incarcerated, among others. Each person could contribute to society if they had access to clean water, food, shelter, education, healthcare, employment, and the assurance of fair and decent treatment. In business language, people are referred to as human capital. Indeed, we are squandering valuable human capital.

Disadvantages faced by BIPOC communities in the United States are systemic. A report commissioned by the UN shows how severe the inequities are. The report, "In the Red: the U.S. Failure to Deliver on a Promise of Racial Equality," (Lynch et al., 2021) indicates that:

> On average, white communities receive resources and services at a rate approximately three times higher, than the least-served racial community (data on Asian, Black, Indigenous, Hawaiian and Pacific Islander, Hispanic, Multiracial and 'Other' racial communities, were used as available). Evidence shows that unequal treatment impacts each of these communities, however, it is most often Black and Indigenous communities that are left the furthest behind. When states are scored on how well they deliver the United Nations Sustainable Development Goals (SDGs) to the racial group least served, no state is even halfway to achieving the SDGs by 2030. (Ibid.)

Globally, countries in the Southern hemisphere are suffering the worst effects of climate change, despite their limited role in bringing it about. "According to the UN, Africa is the continent most vulnerable to the impacts of climate change. This is despite the fact it contributes only 4% of global carbon emissions" (Joice & Ostasiewiecz, 2022). Floods in Pakistan leave hundreds of thousands of people stranded for months, without food and clean water, or sanitation, while death and disease are rampant (Vaidyanathan, 2022). "The tragedy in Pakistan is a stark reminder of climate injustice. Climate breakdown is playing out along colonial lines," says Jason Hickel, cultural anthropologist, author, and professor (Hickel, 2022). In a summary of articles in the newest issue of The Lancet:

> Little attention is given to underlying structural discrimination and the need for racial justice. From vulnerable communities in Puerto Rico coping with the effects of hurricane Fiona, to excessive heat in racially segregated neighbourhoods in the USA, to the tens of millions of people who have been displaced by flooding in Pakistan during 2022, minoritised populations bear the brunt

of the health impacts of climate change, despite being least responsible for it. Racism kills, and climate change kills.
Together, racism and climate change interact and have disproportionate effects on the lives of minoritised people within countries and between the Global North and the Global South. (Abi Deivanayagam et al., 2023)

Even beyond the effects of climate change, scholars have argued that the Global North has profiteered from the Global South long after the official period of colonialism. A research article in the New Political Economy "quantifies the drain from the global South through unequal exchange since 1960:" (Hickel et al., 2021).

We find that in the most recent year of data the global North ("advanced economies") appropriated from the South commodities worth $2.2 trillion in Northern prices—enough to end extreme poverty 15 times over. Over the whole period, drain from the South totaled $62 trillion (constant 2011 dollars), or $152 trillion when accounting for lost growth. (Ibid.)

Migrants, refugees, and asylum seekers often from the Global South also face extreme injustices. The problems will only grow as climate change drives more and more people to seek refuge in more livable places in the North. "In the Global South, extreme climate change will push vast numbers of people from their homes, with large regions becoming uninhabitable," explains Gaia Vince, in her book, *Nomad Century: How Climate Migration Will Reshape our World* (Vince, 2022). Furthermore, she notes that mass migration will only grow. "Over the next fifty years, hotter temperatures combined with more intense humidity are set to make large swathes of the globe lethal for three to five billion of us" (Ibid.).
Global conflicts, sometimes related to competition for resources, also drive migration. According to The World Bank:

A complex web of forces—shocks, stresses, and imbalances—influences migration, environmental shifts, and climate change. Issues related to migration and climate change both involve the discussion of long-term forces, such as global inequalities and geographic differences, as well as sudden, short-term shocks, such as war, conflicts, or natural disasters. (World Bank "Migration", 2022)

In their proposal for a vision for migration in the age of climate change, Deepak Bhargava and Rich Stolz discuss the geopolitical impacts of mass migration. "Climate change and mass migration are reshaping politics, economies, and livelihoods around the world" (Bhargava & Stolz, 2022).

Continuing to marginalize large swaths of people, based on fabricated "reasons" to disguise bias, will make matters worse. Instead, we have an opportunity to embrace and include people of all backgrounds in our efforts to build stronger and healthier communities. This will be good for society and good for business. Healthy, financially empowered, and included people will contribute more to their communities, workplaces, and local and national economies.

Gender Equity Is Fundamental to Build a Better World

Worldwide, women and girls face discrimination, notably in the spheres of education, healthcare, employment, and human rights. Not only is this harmful to them, but economies suffer as well. These systemic challenges are discussed in each of the chapters.

With regard to the effects of climate change, women suffer disproportionately. They are fourteen times more likely to die in climate events and four times more likely to be displaced because of climate. This disparity, and the discrimination that causes it, has had a negative effect on workforce resiliency and bottom lines, according to a report by Task Force for Equity in Climate-related Financial Disclosures (TCFD) and Aon (Aon, 2022; Dickinson, 2022).

Women and girls also experience hunger at higher rates than men. According to the World Food Program, of the 349 million people who are severely hungry in the world right now, nearly 60% are women and girls. "Each cause of unequal treatment reinforces the others, trapping women in a cycle of disadvantage, poverty and hunger" (United Nations "WFP"). The World Bank describes these inequities as well. "In nearly two-thirds of countries around the world, women are more likely than men to suffer from hunger and malnourishment. Deep-rooted gender norms, man-made conflict and a lack of equal rights trap women in a cycle of disadvantage, poverty and hunger." (Ibid.)

Not only are women disadvantaged by the lack of equal rights, but economies suffer as well. "With equal rights, the World Bank estimates women could add $160 trillion dollars to the global economy" (Ibid.).

Despite the value of women's participation in the workforce, job opportunities are often limited. An estimated 2.4 billion women of working age are not afforded equal economic opportunity. 178 countries maintain legal restrictions that prevent their full economic participation. In 86 countries, women face job restrictions, and 95 countries do not guarantee equal pay for equal work, according to The World Bank (World Bank "Women", 2022). Families must endure the consequences. Instead, when more income is put into the hands of women, child nutrition, health and education improve (United Nations, 2012). According to the World Economic Forum (WEF),

> Gender gaps in the workforce are driven and affected by many factors, including long-standing structural barriers, socioeconomic and technological transformation, as well as economic shocks. Geopolitical conflict and climate change both impact women disproportionately. In addition, the projected deepening of the current cost-of-living crisis is also likely to impact women more severely than men, as women continue to earn and accumulate wealth at lower levels. (World Economic Forum, 2022)

According to the World Economic Forum, "Gender parity is not recovering. It will take another 132 years to close the global gender gap. As crises are compounding, women's workforce outcomes are suffering and the risk of global gender parity backsliding further intensifies" (Ibid.).

We will not achieve the goals agreed to by all UN member countries— the UN Sustainable Development Goals (SDGs)—until we understand and address racial inequity and injustice, domestically and worldwide. By depriving people of rights and access to resources, based on their ethnic and racial identities, gender, and sexual orientation, we are perpetuating the very problems that are destructive of both business and society.

Valuable Lessons Have Emerged from Efforts to Address Global Challenges

The past ten years have revealed important lessons for effectively addressing deeply entrenched systemic problems. These lessons are important for companies seeking to drive change. They are discussed in each chapter of the book, and they are illustrated by the case studies.

Collaboration: One business alone cannot solve any one of the issues addressed in this book. With that understanding, businesses have continued to explore a variety of ways to work together with NGOs, governments, and each other. In some cases, companies are part of informal and formal coalitions that tackle a particular problem; in other cases, they establish more structured partnerships. There are examples of coalitions that BSR has formed, including in the Human Rights chapter and Climate and Environment. BSR is a sustainable business network and consultancy focused on creating a world in which all people can thrive on a healthy planet.

A new iteration of collaboration is drawing interest and attention. In some cases, companies that have come together to address an issue are being asked to relinquish control to the people who have experienced the problem. An example can be found in the chapter on Human Rights. In the anti-trafficking movement, there is a focus on "rights-holders," people who have been victims and survivors of trafficking. "There is a shift to engage rights holders not just as voices of victims but also as advisors, employees, and people in positions of power," explains Sara Enright, Director of Sustainability Collaborations at BSR (Enright, 2022). This will be a new experience for companies, with fresh insights and learnings along the way.

Technology innovation: As with most endeavors today, technology is fundamental in addressing systemic problems. This is clear from HP's work advancing digital literacy in schools in Africa and Asia, as well as NGOs that work with corporate partners to prepare young people for futures in engineering and computer sciences. Some examples are in the Education chapter.

Home-grown: Some companies and foundations are recognizing the importance of investing in NGOs that are led by people who have grown up in the communities being served. Kennedy Odede is a strong example. Odede is the Founder and CEO of Shining Hope for Communities (SHOFCO) in Nairobi. (SHOFCO website) He describes the importance of being a grassroots, empowerment organization. Odede explains:

> We know sustained change is not possible without leaders designing the solutions to combat the impacts of the climate crisis in their own communities. Yet these leaders and organizations are systemically left out of the conversation on sustainable climate solutions. It's time we upend the traditional approaches which are frankly grounded in colonialist histories. We see the path forward for climate localization as follows: (1) We want more than a seat at the table, we want local and Indigenous leaders creating the table and co-designing solutions. (2) We need to shift funding and power. (3) We also need trust. (4) And of course we need real commitments with accountability. (Odede, 2022)

The story of SHOFCO is presented in the Education chapter.

People-centered: While the value of stakeholder engagement has been recognized for a while, there is a growing understanding that solutions are best when they are co-created and implemented together with the people who are most affected. A variation on this is the example of "rights-holders" describe above. Another variation is home-grown leadership. More broadly, the idea of being people-centered represents the progression from top-down solutions being imposed on communities by the mighty and powerful. Some companies that seek to advance solutions are adapting to this way of thinking.

An example would be the NGO mothers2mothers (m2m) which is described in the Health chapter. The care system m2m has established to advance the health of women in various countries in Africa centers around "Mentor Mothers." Caregivers from within the communities are trained and employed to provide peer guidance and support to help improve the health and well-being of the women in their care. Originally developed to reduce the incidence of mother-to-child transmission of HIV, the highly effective Mentor Mother model is being expanded to provide additional health services as well. "mothers2mothers (m2m) provides health care to families who need it most, delivered by women who know them best. We're building a healthy, thriving Africa" (Mothers2Mothers website).

Hybrid: This might be the most significant lesson of all. As described by Olufunmilayo Arewa in the Education chapter, this approach eschews parachuting in solutions from the North to the South. The hybrid model recognizes that what works in Ohio, or in a region of France, cannot be expected to yield results if it is dropped into a community in Africa.

Holding up the example of architect Francis Kéré, who won the 2022 Pritzker Prize, Arewa shows that "we need better, more flexible frameworks to harness creativity and innovation that are modified as needed based on local needs and priorities." Born in Burkina Faso, now living in Germany, Kéré designed an elementary school in his hometown of Gando. By engaging local residents in construction, and "drawing blueprints for them in the sand," he builds structures for and with communities, incorporating their materials, their programs, and their unique characters (Heyman, 2016).

The five lessons above complement each other, and sometimes overlap. They reflect the iterative learning by companies, foundations, governments, and NGOs in how to help advance solutions together with the people who will benefit.

Some Companies Invest in Women-Led, Locally Driven Supply Chain Solutions

Sarah Degnan Kambou provides an example of a corporate investment initiative that exemplifies a stakeholder-centric approach to advance women-led, locally driven supply chain solutions. Kambou was President and CEO of the

International Center for Research on Women (ICRW) from 2010 to 2021; Chair of the Board of Capital for Good USA; and Vice Chair Elect of the Board, Global Impact.

With the new millennium, visionary private sector firms began addressing women's and girls' social and economic empowerment in low- and middle-income countries. These initiatives were initially funded through program grants to NGOs, and managed by foundation or corporate social responsibility staff. As evidence mounted on the positive impact of these charitable investments on the lives of women and girls, champions for gender equality began building out the business case—why investing in women and girls is good for business. As that narrative grew more sophisticated and gained traction, and as pathfinder corporations were heralded for their contributions to gender equality and global development, an increasing number of private sector firms began investing core business resources in elements of global value chains, e.g., improving the situation and productivity of women workers; strengthening women vendors in supply chains; and, increasing opportunities for women and girls in local communities.

This discourse has now evolved to widespread global endorsement of environmental, social and governance (ESG) objectives being part and parcel of a stakeholder-centric approach for doing business.

Among post-COVID innovations, of note is the Resilience Fund for Women in Global Value Chains. This is a pooled funding initiative, led by prominent companies, corporate foundations, and private foundations with well-established track records in progressive, collaborative programming for women's empowerment and gender equality. As a collective, the Fund is seeking to disrupt traditional corporate philanthropic approaches, and to invest up to $10M in women-led, locally driven solutions that will ensure the resilience of women who form the backbone of global supply chains. The Fund expects to make its first grants at the end of January 2023. This is an exciting initiative that will surely be monitored for progress and lessons learned by global development stakeholders. As a collective, the Fund is seeking to disrupt traditional corporate philanthropic approaches, and is founded on the principles of shared governance, decolonized philanthropy, and non-linear systemic change. Focusing on the manufacturing, agribusiness, and apparel sectors, where women constitute a majority of workers, the Fund will invest in women-led, locally driven solutions that will ensure the "resilience of women who form the backbone of supply chains." The Fund will soon announce its first direct grants to women-led organizations in Cambodia and Vietnam. As well, the Fund will award an umbrella grant to a regional women's fund for onwarding granting to community efforts in Southeast Asia. This is an exciting initiative that will surely be monitored for progress and lessons learned by global development stakeholders (Kambou, 2023).

Companies Benefit by Addressing Social, Economic, and Environmental Challenges

Many investors today evaluate the asset value of companies based on their impact in addressing climate change and the environment; social issues, including economic development; and the effectiveness of their board governance composition and practices. These expectations fall under the term ESG, for environmental, social, and governance. Such a vision of the role of business in the world would have been unimaginable only twenty years ago.

Some companies are also beginning to look at systemic barriers to diversity, equity, and inclusion (DEI), sometimes adding a B for belonging or a J for justice. While there is an abundance of new literature and business trainings to help companies to improve their DEI practices, critics suggest that there is more lip service than progress up to now. Advocates for DEI call for companies to disclose information regarding their hiring, retention, and promotion rates, as well as salary equity for BIPOC employees and women. This topic is discussed further in the last chapter (Newkirk, 2020).

In the past, companies might have seemed an unlikely source for finding solutions to global problems. Businesses and nonprofits sat at either end of a spectrum, often quite mistrustful of one another. Businesses distinctly stayed on one side, creating products and services for profit, while nonprofits clearly stayed at the other end, pursuing missions for the betterment of the world. Too often, elements of the corporate sector were responsible for creating the human rights abuses, environmental degradation, and economic injustices that continue to plague the world today. In the past, if a business wanted to "do good," it would make a financial contribution to a charity or give its employees a pat on the back for volunteering.

By the 1990s, some corporations became more strategic in their philanthropy, focusing their dollars on charities that related to their businesses (Korngold, 2005). There were a number of drivers for this change. In a weak economy—marked by the stock market crash of 1987, a recession, and high oil prices—and facing increased global competition, companies became more attentive to how they were spending each of their dollars. Businesses began to notice that they had been dispensing charitable funds somewhat idiosyncratically. They realized that these monies could be assets to be invested more strategically in strengthening the communities in which the company operated, while also building corporate goodwill. Perhaps most importantly, corporations saw that they could align their contributions with causes that would enhance their direct business interests, thereby boosting revenues, their brands, and their public image. Newspaper companies began supporting literacy organizations, for example; banks invested in small business development, and some phone companies supported crisis hotlines.

Eventually, even more purposeful companies recognized the value of integrating service—including volunteering, skills-based service, and nonprofit board participation—with philanthropy, in order to advance community relations, marketing, leadership development, and other forms of personal and professional development (Ibid.).

Additional examples are provided in *Leveraging Good Will: Strengthening Nonprofits by Engaging Businesses* (Ibid.). As companies recognized the benefits of community engagement, collaboration, and partnerships, as well as opportunities for social and environmental impact, these issues moved up to the C-suite, and took on names like "corporate social responsibility (CSR)" and "sustainability." These are discussed in the original edition of this book (Korngold, 2014).

Around the turn of the twenty-first century, some leading businesses advanced to a new stage by embracing the concepts of social, environmental, and economic opportunity as part of their core corporate missions. These companies became motivated by three forces. First, they understood that they would thrive only if they operated in a healthy and sustainable environment with customers who had the economic capability and longevity to purchase their products. Second, some businesses recognized that they would increase the likelihood of hiring and retaining the best people, while also motivating employees to be productive. Finally, these companies saw opportunity in developing and producing goods and services for a market that was increasingly demanding sustainable, socially responsible products. These global corporations, therefore, incorporated these values as a key part of their business philosophy and plans. Social issues were no longer a "feel good" or public relations adjunct to the company's core mission. In this way, these leading companies moved toward embracing values held by the NGO sector.

Not only have the missions of some businesses and nonprofits become somewhat aligned, but their operational approaches have also coalesced. Leading companies have realized that they need a purposeful mission, a sustainable environment and supply chain, a healthy, educated, and economically empowered customer base, and a motivated workforce—values traditionally identified with the NGO sector—in order to thrive. Nonprofits have come to understand that they need to make a compelling case for significant resources, create robust business models, demonstrate replicability, see issues in terms of the "win–win," and build effective infrastructures—ideas historically touted by business—in order to achieve scale to address mighty global challenges. Increasingly, companies and nonprofits came to understand a mutuality of interests, and began working as partners to address social, economic, and environmental challenges to improve communities and the world.

The adoption of the United Nations' Sustainable Development Goals (SDGs) in 2015 established a framework for companies, nonprofits, and governments to align their strategies with clear goals to address vital social, economic, and environmental matters. The goals are described as a "shared blueprint for peace and prosperity for people and the planet now and into the future." (United Nations "SDGs") The role of companies is particularly important in advancing the goals. "With the private sector, we have the ability to achieve the United Nations Sustainable Development Goals (SDGs), which envision a world free of poverty, hunger, discrimination, and environmental degradation," says Adam Gordon, Executive Director of the United Nations Global Compact (UNGC) Network USA (Gordon, 2023; United Nations Global Compact Network USA).

The most recent iteration of corporate responsibility is far more serious, especially because it is investor-driven. Companies are evaluated on the basis of their ESG commitments, effectiveness, and disclosure. Additionally, regulatory requirements are becoming more severe. The last chapter of this book focuses on ESG with a particular look at board governance (G), including board composition.

This Book Is Organized According to Major Global Challenges

This book will explore corporate initiatives, sometimes in collaboration with each other, or with NGOs and governments, that provide visionary and innovative solutions to the challenges facing the world now and in the future. These companies recognize that by improving social, economic, and environmental conditions, they will meet the interests of customers, employees, and investors, grow their value, and become more sustainable. As a result, some companies are advancing economic development to reduce poverty and create thriving communities; decarbonizing their operations as well as supply chains, while developing energy efficient products and services for private and public customers; internalizing the costs of natural resources that they consume while producing and marketing environmentally responsible goods; investing in technology-based educational programs to prepare the next generation for twenty-first century jobs; offering access to health-care, medicines, and vaccines—often enabled by mobile technology—to save lives and improve the quality of life for people in underserved regions; and investing in preventing human trafficking and labor abuses, while protecting privacy and freedom of expression on the Internet.

This book features specific approaches that some corporations are taking that appear to be particularly promising. A number of businesses are beginning to emerge as global leaders, while others have demonstrated strength in certain programs but lag in other areas. Importantly, one must remember that some corporate actors have created and continue to perpetuate the threats facing the world; only with such an understanding can we move forward together to find solutions. The purpose of this book is to look ahead by highlighting effective and promising corporate initiatives and to rally the business sector and its stakeholders to continue to think creatively and collaboratively about building a better world.

This book is organized into chapters on climate change and environment, economic development, education, health, and human rights. The final chapter focuses on the role of the board of directors in growing the company's value by finding innovative solutions to the world's most pressing challenges.

Every chapter emphasizes the fundamental importance of understanding and addressing systemic barriers that prevent people from engaging positively in society and the economy. The only way we will advance a vision of a more prosperous world is by recognizing and appreciating all people and welcoming their participation.

Chapter 2 examines climate and the environment, which are inextricably linked. It opens with the warning that unless we change course, we are likely to breach the Paris Agreement's 1.5 °C target in the next two decades, and even breach 2 °C around mid-century. The results will be catastrophic. To achieve the goals of the Paris Agreement, greenhouse gas (GHG) emissions must be halved by 2030—and drop to net-zero by 2050. This is the decisive decade.

The chapter examines market incentives, including investor interests, for corporations to act on climate change. Cases show how some companies are decarbonizing cities, buildings, and transportation; developing smart cities; facilitating the transition to renewable energy with their industrial customers; designing zero plastic waste solutions for their products; and transforming food systems to address climate, food security, and farmer livelihoods. In this way, some corporations are growing value and becoming more sustainable, while also elevating their brands by addressing consumer, employee, and investor concerns.

There is no path for a better future unless it addresses climate and environmental justice. We live on one planet. What happens in one country affects us all. Understanding this is an ethical mandate. It is also fundamental to economics and businesses.

Chapter 3 addresses economic development. Unfortunately, there is a stunning reversal in the trajectory of poverty due to the pandemic. The number of people living in extreme poverty is growing for the first time in three decades. Rising inflation and the effects of the Russian invasion of Ukraine are likely to exacerbate the poverty crisis.

Gender and racial inequities continue to be a steady drag on economies. Global migration, driven by the effects of climate change and geopolitics, will increase. This chapter shows that instead of rejecting people, businesses and society will benefit by making it possible for each person to contribute.

Companies, with nonprofits, train, prepare, and employ people from marginalized communities. And the mobile money innovation has drawn tens of millions of people in the Global South into the economy.

For companies, alleviating poverty presents opportunities, while also addressing a pernicious social issue. By helping to advance people from extreme poverty to the middle class, businesses promote their strategic growth through access to new markets, workforce development, innovation, and product distribution. Inclusion is an imperative and an opportunity. By appreciating the value that all people can contribute, and creating systemic pathways for each person to achieve their potential, companies will help create a more prosperous future for all.

Chapter 4 addresses education, including potential learning losses resulting from the pandemic. Furthermore, gender, racial, and ethnic inequities in education continue to inhibit economic mobility. Some companies are promoting initiatives to accelerate learning, and close the digital divide, for children and young adults from marginalized communities in the United States and in the Global South.

With a focus on science, technology, engineering, and math (STEM), businesses are investing in organizations that prepare young people for twenty-first century careers. This chapter features outstanding nonprofits funded by scores of major companies.

This chapter also examines the advantages of promoting hybrid models for organizations in the Global South—organizations that provide education, healthcare, and other essential services. The hybrid model is co-created by people who live in the community being served—people who are deeply familiar with the needs and the culture. One example is a highly successful grassroots organization whose leader grew up in the community being served. The organization is heavily funded by multinational corporations.

Companies that take an inclusive and systemic approach to solving the global education crisis recognize it is in their own interests, in addition to benefiting societies and economies.

Chapter 5 examines health, where humanitarian concerns intersect with business interests. Regional inequities result in high death rates due to preventable illnesses and diseases, particularly affecting women and children. Climate change and the pandemic have exacerbated the mortality rate worldwide, further exposing the inadequacies of some governments in providing sufficient access to care, medicines, and vaccines.

Quality care can reduce the death rate and improve the world's health. Access to services by all people is essential for moral, practical, and economic reasons. In response to the health crisis, some companies are partnering with NGOs and governments to advance innovative solutions—including mobile technology and drone deliveries. Often, businesses are beginning to understand that solutions must be co-created by people who have grown up in the communities being served.

Healthcare is a vital concern for companies. They require healthy employees to perform their jobs productively. Additionally, when families are healthy, employees can focus on their work rather than caretaking at home. A well population and an efficient healthcare system provide a sound economy in which companies can operate and thrive. In some cases, solving healthcare challenges provides commercial opportunities for companies, including by demonstrating their value, as partners, to advance progress.

Chapter 6 focuses on human rights. Not a day goes by without news of human rights abuses. There is a growing awareness that company products and services might be tainted by human rights abuses of workers in the supply chain. In addition, the horrors of human trafficking continue unabated in cities in which we live and work.

Cybersecurity attacks threaten companies and consumers. For individual consumers, common cyber-related crimes include identity theft, frauds, and scams. Breaches involve invasions of personal health information, stolen or compromised credentials, and ransomware attacks. Furthermore, the spread of misinformation on the Internet related to COVID has cost lives, and the Internet has proven to be a dangerous platform to spread hate and incite violence.

Many of the challenges are system-wide, so some companies join coalitions to drive progress. By collaborating with each other and NGOs, they are becoming potent players in addressing human rights abuses.

Humanitarian interests alone would seem to be sufficient to motivate companies to protect human rights. Increasingly, as well, companies are sensitive to matters that concern customers, employees, investors, and regulators. Businesses are learning that doing the right thing benefits their bottom lines by protecting and building their brands, reducing financial and regulatory risks, elevating employee morale and loyalty, and attracting responsible investors.

Chapter 7 examines the role of boards of directors, with particular attention to board composition. Only highly qualified boards can fulfill their obligations to grow the company's value in the context of the most pressing issues of this and subsequent decades—to identify the challenges and opportunities that are most material to the company, and focus their attention accordingly. The best qualified boards will have directors who bring diverse and relevant experience and expertise, including related to ESG (environmental, social, and governance), climate change, cybersecurity, technology, and the global marketplace.

There has in fact been some progress in transitioning boards with regard to their composition, focus, and attention. Pressure from investors and regulators is helping to drive these important developments.

Creating an Inclusive, Sustainable, and Prosperous Future

Companies have the capacity and self-interest to accelerate progress in addressing climate change and vital social and economic concerns. It is their boards of directors, however, that have the ultimate responsibility and authority to guide and shape their companies. And in order to maximize the company's greater potential in the global marketplace, boards must drive the global agenda for an inclusive, sustainable, and prosperous future.

A number of international companies understand that solving global challenges can increase their profits and long-term sustainability. They are advancing the social, economic, and environmental condition of the world in ways that government cannot. There is much to celebrate and hope for as companies invest in building a better world, and there is a role for every person in every sector to help drive solutions.

The United Nations Global Compact Network USA Board of Directors is a current client of Korngold Consulting LLC.

References

Abi Deivanayagam, T., Selvarajah, S., Hickel, J., Guinto, R. R., de Morais Sato, P., Bonifacio, J. (2023). Climate change, health, and discrimination: Action towards racial justice. *The Lancet, 401*(10370), 5–7. https://www.thelancet.com/journals/lancet/article/PIIS0140-6736(22)02182-1/fulltext. Accessed 26 Jan 2023.

Aon PLC. (2022). *Accelerating the race to Net Zero through gender equity: Strategies for more equitable corporate climate action.* https://climate-gender.aon.com/climate-gender/. Accessed 26 Jan 2023.

Bhargava, D., Stolz, R. (2022, August 24). *The statue of liberty plan: A progressive vision for migration in the age of climate change.* Roosevelt Institute. https://rooseveltinstitute.org/publications/a-progressive-vision-for-migration-in-the-age-of-climate-change/. Accessed 26 Jan 2023.

Dickinson, D. (2022, July 25). *Why climate change disproportionally impacts women.* Fortune. https://fortune.com/2022/07/25/why-climate-change-disproportionally-impacts-women/. Accessed 26 Jan 2023.

Enright, S. (2022, December 23). *Interview with Alice Korngold.*

Gordon, A. (2023, February 2). *Interview with Alice Korngold.*

Heyman, S. (2016, November 16). In Burkina Faso, rebuilding with local touch. *New York Times.* https://www.nytimes.com/2016/10/19/arts/design/in-burkina-faso-rebuilding-with-a-local-touch.html. Accessed 26 Jan 2023.

Hickel, J. (2022, September 4). The tragedy in Pakistan. *Twitter.* https://twitter.com/jasonhickel/status/1566387987235176449?s=27&t=MMEWJF3DTtijlPC7mljZUQ. Accessed 26 Jan 2023.

Hickel, J., Sullivan, D., Zoomkawala, H. (2021). Plunder in the post-colonial era: Quantifying drain from the global south through unequal exchange, 1960–2018. *New Political Economy 26*, 1030–1047. https://doi.org/10.1080/13563467.2021.1899153?journalCode=cnpe20. Accessed 26 Jan 2023.

Horner, W. (2022, September 19). Lack of global collaboration risks COP26 goals, IEA report says. *The Wall Street Journal.* https://www.wsj.com/articles/lack-of-global-collaboration-risks-cop26-goals-iea-report-says-11663628460. Accessed 26 Jan 2023.

Joice, E., Ostasiewiecz, A. (2022, May 14). East Africa drought: "The suffering here has no equal." *BBC News.* https://www.bbc.com/news/world-africa-61437239. Accessed 26 Jan 2023.

Kambou, S. D. (2023, January 31). E-mail to Alice Korngold.

Korngold, A. (2005). *Leveraging good will: Strengthening nonprofits by engaging businesses.* Jossey-Bass, a division of Wiley.

Korngold, A. (2014). *A better world, inc.: How companies profit by solving global problems where governments cannot.* Palgrave Macmillan.

Lynch, A., Bond, H., Sachs, J. (2021). *In the red: The US failure to deliver on a promise of racial equality.* Sustainable Development Solutions Network. https://static1.squarespace.com/static/5dadc6c4073ce72706cd29c6/t/6095554a571d4d08a6edc4d3/1620399440334/In+The+Red-The+US+Failure+to+Deliver+on+a+Promise+of+Racial+Equality-2.pdf

mothers2mothers website. (undated). https://m2m.org/

Newkirk, P. (2020). *Diversity, Inc.: The fight for racial equality in the workplace.* Bold Type Books.

Odede, K. (2022, November 25). Opinion: COP 27 left out Africans, but climate progress still possible. *Devex.* https://www.devex.com/news/opinion-cop-27-left-out-africans-but-climate-progress-still-possible-104483. Accessed 26 Jan 2023.

Partington, R. (2022, October 6). IMF chief warns world heading towards age of greater instability. *The Guardian.* https://www.theguardian.com/business/2022/oct/06/imf-chief-warns-world-is-heading-towards-an-age-of-breakdown. Accessed 26 Jan 2023.

Sen, A. (1999). *Development as freedom.* Anchor Books.

Shining Hope for Communities (SHOFCO) website. (undated). https://www.shofco.org/

The World Bank. (2022, November 2). *Shocks and global imbalances: Conflicts, migration and climate change ("Migration").* https://www.worldbank.org/en/events/2022a/11/02/shocks-and-global-imbalances-conflicts-migration-and-climate-change. Accessed 26 Jan 2023.

The World Bank. (2022, March 1). *Press release: nearly 2.4 billion women globally don't have same economic rights as men ("Women").* https://www.worldbank.org/en/news/press-release/2022b/03/01/nearly-2-4-billion-women-globally-don-t-have-same-economic-rights-as-men. Accessed 26 Jan 2023.

United Nations. (2022). *The sustainable development goals report 2022.* https://unstats.un.org/sdgs/report/2022/. Accessed 26 Jan 2023.

United Nations, Commission on the Status of Women. (2012). *Facts & figures.* https://www.unwomen.org/en/news/in-focus/commission-on-the-status-of-women-2012/facts-and-figures#:~:text=fare%20much%20better.-,Education,urban%20boys%20(60%20percent). Accessed 26 Jan 2023.

United Nations, Department of Economic and Social Affairs. (undated). *The 17 goals ("SDGs").* https://sdgs.un.org/goals. Accessed 26 Jan 2023.

United Nations Global Compact Network USA. (undated). *Webpage.* https://www.globalcompactusa.org/. Accessed 31 Jan.

United Nations Sustainable Development Goals. (undated). *The 17 Goals ("SDGs").* https://sdgs.un.org/goals. Accessed 31 Jan 2023.

United Nations, World Food Program. (undated). *Women are hungrier because of gender inequality ("WFP").* https://www.wfpusa.org/drivers-of-hunger/gender-inequality/. Accessed 26 Jan 2023.

Vaidyanathan, R. (2022, October 4). Pakistan floods: "It's like fighting a war with no end." *BBC News.* https://www.bbc.com/news/world-asia-63080101. Accessed 26 Jan 2023.

Vince, G. (2022). *Nomad century: How climate migration will reshape our world*. Flatiron.

World Economic Forum. (2022, July 13). *Global gender gap report*. https://www.weforum.org/reports/global-gender-gap-report-2022/digest. Accessed 26 Jan 2023.

2

Climate and Environment

When we try to pick out anything by itself, we find it hitched to everything else in the Universe.

—John Muir (1911)

WE HAVE ENTERED INTO A PERILOUS PERIOD WHERE GLOBAL CLIMATE change is causing hardship, suffering, hunger, dislocation, and deaths, resulting from intense droughts, water scarcity, severe fires, rising sea levels, flooding, melting polar ice, catastrophic storms, and declining biodiversity. Recognizing the extreme existential threat of climate change, the Conference of the Parties 21 (COP21), some 196 parties, adopted the Paris Agreement in 2015. This is a legally binding international treaty on climate change. To avoid making the Earth uninhabitable, the goal is to limit global warming to well below 2 °C, preferably to 1.5 °C, compared to pre-industrial levels (United Nations, Climate Change "Paris", n.d.).

In 2018, the Intergovernmental Panel on Climate Change (IPCC) cautioned that to prevent the catastrophic impacts of climate change, global warming must not exceed 1.5 °C (IPCC, 2018). "To achieve this, greenhouse gas (GHG) emissions must be halved by 2030 – and drop to net-zero by 2050," warned the Science Based Targets initiative (SBTi) (Science Based Targets, n.d.). Again, in 2021, the IPCC gave notice that unless we change course, we are likely to breach the Paris Agreement's 1.5 °C target in the next

A. Korngold, *A Better World, Inc.*, https://doi.org/10.1007/978-3-031-31553-4_2

two decades, and even breach 2 °C around mid-century (IPCC, 2021). The 2020s will be the decisive decade. The SBTi called on all businesses to cut emissions at scale (Science Based Targets, n.d.).

Climate change is responsible for 5 million deaths globally every year (Lombrana, 2021). Additionally, global financial losses due to climate change reached $2.56 trillion in 2019–2020 (Eckstein et al., 2021). In the United States alone, 18 disasters caused more than $1 billion each in damage (Ibid.). As climate change worsens, droughts and flooding will drive exponential increases in deaths, hunger, starvation, and mass migration worldwide (Suarez-Orozco, 2019). Sudden shocks like floods and storms, as well as more incremental crises like crop failures and drought, often result in conflicts and violence. Together these conditions drove more than 40 million people from their homes in 2020, primarily people from Asia and Africa (Niranjan, 2021). Women and girls, who constitute the majority of climate refugees, experience the greatest harm from violence, including rape and trafficking (United Nations, Human Rights, 2022).

Furthermore, in the Global South and in fragile nations, climate change is a threat multiplier, raising the risk of violence and jeopardizing global security as people compete for clean water, food, and shelter (Blaine, 2021). These countries are at the greatest risk to suffer the impacts of climate change, despite their being the lowest carbon emitters. Furthermore, the World Bank estimates that the ecological crisis might drive 135 million people into poverty by 2030, which will further exacerbate wealth inequality (World Bank Group, 2020). Those who suffer the most from our human made disasters are BIPOC communities, and their resources to respond and adapt to changes in the climate are often limited (Oxfam, 2023).

Europe and the United States are also experiencing loss of life, livelihoods, and property from deadly floods, storms, droughts, and heat waves (Cornwall, 2021; Hill, 2022). Adding to the trauma caused by the world's catastrophic events, the International Energy Agency's (IEA) Fall 2022 World Energy Outlook notes the increased environmental damage triggered by Russia's invasion of Ukraine (International Energy Agency, 2022). The report describes "a shock of unprecedented breadth and complexity." Nonetheless, it also predicts that fossil fuels will peak—coal demand this very decade, natural gas by 2030, and oil by the mid-30s.

Despite the Paris Agreement, indicators are negative. The global temperature continues to rise; 2022 was the sixth-warmest year on record (NOAA, 2023). Furthermore, in the fall of 2022, the UN Environmental Program warned that "the world is not on track to reach the Paris Agreement goals and global temperatures can reach 2.8 °C degrees by the end of the century" (United Nations Environmental Programme "Emissions", 2022b).

Although climate change's destructive force is underway, there is a way forward. The rate of climate change and its effects can be mitigated. NASA states that "the severity of effects caused by climate change will depend on the path of future human activities. More greenhouse gas emissions will lead to more climate extremes and widespread damaging effects across our planet" (NASA, n.d.). Switching energy systems, however, from fossil fuels to renewables like solar or wind, will reduce emissions driving climate change. To avoid the worst-case scenario, the SBTi warns that:

> Greenhouse gas emissions (GHG) emissions must be halved by 2030 – and drop to net-zero by 2050. We have limited time for action and the private sector has a crucial role to play – every sector in every market must transform. Organizations with science-based targets are already cutting emissions at scale; all businesses must now join them. (Science Based Targets Initiative, n.d.)

Furthermore, and particularly relevant to this chapter, the International Energy Agency (IEA) reports that clean energy is a "huge opportunity for growth and jobs, and a major arena for international economic competition" (International Energy Agency, 2022, Executive Summary). There are financial opportunities for businesses that find innovative solutions for their commercial customers to transition to net zero. "The global market for key mass-manufactured clean energy technologies will be worth around $650 billion a year by 2030 – more than three times today's level – if countries worldwide fully implement their announced energy and climate pledges," according to Energy Technology Perspectives, published by the International Energy Agency (IEA) (International Energy Agency, 2023).

The trajectory of the world is at an inflection point. The future depends on decisions and actions by governments and industry that are made now. Businesses can play a vital role in reducing their own emissions to avoid irreversible and catastrophic climate change. Already, 4052 companies have engaged with SBTi. 2218 have set emissions reduction targets grounded in science. 1669 have made net-zero commitments (Science Based Targets Initiative, n.d.). Furthermore, there are financial benefits and incentives for companies to decarbonize their own operations.

The stakes are high. Climate change and nature are inextricably linked. Nature, in this sense, refers to plants, animals, organisms, and the land and seas. The World Wildlife Fund (WWF) explains:

We will not halt climate change if we allow the crisis in nature to continue unabated. By the same token, if we are unable to limit warming to 1.5°C, climate change is likely to become the dominant cause of biodiversity loss in the coming decades. As the interlinkages between the climate system and nature on land, freshwater systems and in the oceans become ever clearer, so too does the urgent need to bring together our efforts to stop and reverse nature loss and decarbonize the global economy. (Ibid.)

A better future is possible. Perhaps The Nature Conservancy best describes an aspiration we can all share. Its mission is to "conserve the life and waters on which all life depends." Its vision is of "a world where the diversity of life thrives, and people act to conserve nature for its own sake and its ability to fulfill our needs and enrich life" (The Nature Conservancy, n.d.). Achieving this ambition rests on our will to address climate change as well as the degradation of nature and the destruction our planet.

In the face of immense challenges, some global corporations are recognizing the business imperative to be a force for good. These companies realize that their own viability and profitability are at risk. Moreover, they see that they can add to their bottom lines by creating and marketing goods and services to put the Earth on a better course. Although there is a role for governments and NGOs, only international businesses have the vast resources, global reach, and self-interest to drive consequential progress on the climate and nature agendas.

Climate and Nature Are Inextricably Linked

The twin crises of nature loss and climate change are inextricably linked. For too long, however, biodiversity loss and climate change have been discussed and dealt with in siloes. We may, however, be at a turning point," explains Marie Quinney in an article published by the World Economic Forum (Quinney, 2021). Quinney continues by noting a new report that came out of a co-sponsored workshop of fifty climate and biodiversity experts. "The report finds that we can either solve both crises or solve neither. (Ibid.) Population growth adds to the exigency of addressing nature and climate change, since more people will further tax the world's natural resources. The world's population has grown from two billion in 1930, to five billion people in 1987, to eight billion today, to an expected nine billion by 2037, and to ten billion by 2058, thereby doubling in the 71 years from 1987 to 2058 (Worldometer, 2023).

To support consumption since the 1970s, humanity has been extracting more natural resources from the planet than it can renew. At this point, it would take 1.7 years for Earth to regenerate the natural resources that are being consumed in one year. If we make no changes to the rate of consumption, we will need three Earth's worth of resources by 2050 (Population Matters, 2023). This is referred to as "ecological overshoot" (WWF, 2020).

Climate and Environmental Injustice Plague the World

There are ethical and business reasons why companies might focus on providing goods and services to long-neglected BIPOC communities and countries across the globe. First, as citizens of the world, leaving aside the specific history of an individual company, corporations share the moral imperative to achieve justice and to elevate the human condition. Climate and environmental justice is a critical issue requiring redress. These are matters of human rights and racial justice. The UN Sustainable Development Goals (SDGs)' commitment to human rights and racial justice compels a focus on the effects of climate change on BIPOC communities. The Ford Foundation describes the tremendous damage to society in general, and particularly the environment, caused by greed and corruption in the Global South:

> Throughout the Global South, the extraction of natural resources—metals, minerals, forests, and fossil fuels—is growing rapidly, causing severe environmental damage and social harm, particularly to indigenous and rural communities. Added to that, weak governance and corruption mean that revenues from extraction disproportionately benefit big corporations, and all too commonly bypass the communities of origin entirely. (Ford Foundation)

NGOs, such as BSR and the Ford Foundation, are convening businesses along with other stakeholders to "create access to opportunity and resources for everyone within an ecosystem and drive true transformation," as described by BSR. BSR is a "sustainable business network and consultancy focused on creating a world in which all people can thrive on a healthy planet" (BSR "Transformation", 2023a).

> Business is one of many actors critical for the creation of a world in which everyone—regardless of identity or background—has the opportunity for equal participation in all aspects of life, has fair access to resources, and can be confident that systems are operating in ways that improve the quality of life for all, and not a select few. (BSR "EIJ", 2023b)

Moreover, companies can grow their own value by ensuring that the interests of all people are served regarding the use of resources and environmental responsibility. The Global South, the scene of historic discrimination and human rights violations surrounding extractive industries, is the site of natural resource abundance necessary to supply the world. Positive relations with the citizens and countries of these largely BIPOC regions will help companies gain sustainable and equitable access to these resources. Ameliorating the harmful effects of irresponsible environmental degradation in majority BIPOC countries will benefit businesses (Leke & Signe, 2019). The last chapter of the book further addresses these issues.

As with other issues addressed in this book, solutions must come from people in the communities that are most affected. This is especially important given the ignominious history of natural resource exploitation and environmental degradation by sovereigns and companies from the Global North.

As one NGO leader from Kenya states: "It's time to let communities set the agenda for change" (SHOFCO, 2022). This is the model promoted by Shining Hope for Communities (SHOFCO), led by Kennedy Odede. SHOFCO's work is also addressed in the chapter on Education. The NGO, based in Kibera, an impoverished community of Nairobi in Kenya, advances this approach.

Solving complex social problems starts at the grassroots. SHOFCO puts urban settlement residents at the center of our model, because community trust and agenda-setting are essential to unlocking solutions that work.

We therefore believe Governments and the development sector must prioritize the decisions of communities themselves, to drive transformational change.

SHOFCO encourages governments and policy leaders to partner with, listen to, and scale up community-led solutions. In addition, we support immediate shifts in resources and financing towards community-led solutions, moving towards a new development paradigm that promotes racial equity and recognizes deep-rooted community trust as the most powerful tool to deliver impact. (Ibid.)

Climate and environmental injustice are also issues that plague the United States (NAACP, 2023). These are legacies of slavery and Jim Crow. The Equal Justice Initiative (EJI), led by Bryan Stevenson, "believes that reconciliation with our nation's difficult past cannot be achieved without truthfully confronting history and finding a way forward that is thoughtful and responsible" (EJI, 2018).

There are valuable lessons to be learned about ways in which some companies are addressing climate change and ecosystems loss. Below are some illustrative examples.

Climate Change and Ecosystems Loss Are Security Matters

Climate change is regarded as "an accelerant of instability and a threat multiplier" is the conclusion of dozens of reports and articles published by the American Security Project (American Security Project, n.d.). The threat arises from damage caused domestically from extreme weather, in addition to disruption of "US interests in strategically important countries," according to a special report by the Council on Foreign Relations. In the report, author Joshua W. Busby argues that in the United States "extreme weather events, made more likely by climate change, could endanger large numbers of people, damage critical infrastructure (including military installations), and require mobilization and diversion of military assets. Internationally, a number of countries of strategic concern are likely to be vulnerable to climate change, which could lead to refugee and humanitarian crises and, by immiserating tens of thousands, contribute to domestic and regional instability" (Busby, 2007).

Climate change can be a harbinger of the violence (Werrell & Femia, 2013). Anne-Marie Slaughter indicates that "this concept of a 'threat multiplier' is a helpful way to think about climate change and security more broadly." She also notes that other commentators claim that "the consequences of climate change are stressors that can ignite a volatile mix of underlying causes that erupt into revolution" (Slaughter, 2013).

Predictions made in articles published by the Center for American Progress back in 2013 have already come to be. Quoted in the original edition of this book, these warnings by Michael Werz and Max Hoffman are eerily prescient: "We will realize how interconnected the world has become if climate hazards one day disrupt global agriculture, energy, or water systems." They also maintained that migration resulting from environmental degradation, social conflict, and food scarcity are likely to complicate future crisis scenarios. Since these comments were made by Werz and Hoffman, there have been scores of additional articles published by the Center for American Progress with the same warnings (Korngold, 2014).

Businesses Can Gain Opportunities

The first part of this chapter, after assessing the role of governments, focuses on opportunities for companies to grow value by providing market-based solutions to mitigate and postpone the damage to the planet that future generations will inherit. According to the businesses that you will read about in this chapter, we have the technology to transition energy systems and build more resilient cities—with infrastructures that are adaptable to adverse circumstances, particularly to extreme weather and natural disasters. The challenge is not about capability as much as it is about our will to change.

Some businesses are leading the way to change. The featured companies understand that climate change is a severe risk to business and society. They also recognize that reducing and limiting carbon emissions, using renewable energy, designing and manufacturing sustainable products, and constructing resilient buildings and communities is a great opportunity to profit, while helping to improve the world.

The second part of this chapter focuses on ways in which companies can address ecosystems loss and its harmful effects on people and the planet. Market forces present a powerful force to save our planet and all living things. In fact, many businesses are reversing their past practices of harming the environment; some are even taking affirmative steps to build a better world, while burnishing their brands and increasing shareholder value.

Customers, employees, and investors are proving to be the necessary drivers. This chapter will show how twenty-first century companies have the resources, global reach, and self-interest to be leading forces in to advance the vision: "a world where the diversity of life thrives, and people act to conserve nature for its own sake and its ability to fulfill our needs and enrich life" (The Nature Conservancy, n.d.).

Before looking at ways in which some companies are driving innovative approaches to address climate change and ecosystems loss, consider the role that governments can play. There have been three major "conventions of the parties" in 2022, which are global meetings for the world's countries to find and implement solutions. An evaluation of the effect of these meetings would require a book in itself, overall, one might conclude as follows: worthy promises have been made, results are yet to be seen, potentially relationships have been established, but the clock is ticking. Below is a review of these meetings.

Global Governments Convened for Three Conferences of the Parties in 2022

Governments have taken some initial steps toward addressing global problems of climate change and the environment. In the three major convenings in 2022, almost all of the world's countries met and committed themselves to the UN Sustainable Development Goals (SDGs) (United Nations "SDGs", n.d.). These meetings are discussed below.

While it is hoped that the principles adopted in these conferences will yield progress on climate and environmental issues, it is not enough for the business sector to sit on the sidelines. Rather, companies have the vast resources, global footprint, and market incentives to drive innovative solutions, alone and in collaboration with NGOs and governments.

The Conference of the Parties (COP27) Focused on Climate Change

COP27 was the Conference of the Parties (COP) of the United Nations Framework Convention on Climate Change (UNFCC). Governments convened for the purpose of agreeing on policies to limit global temperature rises to below 2 °C degrees and adapt to impacts associated with climate change. COP27 was held in November in Egypt, with more than 92 heads of state and an estimated 35,000 delegates from 190 countries attending. The conference has been held annually since the UN climate agreement in 1992, except in 2020 due to COVID.

COP27 is informed by reports from the Intergovernmental Panel on Climate Change (IPCC), the UN body for assessing the science related to climate change. The IPCC prepares comprehensive Assessment Reports about the state of scientific, technical, and socio-economic knowledge on climate change. The world is warming because of emissions produced by humans, mostly from burning fossil fuels like oil, gas, and coal. According to the IPCC, global temperatures have risen 1.1 °C and are heading towards 1.5 °C. If temperatures rise 1.7 °C to 1.8 °C above 1850s levels, the IPCC estimates that half the world's population could be exposed to life-threatening heat and humidity (IPCC, 2022). To prevent this, 196 parties signed the Paris Agreement in 2015, pledging to "pursue efforts" to limit global temperature rises to 1.5 °C.

What was new at COP27 was the first plan to create a "loss and damage" fund for the Global North to compensate the Global South for billions of dollars in environmental damage. The plan to finance this effort is still unclear.

The World Wildlife Fund (WWF) also reported on new trends at COP27. First, that there was more discussion of the inextricable link between climate change and ecosystems loss. Second, that "food has flown up the climate agenda." WWF views the relationship between climate, the environment, and food security as follows.

> The risks threaten people as well as nature. Human societies, culture and our economy are fundamentally dependent upon nature – for food and water security, for air quality, for protection against disease, for energy, the list goes on. Many Indigenous Peoples and local communities depend directly on ecosystems for their survival. (WWF, 2022)

Diane Holdorf had a similar observation about discussions at COP27 regarding the inextricable link between climate and nature: "Climate is central in most discussions, with integration of nature and biodiversity nearly commonplace particularly in relation to data and finance" (Holdorf "Reflections", 2023a). Holdorf is Managing Director, Food, Land and Water at the World Business Council for Sustainable Development (WBCSD) The WBCSD is a global, CEO-led community of over 200 of the world's leading sustainable businesses working collectively to accelerate the system transformations needed for a net-zero, nature positive, and more equitable future.

The Conference of the Parties (COP15) Focused on Biodiversity

COP15, held in December 2022 in Montreal, Canada, was the fifteenth meeting of Parties to the Convention on Biological Diversity (CBD) (United Nations "Convention", n.d.). CBD is the international legal instrument for "the conservation of biological diversity, the sustainable use of its components and the fair and equitable sharing of the benefits arising out of the utilization of genetic resources" (Ibid.). 196 UN member states, or "Parties," ratified the Convention at the Rio Earth Summit in 1992.

Because of the COVID-19 pandemic, countries had not met for several years. At COP15, governments committed to conserving 30% of the planet's terrestrial, inland water, and coastal and marine areas, and restoring 30% of degraded land and waterways, by 2030; reducing by $500 billion annually harmful government subsidies; cutting food waste in half by 2030; and taking additional measures against biodiversity loss (Convention on Biological Diversity, 2022). The agreement mandates the rights of Indigenous Peoples to their traditional territories (Donnelly et al., 2022). These actions are necessary to mitigate threats to the world's food and water supplies, as well as vast number of species.

The United States is just one of two countries in the world, along with the Holy See, that are not party to the CBD, largely because Republicans blocked US membership (Einhorn, 2022). Nonetheless, in terms of nature finance, the United States is a major donor. It pledged $600 million to the Global Environment Facility, the main UN fund for climate and biodiversity, over the next four years (Weston & Greenfield, 2022).

Biodiversity loss not only threatens food security, habitable land, and health, but it is also an economic matter. According to Bloomberg News, a report by Moody's Investors Services indicates that "nature-related financial risk for some industries is growing at an alarming rate." Moody's warns that $1.9 trillion is at stake as biodiversity loss intensifies nature-related risks (Quinson, 2022).

> High-risk sectors such as coal and metals mining, as well as oil and gas exploration and production, will likely face greater regulatory and investor scrutiny as every day passes. Companies that lack credible management strategies in this arena face the prospect of not only reputational damage, but also serious financial repercussions.

As a result, "risks such as ecosystem health, biodiversity loss and natural resource management are rising up the policy and investor agenda," according to Rahul Ghosh, managing director of ESG issues at Moody's.

The World Economic Forum (WEF) also warns of the catastrophic consequences of biodiversity loss and ecosystems collapse.

> Given that over half of the world's economic output is estimated to be moderately to highly dependent on nature, the collapse of ecosystems will have far-reaching economic and societal consequences. These include increased occurrence of zoonotic diseases, a fall in crop yields and nutritional value, growing water stress exacerbating potentially violent conflict, loss of livelihoods dependent on food systems and nature-based services like pollination, and ever more dramatic floods, sea-level rises and erosion from the degradation of natural flood protection systems like water meadows and coastal mangroves. (World Economic Forum, 2023)

The dangers of a depleted natural world are potentially catastrophic. "A variety of ecosystems are at risk of tipping over into self-perpetuating and irreversible change that will accelerate and compound the impacts of climate change" (Ibid.).

Furthermore, "WEF has estimated that roughly half of global gross domestic product, or about $44 trillion worth of economic value, depends on the natural world in some way, meaning its destruction represents an enormous financial loss" (Quinson, 2022).

> Companies that are dependent on "ecosystem services," such as protein and agriculture, are also vulnerable. In fact, forestry, agriculture, fishing, and tourism are among the sectors most at risk.

Most investors and intermediaries are only just beginning to include nature-related risks in their assessments. It is estimated that the market for biodiversity investments may reach as much as $93 billion by 2030, up from about $4 billion in 2019.

The Conference of the Parties (CoP19) Focused on Endangered Species

The 19th meeting of the Conference of the Parties of the Convention of International Trade in Endangered Species of Wild Fauna and Flora (CITES CoP19) took place in Panama City, Panama in November 2022 (CITES, 2022). CITES is an international agreement between governments, with the purpose of ensuring that international trade in specimens of wild animals and plants does not threaten the survival of the species. 365 decisions came out of CoP19 with the parties "agreeing that they need to enforce measures that allow international trade to continue but only in ways that are sustainable and legal to safeguard its benefits and existence for future generations" (Higuero, 2023).

The World Watches to See the Extent to Which COP Agreements Are Fulfilled

There are reasons to be concerned about the likelihood that agreements made at the various COP meetings will be achieved. The UN Environmental Programme shares its assessment:

> It is unclear which commitments made, at either COP27 regarding the climate, or COP15 regarding the environment, will be met. Countries failed to decisively move away from fossil fuels.

Countries repeated the 'phase-down-of-coal' phrase featured in last year's agreement at COP26 in Glasgow. While the final text does promote renewables, it also highlights 'low emission' energy, which critics say refers to natural gas – still a source of GHG emissions. (United Nations Environment Programme "COP27", 2022a)

Furthermore, according to the UNEP, "there were concerns that no real progress was made on raising ambition or cutting fossil fuel emissions since COP26" (Ibid.).

Another important decision made at COP27 is worth watching to see if it has the potential to be achieved. Countries reached a decision to establish and operationalize a loss and damage fund, particularly for nations in the Global South that are most vulnerable to the climate crisis (Ibid.).

"Loss and damage" refers to the negative consequences that arise from the unavoidable risks of climate change, like rising sea levels, prolonged heatwaves, desertification, the acidification of the sea and extreme events, such as bushfires, species extinction and crop failures. As the climate crisis unfolds, these events will happen more and more frequently, and the consequences will become more severe. (Ibid.)

The African continent for example, contributes the least to climate change yet is the most vulnerable to its impacts. African countries that contribute so little will have to spend up to five times more on adapting to the climate crisis than on healthcare. G20 countries, meanwhile, represent around 75 per cent of global greenhouse emissions. Meanwhile, Pakistan has seen US$30 billion in damages from severe flooding but emits less than 1 per cent of global emissions. (Ibid.)

The World Resources Institute (WRI) describes loss and damage as a "matter of climate justice." It shares its concerns that "while developed countries agreed at the COP27 UN climate summit in 2022 to create a fund for addressing losses and damages in particularly vulnerable nations, many questions remain around how it will work and how much money wealthy nations will provide" (Ibid.). WRI is a global research NGO that works with governments, businesses, multilateral institutions, and civil society groups to develop practical solutions that improve people's lives and ensure nature can thrive.

The bottom line is that "the world is falling short on reducing greenhouse gas emissions and in efforts to adapt to the changing climate. Actions and support to developing countries remain insufficient as climate risks grow and impacts increasingly devastate the lives and livelihoods of vulnerable countries and communities" (United Nations, Climate Action, n.d.). Furthermore, with regard to COP15, "a previous 10-year agreement failed to fully achieve a single target at the global level, according to the body that oversees the Convention on Biological Diversity, the United Nations treaty that underpins the old agreement and the new one reached [in Montreal in December 2022]" (Einhorn, 2022).

Governments face a variety of challenges in attempting to restore and protect the world's ecosystems. First, governments represent nation-states with clearly defined borders; officials are accountable to their constituents who often focus on immediate and parochial interests. Second, governments have an array of stakeholders to manage and many issues to balance. When people are out of jobs, concerns about protecting ecosystems can seem to the voting public as conflicting with what appear to be more immediate needs. Third, government leaders are usually not in office long enough to establish and implement long-term visions and strategies, while ecosystem planning requires longer-term thinking and investments. Finally, many governments are composed of coalitions of parties with a variety of interests and constituents.

If governments have a mandate that is too short-term and parochial to mitigate the rapid acceleration of climate change and protect ecosystems in a meaningful way, then perhaps corporations spanning borders, driven by market interests, can help us reach the promised land.

Some National and Local Governments Are Advancing Progress

Although it can be difficult to find and implement agreements among nearly two hundred parties—countries—there is meaningful work being done at regional levels. For example, some countries and cities are providing added incentives for companies to act on climate change and ecosystems loss.

Not only are these governments trying to increase the resilience and diversity of clean energy supply chains, but they are also competing for huge economic opportunities. They are aware that if "we take decisive action now, there is potential to gain $43 trillion in net present value to the global economy by 2070, as shown by the World Economic Forum" (World Economic Forum, 2022). As a result, major economies are acting to combine their climate, energy security, and industrial policies.

The Inflation Reduction Act (IRA) in the United States is an example. In case studies about Trane and Intel below, IRA is regarded as a meaningful incentive by companies, as well as their customers—building owners and cities. In addition, there are two plans in the EU: one is the Fit for 55 package, designed to reduce the European Union's greenhouse gas emissions by 55% by 2030, and the REPowerEU plan to rapidly reduce dependence on Russian fossil fuels by 2027. The Production Linked Incentive plan in India encourages manufacturing of solar PV and batteries, and China is working to meet and even exceed the goals of its latest Five-Year-Plan (International Energy Agency, 2023).

An example at the city level is Local Law 97 (LL97), part of New York City's Climate Mobilization Act, passed by the City Council in April 2019. Buildings account for an estimated two-thirds of greenhouse gas emissions in New York City (NYC). Under LL97, most buildings over 25,000 square feet will be required to meet new energy efficiency and greenhouse gas emissions limits by 2024, with stricter limits coming into effect in 2030. The goal is to reduce the emissions produced by the city's largest buildings 40% by 2030 and 80% by 2050 (New York City, 2023). As shown below, LL97 is resulting in greater demand for Trane to decarbonize NYC buildings. Trane is a manufacturer of heating, ventilation, and air conditioning systems, along with building management systems and controls.

In Boston, the Building Emissions Reduction and Disclosure Ordinance (BERDO) requires large buildings to reduce their emissions (City of Boston, 2023). In the state of Washington, the Climate Commitment Act (CCA) caps and reduces greenhouse gas from the state's largest emitting sources and industries, making it possible for businesses to find efficient models to lower carbon emissions. This program complements other climate policies to help Washington State achieve its commitment to reducing GHG emissions by 95% by 2050 (State of Washington, n.d.).

Globally, NGO C40 is a network of mayors "taking urgent action to confront the climate crisis and create a future where everyone can thrive." C40 includes 96 member cities that make up one-fifth of the world's economy (C40Cities "WHO", 2023b). Sadiq Khan, Chair of C40 and Mayor of the City of London describes the NGO's work in 2022:

From São Paulo to Seoul, Accra to Dhaka, Buenos Aires to Bogotá, and Milan to Montréal, C40 cities are stepping up and showing that ambitious climate action is possible. Mumbai, for example, is…introducing climate budgeting. Tokyo is collaborating with Kuala Lumpur to develop low-carbon building standards. Lagos is decarbonising its energy supply by installing solar panels on schools and health centres. And in London, we've announced that we will expand our world-leading Ultra Low Emission Zone – to cover all of Greater London – ensuring that almost five million more Londoners will breathe cleaner air. (Khan, 2022)

Government-sponsored initiatives in cities further add to the financial incentives for companies to decarbonize cities and industries worldwide. Below are examples of ways in which investors and businesses are driving progress to address climate change and environmental degradation.

Markets Create Incentives for Companies to Act on Climate Change

Some businesses are realizing market opportunities by advancing solutions to decarbonize economies, including cities, buildings, and transportation, to thus mitigate and postpone the worst impacts of climate change. Examples include information and communications technology (ICT) companies that are developing innovative technologies to pioneer energy solutions that they use in their own operations and sell to other businesses. Other companies are driving revenues by making buildings better for people, the environment, and their bottom lines (Trane website, 2022). Still other businesses integrate sustainability in their core strategies, which affects every aspect of the company from operations, to financial planning and reporting, investments, mergers, and acquisitions.

Driving such changes are employees, customers, investors, and nonprofit organizations. An important consideration for companies is the growing demand to disclose information about their climate and environmental impacts. Some corporations are doing so. One of the most significant initiatives is led by CDP that scores companies according to their environmental impacts; each company's score is indicated directly on its NYSE stock listing. CDP is an NGO formerly known as the Climate Disclosure Project. As described further in this chapter, 680 investors with over $130 trillion in assets have requested that corporations disclose through CDP on climate change, water security, and forests; 18,700 companies are doing so (CDP website, 2023).

While this chapter describes the efforts of some companies that are advancing the global decarbonization of industries and cities, most businesses are still not doing their part to reduce emissions and are missing opportunities. According to the CDP, "greenhouse gas (GHG) emissions reduction targets publicly disclosed by companies in G7 economies are still only ambitious enough to align with a 2.7 °C decarbonization pathway." This is "well above the Paris Agreement's goal to keep Earth's temperature rise at or below 1.5 °C—the upper temperature limit that science demands to avoid the most catastrophic environmental impacts" (CDP, 2022). Furthermore, the best performing corporate sectors among the G7 countries are in Europe. Adherence to the Paris limit is vital. The difference between 1.5 °C and 2 °C means 2.6 times more people are likely to be exposed to extreme and potentially dangerous heat events (World Meteorological Organization, 2022a).

Businesses have an opportunity to grow value by leading the way in transitioning the economy to mitigate climate change. "The global market for key mass-manufactured clean energy technologies will be worth around $650 billion a year by 2030 – more than three times today's level – if countries worldwide fully implement their announced energy and climate pledges," according to Energy Technology Perspectives, published by the International Energy Agency (IEA) (International Energy Agency, 2023). The report is the world's first global guidebook for the clean technology industries of the future. "The related clean energy manufacturing jobs would more than double from 6 million today to nearly 14 million by 2030 – and further rapid industrial and employment growth is expected in the following decades as transitions progress" (Ibid.).

By decarbonizing industries and cities, it is possible for us to mitigate and postpone the damage to the planet that future generations will inherit. According to the businesses featured in this chapter, the technology exists to build more resilient cities—with structures and infrastructures that are adaptable to adverse circumstances, particularly to extreme weather and natural disasters. Moreover, some corporations recognize that reducing and limiting carbon emissions, using renewable energy, designing and manufacturing sustainable products, and constructing resilient buildings and communities is an opportunity to profit, while helping to improve the world. The challenge is not about capability as much as it is about our will to change.

Investors and Companies Grow Value by Driving Decarbonization

The perils of climate change are the direct result of there being too much carbon dioxide in the atmosphere. Reducing emissions will require scaled and concerted efforts across all major systems, economic sectors, and geographies. This includes accelerating the shift to renewable energy, driving innovation and new technology development to decarbonize industry, redesigning cities and low carbon transportation infrastructures, and transforming food systems.

Companies have the vast resources, global footprints, and market incentives to drive change. Companies featured in this section recognize the opportunities to grow value by decarbonizing cities, while also improving living conditions worldwide.

The Opportunity for Companies to Decarbonize Cities

"The world is undergoing the largest wave of urban growth in history. More than half of the world's population now lives in towns and cities, and by 2030 this number will swell to about 5 billion," according to the United Nations Population Fund (United Nations Population Fund, 2022). Furthermore, it is estimated that the global urban population will double by 2050. Importantly, "more than 80% of global GDP is generated in cities, urbanization can contribute to sustainable growth through increased productivity and innovation if managed well" (World Bank, 2022).

The growth of cities has major implications for climate change, since cities already account for more than 70% of global carbon emissions (Dasgupta et al., 2022). Buildings are responsible for almost 40% of global energy-related carbon emissions. On the current path, carbon emissions related to buildings are expected to double by 2050 (Economist, 2022). As a result, the transition from fossil fuels to renewable energy and green building solutions is fundamental to slow down climate change and its effects (C40 Cities "What", 2023a).

Given the large amount of carbon emitting from cities and buildings, there is a tremendous market opportunity for companies to find innovative solutions. In fact, a number of companies are providing smart solutions for cities, transportation, and buildings, thereby producing a triple bottom line for urban communities—advancing social, economic, and environmental development. A "smart city" has networked, digital, and communications technologies that support the community's information needs, creating streamlined and improved services for energy efficiency, traffic and transportation, emergencies, sanitation, pollution mitigation, education, and healthcare.

Many of the smart city solutions that are being applied, however, are focused on cities in developed countries, while most of the growth in the world's cities will be concentrated in Africa and Asia (United Nations Population Fund, 2022). According to the UN Population Fund:

The urbanization process – which is particularly pronounced in Africa and Asia, where much of the world's population growth is taking place – is also an enormous opportunity for sustainability, if the right policies are put in place. Urban living has the potential to use resources more efficiently, to create more sustainable land use and to protect the biodiversity of natural ecosystems. (Ibid.)

That is an optimistic view. Extensive reforms would need to take place in order to realize such a hopeful vision. In reality, "the face of inequality is increasingly an urban one. Too many urban residents grapple with extreme poverty, exclusion, vulnerability, and marginalization" (Ibid.). Data reveal that "as of 2020, over 24% of global urban population lived in slums."

This urban crisis is particularly pronounced in Africa: the population in the slums of sub-Saharan Africa "amounted to 50.2% of the total population which is the highest out of all major regions [worldwide]" (Statistica, 2022). A researcher describes the broader implications of urban poverty in African cities:

One of the most enduring physical manifestations of social exclusion in African cities is the proliferation of slums and informal settlements. People living in these settlements experience the most deplorable living and environmental conditions. They are also excluded from participating in the economic social, political, and cultural spheres of the city. (Arimah, n.d.)

A report by the UN Human Settlements Program (UN-HABITAT, 2020) explains that, as a result, developing countries face very different challenges than developed countries.

Urban priorities for the future are rising levels of poverty, providing adequate infrastructure, affordable and adequate housing and addressing challenge of slums, high levels of youth unemployment, and investing in secondary cities. How these challenges are addressed will lead to a range of future scenarios. (UN-HABITAT, 2020)

As shown by Olufunmilayo Arewa in her book, *Disrupting Africa: Technology, Law, and Development* (Arewa, 2021), exclusion and poverty in Africa are the legacies of colonialism and postcolonialism. Some approaches to address the severe challenges facing the most marginalized communities in Africa are described in the chapter on Economic Development. That chapter shows that most of the successful models tend to be organized at the grassroots, like Shining Hope for Communities (SHOFCO). While strong organizations are sometimes initiated by companies based in the Global North, the efforts can potentially be most effective when local communities are fully engaged in leadership, planning, and implementation. Moreover, companies must avoid the past mistake of building infrastructures to extract resources from Africa (leaving behind environmental problems) and deploying people from other countries as workforces—as these bear the hallmarks of colonialism.

Instead, there are commercial opportunities for companies to partner with the people of Africa who offer a great wealth of the human capital. Companies can enhance the lives of the people of Africa, promote economic development, and increase the companies' productivity by providing access to healthcare services, education, and workforce development. Some companies are in early planning stages of such efforts; these stories might be written in just one or two years.

In the meantime, some of the best examples of companies driving change to mitigate the effects of climate change can be found in the Global North. Below are some effective models.

Trane Creates Business Value by Advancing Decarbonization

Institutional investors are compelling the private sector to address material ESG issues, like climate change. As a result, to attract and satisfy their investors, some boards of directors and C-suite executives are leading change. These new expectations present profitable business opportunities for other companies providing services and products to help in a decarbonization initiative.

"As more and more companies set ambitious climate goals, they require expertise and services to help them create and implement a roadmap to decarbonization—to move from strategic to tactical to implementation. There are untapped opportunities in the marketplace to solve these challenges for customers," explains Scott Tew, Vice President of Sustainability and Managing Director, Center for Energy Efficiency and Sustainability at Trane Technologies (Tew, 2023). The company is a global climate innovator that brings efficient and sustainable climate solutions to buildings, homes, and transportation. With 37,000 employees at hundreds of locations around the world, Trane Technologies has annual sales of more than $14 billion.

In response to growing market demand over the past decade, Trane has evolved from an equipment manufacturer to become a global climate innovator, serving as consultants to advance decarbonation. Their process leverages two integrated engineering competencies to deliver solutions that can be effectively implemented and scaled: facility engineering and financial engineering. Furthermore, because decarbonization is now at the top of board agendas, Trane's strategy to address customer interests has shifted. Instead of going to market through facilities managers as in the past, Tew and his team have become advisors at the C-suite level in companies, including helping to prepare board meeting presentations. "The demand is staggering," shares Tew.

Trane's energy decarbonization services have become a compelling revenue source for the company. As a result, sustainability has the attention of the board of directors. Furthermore, says Tew, "sustainability discussions at the board level have shifted focus from risk to opportunity." Tew also explains that every board committee has a facet of responsibility related to sustainability. Here are examples of some of the responsibilities of two of the board committees at Trane (Trane Technologies, 2023). Note how the remit of some companies has expanded from traditional areas to include emerging areas, such as Nominating now encompassing Sustainability.

Sustainability, Corporate Governance and Nominating Committee:

1. Oversee the Company's sustainability efforts including the development and implementation of policies relating to environmental, social and governance ("ESG") issues.
2. Monitor the Company's performance against its sustainability and ESG objectives including the impacts of climate change.
3. Evaluate social and environmental trends and issues in connection with the Company's business activities and make recommendations to the Board regarding those trends and issues.

Technology and Innovation Committee:

1. The Committee shall review the Company's technology and innovation strategy and approach, including its impact on the Company's performance, growth, and competitive position.
2. The Committee shall review with management technologies that can have a material impact on the Company, including product and process development technologies, manufacturing technologies and practices, and the utilization of quality assurance programs.
3. The Committee shall assist the Board in its oversight of the Company's investments in technology and innovation, including through acquisitions and other business development activities.

4. The Committee shall review technology trends that could significantly affect the Company and the industries in which it operates.
5. The Committee shall assist the Board in its oversight of the Company's technology and innovation initiatives, and support, as requested, the Sustainability, Corporate Governance and Nominating Committee in its review of the Company's environment, health and safety policies and practices, and the Audit Committee in its review of the Company's information technology and cybersecurity policies and practices.
6. The Committee shall assist the Board in its oversight of the Company's responses to certain environmental matters including climate change, greenhouse gas emissions, energy-efficient and low-emissions products and product life cycle and materials, and support as needed, the Sustainability, Corporate Governance and Nominating Committee in its review of environmental and sustainability practices.
7. The Committee shall oversee the direction and effectiveness of the Company's research and development operations.
8. The Committee shall assist the Board in its oversight of the processes by which the Company ensures the transparency and performance of its supply chains.
9. The Committee shall assist the Board in its oversight of the processes by which the Company ensures the reliability and safety of the Company's products.

Companies are responding to investors who recognize that decarbonization reduces business risks related to energy prices and climate disasters, creates shareholder value and brand equity, and reduces operational costs. The Inflation Reduction Act (IRA) of 2022 also provides financial incentives to real estate owners to transition from fossil fuels to clean energy (The White House, 2023).

Examples of specific solutions Trane has brought forward to help deliver decarbonization to corporations include:

- **Energy Efficiency**: Introduction of artificial intelligence software to a building automation system for 100+ plasma donation centers. The artificial intelligence continuously drives down energy use, cost and associated emissions by creating optimized operational sequencing to respond to advanced internal and external data.
- **Electrification**: Utilization of heat recovery for a high-tech industrial manufacturer to reduce natural gas use and emissions at a plant in Texas. This solution effectively captured heat from process cooling to be utilized for space heating.

- **Refrigerant Management:** Development of a full inventory of installed refrigerants and associated global warming potentials for a global food distribution company. This included a glidepath for global warming potential based on asset life and available alternatives.
- **Renewable Energy:** Provide design support, equipment, controls, and monitoring for a large, global restaurant chain establishing a flagship Net Zero design and location. The solution included a VRF-based HVAC system, which is an all-electric system that runs at ultra-high efficiencies. This design enabled for facility to be supplied by 100% renewable energy (Joelson, 2023).

In each case, Trane delivered a solution that enabled the corporation to advance towards their publicly stated climate goals by reducing their carbon emissions, saving money, and creating safer and healthier buildings for employees, consumers, and visitors.

Trane's work in accelerating energy efficiency extends beyond the United States. One major project is with the largest hospital in Malta, Mater Dei. Its infrastructure challenges have been compounded by its proximity to the sea, which is corrosive. Additionally, as an island nation in the Mediterranean Sea, The Republic of Malta has limited natural resources; therefore, scarcity is a pressing concern for development. The institution's goals have been to reduce emissions, and achieve cost savings, while also investing in indoor environmental quality (IEQ) improvements (Trane Technologies, 2022). Trane addressed the hospital's interests with a combination of electric technologies, including air-cooled chillers, water-to-water heat pumps, and building automation system to control comfort & energy efficiency. Mater Dei Hospital can now meet strict IEQ standards, while also monitoring and reducing energy use.

While Trane Technologies' work is highly effective in decarbonizing buildings for the betterment of people and planet, the company is also growing profits and value. Driven by the interests of investors and led by the board of directors and C-suite executives, the company is leading the way for others to follow.

Intel Creates Business Value with Energy Solutions

A major advance in reducing urban carbon levels has come through the development of smart cities, meaning cities that are energy efficient with sustainable infrastructures. Intel has developed technologies and thoughtware essential for the emergence of smart cities.

Energy producers and providers are shifting from large, centralized infrastructures to smaller, more flexible, decentralized, and intelligent models, known as microgrids. Microgrids offer various benefits that allow customers to access power more efficiently, thus reducing carbon output by:

- Operating "at the edge"—locally—and, if necessary or beneficial, without connection to the main grid.
- Accessing and consuming energy more sustainably.
- Tracking their energy consumption to manage it like a budget.
- Solving for the intermittent nature of wind and solar energy, allowing users to switch easily to wind and solar sources, thereby facilitating the transition from fossil fuels to alternative energy sources without service disruption.

Microgrids are also better suited for conditions like fires and floods caused by climate change. Energy can be accessed as and where needed despite episodic catastrophes.

Intel has developed architecture to run microgrids. This technology can be installed by a utility to power an entire smart city, or by a single major user (such as a hospital or university) to manage its own energy needs. The smart city system facilitated by the microgrid can yield more efficient use of carbon resources and increased use of non-carbon energies.

Intel also provides technology to make urban transportation more efficient and to reduce carbon. The largest source of carbon emissions in the United States is in the transportation sector; 83% from cars and trucks, according to the Congressional Budget Office (CBO, 2022). Greater use of electric vehicles, along with tighter standards for fuel economy and emissions, are projected to moderately reduce emissions over the next decade. At the same time, Intel's smart city Internet of Things (IoT) technologies improve mobility, save energy, and reduce pollution.

Smart cities track data from many inputs embedded throughout a city's infrastructure, then analyze the data with AI and share it through open data pools. For example, smart traffic signals can respond to traffic conditions and retime themselves to relieve congestion. Smart streetlights with cameras, microphones, and sensors can dim themselves when no one is around and gather intelligence on traffic, public safety, and air quality. Smart public transportation can count passengers, track vehicle locations, and share status. This creates a constant awareness of conditions that can be used for traffic management, route planning, public safety, and emergency response (Intel "Smart", n.d.-c). And these various adjustments in a smart city can reduce energy demand and resulting carbon production.

Fundamental to this model is software to analyze data at the edge, to frame out what end users need. By enabling AI at the edge, decision-making time is faster and more efficient. An example is provided by Sameer Sharma, General Manager, Smart Cities and Intelligent Transportation at Intel. "Many cities have fixed cameras. But a subset of cities has programable cameras. The advantage is the ability to respond to a situation you could not plan for. For example, programable cameras make it possible for cities to evaluate the extent to which people are socially distancing, thereby allowing cities to plan further public health education accordingly" (Sharma, 2023).

Embedded smart city technologies (sensors, cameras, and edge computing) can now provide near real-time awareness of issues requiring attention, and data collected and analyzed from these devices can be used to optimize city operations. Smart city solutions can improve basic services, enhance public safety, increase sustainability, and inform planning and policy making. (Intel "Resilient", n.d.-b)

Furthermore, "if your data center is smart enough, it can make decisions to determine which of the many workloads it's running are more urgent, and which can be delayed or shifted," explains Michael Bates, General Manager, Intel Energy Centre of Excellence (Bates Interview, 2023).

Intel's work with the Chicago Transit Authority (CTA) is illustrative of the value of IoT technology to transition a city's transportation system for greater efficiency—for passenger use, management and operators, and carbon emissions.

The CTA operates the nation's second largest public transportation system. New IoT technology—sensors and onboard Wi-Fi beacons—is installed and integrated with existing fare systems and onboard video feeds. AI aggregates and analyzes data at the edge, then shares the data with CTA operators in near–real time. A machine learning algorithm helps CTA operators deploy city buses more effectively without needing to replace their current fleet management system. This flexible, open-architecture solution can be easily expanded to other vehicles to deliver long-term improvements citywide. (Intel "CTA", n.d.-a)

The CTA example also shows the power of collaboration. In addition to working with the CTA, Intel worked with City Tech Collaborative, a nonprofit urban solutions accelerator, and Genetec, a security company.

Sharma and Bates emphasize the importance of Intel's fundamental approach to create nonproprietary solutions that are interoperable. Customers are far less likely to purchase systems that lock them into one provider, or limit access to members of the public. Bates explains that "Intel's competitive advantage is its ability to convene a global ecosystem to address the biggest challenges in the energy transition toward an open solutions platform that ensures trust, choice, and interoperability for our industry and partners. This allows us to commercialize these platforms more efficiently when deploying groundbreaking solutions to critical challenges and enables us to disrupt and create new markets" (Bates Email, 2023).

Scores for Climate Impacts Displayed in Google's Market Summary Snapshot

In order to determine the monetary value of current and prospective holdings, investors require an accurate assessment of a company's impact on climate change, water security, and forests. CDP, an NGO formerly known as the Climate Disclosure Project is highly regarded for collecting, analyzing, and scoring companies based on their climate and environmental impact. The score that CDP determines for each company is so important that for some stocks, it is included as a line item on Google's Market Summary of NYSE-listed companies, alongside traditional financial metrics like market capitalization and price-to-earnings ratio. Achieving an A score reflects a company's environmental leadership position. A B-/B score reflects good environmental management, but not leadership. A C-/C rating indicates awareness-level engagement. A D-/D score shows that the company needs to have disclosed more extensive information. An F score is for failure to disclose (CDP, "Explained", n.d.-a).

Because the scores have such significant ramifications for a company's investment profile, corporations are highly motivated to achieve a good score by CDP. Furthermore, when a company has a grade decline, this causes consternation among the C-suite executives and the board of directors. "The annual publication of CDP's ratings has become a major event for companies and their investors," explains Trevor Joelson, Business Development Manager—Key Accounts, Trane.

At the time that the first edition of this book was published, CDP had engaged hundreds of investors with $87 trillion in assets in monitoring how companies and their suppliers manage and reduce their carbon emissions and their environmental footprint. Today, nearly a decade later, CDP has expanded its work to serve as the global disclosure system for thousands of cities, states, and regions, as well as companies, to manage their environmental impacts. CDP provides this information at the request of investors, purchasers, and city stakeholders. CDP's scope and influence has grown to the point that in the past two decades, over.

- 680 investors with over $130 trillion in assets requested companies to disclose through CDP on climate change, water security, and forests.
- 280 major buyers, with a combined purchasing power of $6.4 trillion, asked their suppliers to disclose through CDP.
- 18,700 companies reported through CDP on climate change, water security, and forests.
- 1100 cities, states, and regions disclosed environmental information through CDP (CDP website, n.d.).

The companies on CDP's A-list actually outperform the rest of the market, according to an analysis by STOXX, a Swiss globally integrated index provider, covering the world markets across all asset classes (STOXX, n.d.). Two hundred of the 13,126 companies that filed CDP disclosures on Climate Change received an A score; these companies outperformed the reference index by 5.8% per annum from 2011 to 2021.

Companies that measure, manage, disclose, and reduce their greenhouse gas emissions demonstrate their commitment to address environmental challenges, while growing the company's value. The effectiveness of their efforts matters to investors and the public.

Carbon Pricing Allows a Company to Translate Goals into Financial Terms

"The next iteration of maturity for corporations in the sustainability space is carbon pricing," explains Joelson at Trane. Carbon pricing allows a company to put a value on each aspect and phase of their strategy to reduce their CO_2 emissions. The carbon price is set at the C-suite level. With this information, facilities managers can translate goals in quantifiable, financial terms. Increasingly, ratings agencies like CDP are asking companies if they have a carbon price.

Below are a few of the key findings published in CDP's report, "Putting a Price on Carbon." The report is informed by over 5900 corporate disclosures to CDP in 2020 (CDP, 2021).

- There is an "80% increase in the number of companies planning or using an internal carbon price in just five years."

- "Most companies use internal carbon pricing to achieve one or more of key objectives: driving low-carbon investment, driving energy efficiency; and changing internal behavior."
- "Internal carbon pricing goes hand in hand with emissions reduction activities."
- "The median internal carbon price disclosed by companies in 2020 was $25 per metric ton of CO_2e."
- "More than double the number of companies use evolutionary prices which adjust over time in comparison to static prices."
- "Companies can use an internal carbon price to plan for carbon pricing regulation" (Ibid.).

While this chapter describes the efforts of some of the companies seeking to advance decarbonization, the private sector as a whole is not doing enough. According to the CDP, "greenhouse gas (GHG) emissions reduction targets publicly disclosed by companies in G7 economies are still only ambitious enough to align with a 2.7 °C decarbonization pathway." This is "well above the Paris Agreement's goal to keep Earth's temperature rise at or below 1.5 °C — the upper temperature limit that science demands to avoid the most catastrophic environmental impacts" (CDP, 2022). Furthermore, the best performing corporate sectors among the G7 countries are in Europe. Adherence to the Paris limit is vital. The difference between 1.5 °C and 2 °C means 2.6 times more people are likely to be exposed to extreme and potentially dangerous heat events (World Meteorological Organization "Science", 2022b).

Companies described here, as well as other businesses, understand the opportunity to grow their value exponentially by finding and implementing innovative solutions to reduce carbon emissions in cities, buildings, transportation, and their own operations. Their boards of directors and C-suite executives are leading the way, together with their investors who seek to increase their own profits. At the same time, these advances are driving important progress in addressing climate change and the degradation of natural resources.

Markets Create Incentives for Companies to Conserve the Natural Environment

Climate and Environment Are Inextricably Linked

Clean air, water, and arable land are essential for human sustenance; without them, we would all perish. The degradation of essential resources, including water (for drinking, sanitation services, health, and economic development) and the destruction of the ecosystems and biodiversity (necessary to maintain the food chain and natural resources) pose great challenges to Earth and humankind. Unfortunately, however, given the growth in the world's population from five billion people in 1987, to eight billion today, to an expected nine billion by 2027, the consumption of natural resources exceeds the Earth's capacity. Referred to as Earth Overshoot Day, July 28, 2022, marked the day when humanity expended all the biological resources that Earth regenerates during the entire year (Earth Overshoot Day website, 2023).

The gap in and competition for resources, combined with the negative effects of COVID-19, cause severe deprivation and conflict in many regions. Two billion people do not have access to clean drinking water (CDC, 2022), and over 1.7 billion people do not have basic sanitation services (Ibid.). Safe and readily available water is essential for public health, whether it is used for drinking, domestic use, food production, or recreational purposes. Poor sanitation and contaminated water cause life-threatening diseases such as cholera, diarrhea, dysentery, hepatitis, typhoid, and polio (WHO, 2021). "Cascading and interlinked crises are putting the 2030 Agenda for Sustainable Development in grave danger, along with humanity's very own survival," according to the 2022 Sustainable Development Goals (SDGs) report, in reference to COVID-19, climate change, and violent conflicts (United Nations "SDG Report", 2022). These threats severely impede progress towards a number of SDGs, including food and nutrition, health, education, the environment, and peace and security.

Water and sanitation are not only fundamental for people's health and well-being, but these are also economic matters. Addressing these issues can advance economic growth and reduce poverty. The UN reports that "economies are embedded in nature and depend profoundly on the flow of goods and services it generates, such as food and raw materials, pollination, water filtration, and climate regulation" (Ibid.).

Furthermore, environmental degradation and the decline of biodiversity threaten the food chain and important natural resources. According to The World Bank, "the global decline of biodiversity and ecosystem services" could lead to a "collapse in select services such as wild pollination, provision of food from marine fisheries and timber from native forests," which could cause a decline in global GDP of $2.7 trillion in 2030.

"Nature-smart policies can reduce the risk of ecosystem collapse," thereby promoting success for both biodiversity and economic outcomes. The World Bank recommends a set of policies to reverse the damage, resulting in an "increase in global real GDP in 2030 that is estimated to be in the order of $50 billion to $150 billion," and recommends a plan for global cooperation (World Bank Group, 2021).

Human effects on the environment can lead to the loss of arable land and food production. The World Meteorological Organization presents a potentially bleak picture of the future. It shows that human activities can jeopardize a healthy planet, by leading to a "a lack of precipitation for extended periods and uncontrolled land use," which will result in desertification. "It is estimated that one-third of the Earth's surface and one-fifth of the world's population are threatened by desertification" (World Meteorological Association "Environment", 2022a).

There is evidence of this negative trend. "While the global prevalence of moderate or severe food insecurity has been slowly on the rise since 2014, the estimated increase in 2020 was equal to that of the previous five years combined. Nearly one in three people in the world (2.37 billion) did not have access to adequate food in 2020 – that's an increase of almost 320 million people in just one year" (United Nations, Food and Agriculture Organization, 2021).

Companies in the food production sector will also face severe consequences, if they take insufficient action. Extreme and frequent changes in weather, as well as severe floods and droughts will affect land use and crop production. Food and agriculture companies and well as consumer-packaged goods companies (CPGs) will see these threats reflected in their bottom lines.

Planet Earth is on the wrong course. An expanding consumer population has demonstrated a growing appetite for goods and products, using natural resources in increasing amounts. Moreover, too many companies have exploited and managed resources irresponsibly, degrading and depleting the world's water, forests, and soil. Unfortunately, governments, which are entrusted to protect the interests of the people, have not succeeded in addressing the challenges of the world's ecosystems.

A better future is possible. Perhaps The Nature Conservancy best describes an aspiration we can all share. Its mission is to "conserve the life and waters on which all life depends." Its vision is of "a world where the diversity of life thrives, and people act to conserve nature for its own sake and its ability to fulfill our needs and enrich life" (The Nature Conservancy, n.d.).

Market forces present a powerful force to save our planet and all living things. In fact, some businesses are reversing their past practices of harming the environment, and even taking affirmative steps to advance the Earth toward a more promising future. Customers, employees, and investors are proving to be important drivers.

Diane Holdorf at the WBCSD asserts that "all businesses depend on nature, which we can think about as natural capital assets. The rapid loss of biodiversity puts business resilience at risk, creating the business case for developing plans which take action to halt the loss of nature" (Holdorf "Accelerating", 2022). She puts the risk in financial terms related to the global economy: "Nature and biodiversity are degrading quickly, with 70% of the world's ice-free land surface and 66% of our marine environment significantly altered through human activity, and species populations down almost 70% since 1970. More than half of the world's GDP, USD $44 trillion, is at risk from nature loss by 2030" (Ibid.).

This chapter will show how some companies are working in partnership with NGOs and governments to address ecosystems loss to ensure a better future for humanity and our planet, along with their own fortunes. It will also describe some industry-wide collaborations among corporations to explore and develop innovative solutions.

Colgate-Palmolive Was an Early Adopter for Water Security and Climate

Colgate-Palmolive was an early adopter, working to address climate change and the impact on our environment for over twenty years. As early as 2002/2003, the company began tracking and disclosing its carbon emissions data as a responder to the CDP in its first year of operation. CDP, the Carbon Disclosure Project, is an NGO that runs the global disclosure system for investors, companies, cities, states, and regions to manage their environmental impacts (CDP website, n.d.). By 2022, Colgate-Palmolive's net zero climate targets were approved by the Science Based Targets initiative (SBTi), the NGO that independently assesses and approves companies' Net Zero carbon emissions targets according to the criteria of UN Global Compact (UNGC) Business Ambition Climate pledge (Science Based Targets initiative, n.d.; United Nations Global Compact, n.d.). Colgate-Palmolive has also earned the highest score for water security and climate change—an A—from CDP, for the past three years (CDP "Search", n.d.-b).

Colgate-Palmolive sells its products in more than 200 countries and territories and is focused on Oral Care, Personal Care, Home Care, and Pet Nutrition. Its alignment with stringent sustainability and social impact goals has a significant impact in addressing climate change and its threat to disrupt our lives—from environmental impacts like weather events, water security and biodiversity, to food supply, to socioeconomic stability.

The Colgate brand is in more homes than any other. Since 80% of the company's GHG emissions are attributable to the use and disposal of its products, its strategy is to seek to avoid emissions by providing consumers with more sustainable products which often have lower carbon footprints, such as a recyclable toothpaste tube. Colgate-Palmolive also seeks to eliminate plastic waste. Specifically, it commits to eliminate a third of new plastics and achieve 100% recyclable, reusable, or compostable plastic packaging by 2025. The company also engages with NGOs, such as The Recycling Partnership to encourage recycling. For residual amounts of emissions that originate from its business activities, the company seeks to use carbon removal and mitigation tactics based on proven nature-based solutions, such as forest protection and reforestation initiatives (Colgate-Palmolive, 2022).

Furthermore, since the sourcing of ingredients and packaging accounts for 80% of the company's purchased goods and services emissions, Colgate-Palmolive is working with its suppliers "to encourage them to set science-based climate targets, assess their climate and water risks, improve their energy and water efficiency and increase their use of renewable energy" (Ibid.).

Colgate partners with numerous NGOs, governments, and companies to advance climate justice and equity. We recognize that the burdens imposed by climate change are unequal across social groups. Often those with the smallest contribution to climate change are the worst affected by it. The livelihoods of the world's most vulnerable are often threatened by the adverse effects of climate change. Through work that it conducts with its partner Earthworm Foundation supporting our Palm Oil Program, Colgate engages with small holder farmers, communities and local governments in Indonesia, Malaysia and Latin America. These projects focus on building capacity with farmers and communities to implement good forest management practices, implementing conservation practices for existing forests and engaging with governments to ensure beneficial land use planning to protect standing forests (Tracy Email, 2023). Additionally, Colgate-Palmolive works with GlobeScan on the Nature Agenda Project, "which is a shared research and engagement program that is supported by 26 member companies" (Colgate-Palmolive, 2022).

Importantly, the company's board of directors regards sustainability as being critically important to the company's overall business and growth strategy and plays an essential role providing guidance and oversight. The new independent board chair, Lorrie Norrington, brings significant ESG expertise to the Nominating, Governance and Corporate Responsibility Committee. She is the Operating Partner with Lead Edge Capital, and formerly led global operations for eBay. Ann Tracy, Chief Sustainability Officer, Colgate-Palmolive, share the company's perspective.

> At Colgate-Palmolive, our purpose to reimagine a healthier future for all people, their pets, and our planet inspires our people and drives our business strategy. While we've been focused on sustainability and social impact for over two decades, we recognize that ESG efforts are increasingly important to investors, retailers, and consumers, which is why this work is embedded into our strategy. We're committed to continue innovating and leading in this space. And to tackle the biggest, most complex challenges, we plan to continue focusing on partnerships between the public and private sectors, as well as academic and industry associations. Together, we will work to build a better future. (Tracy, 2023)

An Industry-Led Collaboration for Sustainable Production and Sourcing of Commodities

"Private-sector collaboration for sustainable development is essential to making progress with the global roadmap provided by the SDGs," according to a research report published by The Rockefeller Foundation with BSR (Enright et al., 2018). Given the daunting challenges described in the Global Risks Report 2023 report, issued by the World Economic Forum (WEF), it is clear that collaboration is required to address newly emerging and rapidly accelerating economic, environmental, societal, geopolitical, and technological risks (World Economic Forum, 2023). WEF's analysis talks about a potential "polycrisis," "relating to shortages in natural resources, such as food, water, and metals and minerals."

BSR has been a leader in forming and sometimes spinning off industry-led collaborations that have resulted in progress addressing social, economic, and environmental challenges. The organization's recipe for successful corporate collaboration is based on its experience iteratively assessing and enhancing 56 initiatives. "We constantly examine ways to incentivize companies to engage productively to drive the best results," explains Sara Enright, Director of BSR's collaborative programs. BSR works with hundreds of businesses and stakeholders to design, implement, and scale collaborative initiatives to strengthen company performance, improve markets and industries, and contribute to systemic change for a more just and sustainable world (Enright et al., 2018).

Formed in 2019, Action for Sustainable Derivatives (ASD) is a collaborative initiative, co-managed and co-facilitated by BSR and Transitions, two organizations with extensive experience and expertise in supply chain sustainability and business collaborations. Together, the two NGOs bring together participants in the palm oil derivatives supply chain to "transform supply chains by increasing transparency, monitoring risks, reengaging the sector, and generating on-the-ground impacts." The mission of ASD is to "achieve a palm derivative supply chain that upholds No Deforestation, No Peat, No Exploitation principles (NDPE), respects human rights, and supports local livelihoods" (Action for Sustainable Derivatives, 2021).

The industry-led platform brings together companies in the palm derivatives and oleochemical sectors to collectively tackle supply chain issues around palm oil and palm kernel oil derivatives. Originally focusing on palm derivatives, ASD has begun expanding its work to other commodities, including coconut and soy derivatives (Action for Sustainable Derivatives website, 2021).

Palm oil is an edible vegetable oil derived from the fruit of oil palm trees. The oil is used in food manufacturing, in beauty products, and as biofuel. In fact, palm oil is in close to fifty percent of the packaged products found in supermarkets (WWF, n.d.). The trees are native to Africa but were brought to South-East Asia more than a hundred years ago as an ornamental tree crop. Now, Indonesia and Malaysia provide over 85% of global supply but there are 42 other countries that also produce palm oil (Ibid.).

Palm oil drives deforestation of some of the world's most biodiverse forests. Forest loss coupled with conversion of carbon rich peat soils releases millions of metric tons of greenhouse gases into the atmosphere, thereby accelerating climate change. Additionally, this is an industry that exploits workers and child labor (Scott & Kusbiantoro, 2021).

"Boycotting palm oil is not the answer," according to the World Wildlife Fund (WWF). There are millions of smallholder farmers who depend on producing palm oil for their livelihoods. "Instead, we need to demand more action to tackle the issues and go further and faster. The best thing we can do is support sustainable palm oil" (WWF, n.d.).

ASD facilitates the sharing of information, data, constraints, and solutions to achieve a wholescale transformation of the complex palm derivatives sector. Achievements of this industry-led initiative in 2022 include collective transparency for 825,000 tons of palm-based materials—nearly double the volume covered during the first year of ASD (Action for Sustainable Derivatives, 2022). ASD's work helps to advance four UN Sustainable Development Goals (SDGs), including SDG12: Responsible consumption and production, SDG13: Climate action, SDG15: Life on land, and SDG17: Partnerships for the goals.

There is an additional aspect of ASD that makes it particularly unique. ASD launched a collective social impact fund that enables ASD members to coordinate on social and environmental philanthropic support, in addition to the transparency mapping. Companies contribute to the pooled fund, which aims to address root causes of social and environmental inequalities and injustices in source regions. As described in ASD's 2022 Progress Report:

[The Impact Fund is] aimed at driving positive impact in priority production landscapes, moving beyond risk mitigation, and working as a lever for positive change. Developed in partnership with the Tides Foundation, the ASD Impact Fund enables ASD members to pool funding and collectively support projects on the ground. The ASD Impact Fund kicked off its impact work with support for the Kaleka Mosaik Initiative. This five-year project aims to sustainably restore the landscape and drive economic growth in two of the largest palm producing districts in Central Kalimantan, Indonesia, from which contributing ASD members source an average of 2% of their palm derivatives. Project activities include certification of smallholder farmers, incentivizing community conservation of natural forests, community-based restoration and forestry, enhancing use of fire-free agriculture, encouraging protection of natural forests, and restoration of forests. (Ibid.)

Food Systems Summits Address Hunger, Farmer Livelihoods, and Climate Change

As many as 828 million people across the world go hungry every day. The number of people suffering from hunger has grown by 150 million since 2019, largely due to the COVID pandemic, global conflict, and the climate crisis. 45% of child deaths are attributed to hunger and related causes. The vast majority of people who go hungry live in developing countries, where extreme poverty and lack of access to nutritious food often leads to malnutrition. Women and children are particularly vulnerable (Action Against Hunger, 2023).

In the United States, over 34 million people, including 9 million children, are food insecure, which is defined as a lack of consistent access to enough food for every person in a household to live an active, healthy life. Causes of food insecurity include poverty, unemployment, or low income; lack of affordable housing; chronic health conditions or lack of access to healthcare; and systemic racism and racial discrimination. According to Feeding America, the largest charity working to end hunger in the United States, "hunger in the African American (Feeding America "Black Communities", 2023a) Latino, (Feeding America "Latino Communities", 2023c), and Native American (Feeding America "Native American Communities", 2023b) communities is higher because of systemic racial injustice. To achieve a hunger-free America, we must address the root causes of hunger and structural and systemic inequities" (Feeding America website, 2023).

There are costs to business as well as humanity. According to the Intergovernmental Science-Policy Platform on Biodiversity and Ecosystem Services (*IPBES*), "land degradation has reduced the productivity of 23% of the global land surface, up to $577 billion in annual global crops are at risk from pollinator loss and 100–300 million people are at increased risk of floods and hurricanes because of loss of coastal habitats and protection" (IPBES, 2019).

Moreover, it is important to recognize the role of violent conflict, which in 2021 "was the primary driver of food insecurity around the world, with 99 million people in 23 countries experiencing acute food insecurity due to unrest and insecurity" (World Food Programme, n.d.). Violence and hunger are inextricably linked. Drought often forces mass numbers of farmers from their lands to the cities, where there are insufficient jobs and infrastructure and a lack of government response. It has been argued that drought and the poor governmental response were contributing factors leading to Syria's civil war (Friedman, 2013).

Zero hunger, which is the first of the UN Sustainable Development Goals (SDG1), established in 2015, cannot be achieved without stability. The World Food Program (WFP) points out that "food insecurity inevitably worsens when fighting drives large numbers of people from their homes, land and livelihoods, and when it restricts access to people in need of life-saving assistance." Together with the Stockholm International Peace Research Institution (SIPRI), the WFP conducted research to determine best practices in advancing peace. Their recommendations included "enhancing access to contested natural resources (e.g., water, land); bolstering social cohesion and resolving grievances within and between communities; increasing opportunity and inclusion, including for youth; and increasing citizen-state trust by contributing to strengthening state accountability and service delivery" (World Food Programme, n.d.).

Over the course of three "Summit Dialogues" attended by Alice Korn-gold in 2022 and early 2023, a variety of stakeholders convened to plan and commit to solutions to the world's food crisis. Sponsors included Bayer, a global enterprise with core competencies in the life sciences fields of health-care and agriculture, and Clim-Eat, an NGO think-and-do tank that aims to accelerate food systems transformation under climate change; and the World Farmers Association. In each of the three summit dialogues, approximately 65 participants from companies, including Unilever and DSM; NGOs, including the World Business Council for Sustainable Development (WBCSD) and the Global Foodbanking Network; research institutions; and intra-governmental organizations joined in large and small group discussions.

Topics included pressing issues on the climate change and food security agenda such as equitable livelihoods, smallholder farmers, nature-positive production, research and science for innovation, sustainable consumption patterns, safe and nutritious food for all, soil health, finance for resilient supply chains, tech solutions for climate-smart regenerative food systems, youth as a driving force, and market demand for nutritious and healthy, environmentally sustainable consumption.

Diane Holdorf from the WBCSD stressed the important role for companies, in their own interests as well as the interests of society: "Frontrunners have shown that businesses which do take action can successfully reverse their negative impact on nature and generate business benefits: the potential finan-cial upside for business is currently estimated at USD $10 trillion annually by 2030" (Holdorf, 2022).

David Nabarro served as moderator at the January 2023 Summit. Nabarro is Co-Director, Institute of Global Health Innovation, Imperial College of London. Agnes Kalibata was a featured speaker. She is President, Alliance for Green Revolution in Africa (AGRA). Additional speakers and facilita-tors included Tania Strauss, Head of Strategy and Global Projects, Food Systems Initiative, World Economic Forum (WEF); Rodrigo Santos, Presi-dent, Bayer Crop Science Division, Bayer; Arnold Puech d'Allisac, President, World Farmers Association; and Natasha Santos, Head of Global Stake-holders Affairs and Strategic Partnerships, Vice President, Bayer. At the prior two Summits, Danush Dinesh served as the moderator. Dinesh is Founder, Clim-Eat.

Participants focused on ways to transform food systems to become climate-smart and nature-positive to benefit people and nature; improve soil health and increase yields, reduce food loss and food waste; maximize biodiver-sity and ecosystem functions; improve livelihoods; address gender inequities;

engage the next generation; and enhance resilience to climate change. Solutions developed during the summits emphasized the needs of low- and middle-income countries, and the needs of smallholder farmers. Action plans addressed ways to engage the private sector and accelerate the adoption of regenerative management practices.

Dr. Agnes Kalibata addressed two of the summits convened by Bayer and Clim-Eat reported on the hundreds of Independent Dialogues of the UN Food Systems Summit. "From discussions on the rights of women, youth and Indigenous Peoples to support for small businesses and smallholders, the results of the Independent Dialogues show that we all share the same goal of a stronger, healthier and more inclusive food system." Agnes Kalibata, is the UN Secretary-General's Special Envoy for the 2021 Food Systems Summit (Kalibata, 2021).

Some companies recognize that businesses bring vital resources to drive change. They also understand that challenges are systemic, so solutions must be as well. As a result, collaboration is essential, including with partners on the ground. According to Rodrigo Santos, Member of the Board of Management of Bayer AG, and President of Bayer's Crop Science Division:

> With their expertise, innovation and customer focus, businesses are uniquely positioned to lead the change to a better future. Take agriculture: Farming is central to food security and climate challenge, especially in some rural areas across Africa, Southeast Asia or Latin America, where resources are scarce and access to training limited. While companies like Bayer offer much-needed solutions to curb greenhouse gases and better produce food using less resources, partners are crucial, both internationally and on the ground, to combine strengths, accelerate impact and deliver at scale. (Santos, 2023)

Diane Holdorf, of the WBCSD, shares a similar perspective. "Leading companies of all sizes continue to show how innovation and operationalizing sustainability drive solutions to address climate change, protect nature, and advance equity and inclusion. Working together across value chains and sectors scales these solutions. Accelerating these transitions is even more urgent now" (Holdorf, 2023b).

Participants work together in between summits to plan and implement specific initiatives to which they have committed. Gabriela Burian explains below. Burian is the Global Head of Multi-Stakeholder Partnerships at Bayer Crop Science, and Liaison Delegate with the World Business Council for Sustainable Development (WBCSD) (Burian, 2023).

Although each company and organization must be ambitious in its own goals, we know that we can accomplish more when we work in collaboration. So, together with Clim-Eat and the World Farmers Organization, we have assembled a group of diverse leaders from a variety of organizations – businesses, NGOs, farmer groups, academic institutions, and governments – from across the world. Together, we explore different perspectives and co-create new solutions for more sustainable food systems – systems that can be adapted to the reality in each region, and with farmers at the center.

"Ultimately, the test will be in the results. We must hold ourselves accountable for measurable progress in advancing food security, mitigating climate change, and protecting vital natural resources," she adds (Ibid.).

Businesses Can Lead in Addressing Climate and Environment Challenges

"The current global energy crisis is a pivotal moment for clean energy transitions worldwide, driving a wave of investment that is set to flow into a range of industries over the coming years" (International Energy Agency, 2022). This is the prediction of the International Energy Agency in its report, Energy Technology Perspectives 2023.

There is a global market opportunity for key mass-manufactured clean energy technologies worth around $650 billion a year by 2030, more than three times today's level. Related clean energy manufacturing jobs would more than double from 6 million today to nearly 14 million by 2030, with over half of these jobs tied to electric vehicles, solar PV, wind, and heat pumps. As clean energy transitions advance beyond 2030, this would lead to further rapid industrial and employment growth. (Ibid.)

The companies featured in this chapter are profiting by reducing costs through energy efficiencies, and by creating and selling products and services to meet the demands of businesses and consumers seeking to reduce their expenses and carbon footprint. These companies are benefiting while improving the world. Although governments have endorsed the principle that global warming must be contained, more is needed. Customers, employees, and investors can continue to play an important role in driving the sustainability agenda, by voting with their dollars and feet for companies who share their values.

Bayer is a current client of Korngold Consulting LLC.

References

Action Against Hunger. (2023). World hunger facts. https://www.actionagainsthu nger.org/the-hunger-crisis/world-hunger-facts/. Accessed 31 Jan 2023.

Action for Sustainable Derivatives. (2021). About us. https://sustainablederivatives. org/about. Accessed 31 Jan 2023.

Action for Sustainable Derivatives. (2022, November). Annual update on progress 2022: Driving action on derivatives. https://static1.squarespace.com/static/ 6166ce0aec25090d097ac817/t/637e62b274e61a222ed78eec/1669227245749/ ASD+Annual+Update+on+Progress+2022.pdf. Accessed 31 Jan 2023.

Action for Sustainable Derivatives website. (2021). https://sustainablederivatives. org/. Accessed 31 Jan 2023.

American Security Project. (n.d.). Climate security is national security. https://www. americansecurityproject.org/climate-security/. Accessed 31 Jan 2023.

Arewa, O. B. (2021). *Disrupting Africa: Technology, law, and development.* Cambridge University Press.

Arimah, B. C. (n.d.). Slums as expressions of social exclusion: Explaining the preva-lence of slums in African countries. https://www.oecd.org/dev/pgd/46837274. pdf. Accessed 31 Jan 2023.

Bates, M. (2023, January 12). Interview with Alice Korngold.

Blaine, T. (2021, July 19). Climate change risks new violence conflict. How to respond? United States Institute of Peace. https://www.usip.org/publications/ 2021/07/climate-change-risks-new-violent-conflict-how-respond. Accessed 31 Jan 2023.

BSR. (2023a). Business transformation for a just and sustainable world ("Transfor-mation"). https://www.bsr.org/. Accessed 31 Jan 2023a.

BSR. (2023b). Equity, inclusion, and justice: Driving social justice at an individual and systematic level ("EIJ"). https://www.bsr.org/en/focus/equity-inclusion-and-justice. Accessed 31 Jan 2023b.

Burian, G. (2023, January 18). Interview with Alice Korngold.

Busby, J. W. (2007). Climate change and national security: An agenda for action. Council of Foreign Relations Press. https://www.cfr.org/report/climate-change-and-national-security. Accessed 28 Jan 2023.

C40Cities. (2023a). What we do ("What"). https://www.c40.org/what-we-do/sca ling-up-climate-action/energy-and-buildings/#:~:text=Buildings%20are%20resp onsible%20for%20more,part%20of%20all%20climate%20action. Accessed 31 Jan 2023a.

C40Cities. (2023b). Who we are ("Who"). https://www.c40.org/about-c40/. Accessed 31 Jan 2023b.

CDP. (2021). Putting a price on carbon: The state of internal carbon pricing by corporates globally. https://cdn.cdp.net/cdp-production/cms/reports/documents/ 000/005/651/original/CDP_Global_Carbon_Price_report_2021.pdf?161893 8446. Accessed 31 Jan 2023.

CDP. (2022, September). Missing the mark: 2022 analysis of global CDP temperature ratings. https://cdn.cdp.net/cdp-production/cms/reports/documents/000/006/544/original/Missing_the_Mark_-_CDP_temperature_ratings_analysis_2022.pdf?1662412411. Accessed 31 Jan 2023.

CDP. (n.d.-a). CDP scores explained ("Explained"). https://www.cdp.net/en/scores/cdp-scores-explained. Accessed 31 Jan 2023.

CDP. (n.d.-b). Search and view past CDP responses—Colgate-Palmolive ("Search"). https://www.cdp.net/en/responses?page=2&per_page=5&queries%5Bname%5D=colgate+palmolive&sort_by=project_year&sort_dir=desc. Accessed 31 Jan 2023.

CDP website. (2023). https://www.cdp.net/en. Accessed 31 Jan 2023.

Centers for Disease Control and Prevention (CDC). (2022, May 31). Global WASH fast facts. https://www.cdc.gov/healthywater/global/wash_statistics.html#:~:text=Find%20information%20on%20how%20safe,hygiene%20service%20levels%20are%20defined.&text=2%20billion%20people%20lack%20access,have%20basic%20drinking%20water%20service. Accessed 31 Jan 2023.

CITES. (2022). Nineteenth meeting of the Conference of the Parties. https://cites.org/eng/cop19. Accessed 31 Jan 2023.

City of Boston. (2023). Building emissions reduction and disclosure. https://www.boston.gov/departments/environment/building-emissions-reduction-and-disclosure. Accessed 31 Jan 2023.

Colgate-Palmolive Company. (2022). Climate transition and net zero action plan. https://www.colgatepalmolive.com/content/dam/cp-sites/corporate/corporate/common/pdf/2022-climate-transition-net-zero-action-plan.pdf. Accessed 31 Jan 2023.

Congressional Budget Office. (2022, December). Emissions of carbon dioxide in the transportation sector. https://www.cbo.gov/publication/58566. Accessed 31 Jan 2023.

Convention on Biological Diversity. (2022, December 19). Press release—COP15: Nations adopt four goals, 23 targets for 2030 in landmark UN biodiversity agreement. https://www.cbd.int/article/cop15-cbd-press-release-final-19dec2022. Accessed 31 Jan 2023.

Cornwall, W. (2021, July 20). Europe's deadly floods leave scientists stunned. Science. https://www.science.org/content/article/europe-s-deadly-floods-leave-scientists-stunned. Accessed 31 Jan 2023.

Dasgupta, S., Lall, S., & Wheeler, D. (2022, January 5). Cutting global carbon emissions: Where do cities stand? World Bank. https://blogs.worldbank.org/sustainablecities/cutting-global-carbon-emissions-where-do-cities-stand. Accessed 31 Jan 2023.

Donnelly, L., Pugliesi, J., & Leitheiser, E. (2022, December 20). COP15: A historic deal to halt biodiversity loss by 2030. BSR. https://www.bsr.org/en/blog/cop15-a-historic-deal-to-halt-biodiversity-loss-by-2030. Accessed 31 Jan 2023.

Earth Overshoot Day website. (2023). https://www.overshootday.org/. Accessed 31 Jan 2023.

Eckstein, D., Kunzel, V., & Schafer, L. (2021). Global climate risk index 2021—who suffers the most from extreme weather events? Weather-related loss events in 2029 and 2000–2019. German Watch. https://www.germanwatch.org/sites/def ault/files/Global%20Climate%20Risk%20Index%202021_2.pdf. Accessed 31 Jan 2023.

Economist. (2022, June 15). The construction industry remains horribly climate-unfriendly. https://www.economist.com/finance-and-economics/2022/06/15/ the-construction-industry-remains-horribly-climate-unfriendly. Accessed 31 Jan 2023.

Einhorn, C. (2022, December 19). Nearly every country signs on to a sweeping deal to protect nature. *New York Times*. https://www.nytimes.com/2022/12/19/ climate/biodiversity-cop15-montreal-30x30.html. Accessed 31 Jan 2023.

Enright, S., Oger, C., Pruzan-Jorgensen, P. M., & Farrag-Thibault, A. (2018, February 28). Private-sector collaboration for sustainable development. BSR. https://www.bsr.org/en/reports/private-sector-collaboration-for-sustainable-development. Accessed 31 Jan 2023.

Equal Justice Initiative (EJI). (2018). Slavery in America: The Montgomery slave trade. https://eji.org/report/slavery-in-america/. Accessed 31 Jan 2023.

Feeding America. (2023a). Hunger hits Black communities harder ("Black communities"). https://www.feedingamerica.org/hunger-in-america/black-communities. Accessed 31 Jan 2023a.

Feeding America. (2023b). Hunger impacts Native American families and communities ("Native American communities"). https://www.feedingamerica.org/hun ger-in-america/native-american. Accessed 31 Jan 2023b.

Feeding America. (2023c). Latino communities experience hunger at a much higher rate ("Latino communities"). https://www.feedingamerica.org/hunger-in-america/latino-hunger-facts. Accessed 31 Jan 2023c.

Feeding America website. (2023). https://www.feedingamerica.org/. Accessed 31 Jan 2023.

Ford Foundation. (2023). Natural resources and climate change. https://www.for dfoundation.org/work/challenging-inequality/natural-resources-and-climate-cha nge/. Accessed 31 Jan 2023.

Friedman, T. (2013, May 18). Without water, revolution. *New York Times*. https:/ /www.nytimes.com/2013/05/19/opinion/sunday/friedman-without-water-revolu tion.html?pagewanted=1&_r=3&hpw%20(June%209,%202013). Accessed 28 Jan 2023.

Higuero, I. (2023, January 9). SG's reflections on CITES, COP19 outcomes. CITES. https://cites.org/eng/news/sg/reflection-on-cites-cop19-outcomes#:~: text=The%20record%2Dbreaking%20365%20decisions,and%20existence% 20for%20future%20generations. Accessed 31 Jan 2023.

Hill, A. C. (2022, October 4). The United States needs to prepare for more billion-dollar climate disasters like Hurricane Ian. Council of Foreign Relations. https://www.cfr.org/in-brief/us-hurricane-ian-billion-dollar-damage-cli mate-change-disaster. Accessed 31 Jan 2023.

Holdorf, D. (2022, December 8). Accelerating business along the road to a nature-positive future ("Accelerating"). https://www.wbcsd.org/Overview/News-Insights/WBCSD-insights/Accelerating-business-along-the-road-to-a-nature-positive-future Accessed 31 Jan 2023.

Holdorf, D. (2023a). Closing reflections from Davos2023a ("Reflections"). https://www.linkedin.com/posts/diane-holdorf_davos2023a-cop28-activity-7022199254630723584-LdD1?utm_source=share&utm_medium=member_desktop. Accessed 31 Jan.

Holdorf, D. (2023b, February 3). Email to Alice Korngold.

Integrated Panel on Climate Change (IPCC). (2018). Global warming of 1.5C. https://www.ipcc.ch/sr15/. Accessed 31 Jan 2023.

Integrated Panel on Climate Change (IPCC). (2021). Climate change 2021: The physical science basis. https://www.ipcc.ch/report/ar6/wg1/. Accessed 31 Jan 2023.

Intergovernmental Panel on Climate Change (IPCC). (2022). Climate change 2022: Impacts, adaption and vulnerability. https://www.ipcc.ch/report/ar6/wg2/. Accessed 31 Jan 2023.

Intel. (n.d.-a). CTA: Driving the future of public transportation ("CTA"). https://www.intel.com/content/www/us/en/customer-spotlight/stories/chicago-transit-authority-customer-story.html. Accessed 31 Jan 2023a.

Intel. (n.d.-b). Smart city solutions for safer, more resilient communities ("Resilient"). https://www.intel.com/content/www/us/en/internet-of-things/smart-cities.html. Accessed 31 Jan 2023b.

Intel. (n.d.-c). Urban mobility and the future of smart transportation ("Smart"). https://www.intel.com/content/www/us/en/transportation/urban-mobility.html. Accessed 31 Jan 2023.

International Energy Agency. (2022, November). World energy outlook 2022. https://iea.blob.core.windows.net/assets/830fe099-5530-48f2-a7c1-11f35d510983/WorldEnergyOutlook2022.pdf. Accessed 31 Jan 2023.

International Energy Agency. (2023, January). Energy technology perspectives 2023. https://www.iea.org/reports/energy-technology-perspectives-2023. Accessed 31 Jan 2023.

International Science-Policy Platform on Biodiversity and Ecosystem Services (IPBES). (2019, May 6). Media Release—Nature's dangerous decline "unprecedented;" species extinction "accelerating". https://ipbes.net/news/Media-Release-Global-Assessment. Accessed 31 Jan 2023.

Joelson, T. (2023, January 13). Email to Alice Korngold.

Khan, S. (2022). C40: 2022 highlights. C40. https://www.c40.org/news/c40-2022-in-focus/. Accessed 31 Jan 2023.

Korngold, A. (2014). *A better world, inc.: How companies profit by solving global problems where governments cannot*. Palgrave Macmillan.

Leke, A., & Signe, L. (2019, January 11). *Spotlighting opportunities for business in Africa and strategies to succeed in the world's next big growth market*. Brookings. https://www.brookings.edu/research/spotlighting-opportunities-for-business-in-africa-and-strategies-to-succeed-in-the-worlds-next-big-growth-market/. Accessed 31 Jan 2023.

Lombrana, L. M. (2021, July 7). *Climate change linked to 5 million deaths a yar, new study shows*. Bloomberg. https://www.bloomberg.com/news/articles/2021-07-07/climate-change-linked-to-5-million-deaths-a-year-new-study-shows. Accessed 31 Jan 2023.

Muir, J. (1911). *My first summer in the Sierra*. Houghton Mifflin.

NAACP. (2023). Environmental and climate justice. https://naacp.org/know-issues/environmental-climate-justice. Accessed 31 Jan 2023.

National Aeronautics and Space Administration (NASA). (n.d.). The effects of climate change. https://climate.nasa.gov/effects/. Accessed 31 Jan 2023.

National Oceanic and Atmospheric Administration (NOAA). (2023, January 12). 2022 was world's 6th-warmest year on record. https://www.noaa.gov/news/2022-was-worlds-6th-warmest-year-on-record. Accessed 31 Jan 2023.

New York City. (2023). Sustainable buildings: Local Law 97. https://www.nyc.gov/site/sustainablebuildings/ll97/local-law-97.page. Accessed 31 Jan 2023.

Niranjan, A. (2021, May 20). Extreme weather forces people to flee homes. *DW*. https://www.dw.com/en/climate-refugees-migration-displacement/a-57585752. Accessed 31 Jan 2023.

Oxfam. (2023). How does climate change affect poverty and inequality? https://www.oxfamamerica.org/explore/issues/climate-action/climate-change-and-inequality/. Accessed 31 Jan 2023.

Population Matters. (2023). Resources and consumption. https://populationmatters.org/resources-consumption. Accessed 31 Jan 2023.

Quinney, M. (2021, June 2021). *New report shows why fighting climate change and nature loss must be interlinked*. World Economic Forum. https://www.weforum.org/agenda/2021/06/new-report-shows-biodiversity-key-to-fighting-climate-change/. Accessed 1 Jun 2023.

Quinson, T. (2022, September 28). *Moody's has a $1.9 trillion warning over biodiversity*. Bloomberg. https://www.bloomberg.com/news/articles/2022-09-28/moody-s-1-9-trillion-warning-over-biodiversity-green-insight#xj4y7vzkg?leadSource=uverify%20wall. Accessed 31 Jan 2023.

Santos, R. (2023, February 2). Email to Alice Korngold.

Science Based Targets. (n.d.). Ambitious corporate climate action. https://sciencebasedtargets.org/. Accessed 31 Jan 2023.

Scott, K., & Kusbiantoro, R. (2021, August 31). *Creating opportunities for action: Advancing children's rights in the palm oil industry*. BSR. https://www.bsr.org/en/blog/opportunities-for-action-children-rights-in-the-palm-oil-industry. Accessed 31 Jan 2023.

Sharma, S. (2023, January 12). Interview with Alice Korngold.

Shining Hope for Communities (SHOFCO). (2022). Shifting the development paradigm. https://www.shofco.org/new-system-change1-3/. Accessed 31 Jan 2023.

Slaughter, A.-M. (2013, February). Preface. In C. E. Werrell & F. Femia (Eds.), *The Arab spring and climate change* (pp 1–6). Center for American Progress. https://www.americanprogress.org/wp-content/uploads/2013/02/ClimateChangeArabSpring.pdf

State of Washington, Department of Ecology. (n.d.). Climate Commitment Act. https://ecology.wa.gov/Air-Climate/Climate-Commitment-Act. Accessed 31 Jan 2023.

Statistica. (2022, August 5). Share of urban population living in slums in 2020, by region. https://www.statista.com/statistics/684694/percentage-of-world-urban-population-in-slums-by-region/. Accessed 31 Jan 2023.

STOXX. (n.d.). Global climate change leaders index. https://www.stoxx.com/document/Bookmarks/CurrentFactsheets/SXCCLEG.pdf. Accessed 31 Jan 2023.

Suarez-Orozco, M. (Ed.). (2019). *Humanitarianism and mass migration: Confronting the world crisis.* University of California Press.

Tew, S. (2023, January 15). Interview with Alice Korngold.

The Nature Conservancy. (n.d.). Mission. https://www.nature.org/en-us/about-us/who-we-are/. Accessed 31 Jan 2023.

The White House. (2023). Clean energy economy: A guidebook to the Inflation Reduction Act's investments in clean energy and climate action, version 2. https://www.whitehouse.gov/wp-content/uploads/2022/12/Inflation-Reduction-Act-Guidebook.pdf. Accessed 31 Jan 2023.

Tracy, A. (2023, January 26). Interview with Alice Korngold.

Trane Technologies. (2022, March 28). Sustainability in action: Mater Dei Hospital in Malta. https://blog.tranetechnologies.com/en/home/solutions-innovation/mater-dei-hospital-in-malta.html. Accessed 31 Jan 2023.

Trane Technologies. (2023). Corporate governance committees and charters. https://www.tranetechnologies.com/en/index/company/corporate-governance/corporate-governance-committees.html. Accessed 31 Jan 2023.

Trane website. (2022). https://www.trane.com/index.html. Accessed 31 Jan 2023.

United Nations. (2022). The sustainable development goals report 2022 ("SDG Report"). https://unstats.un.org/sdgs/report/2022/. Accessed 26 Jan 2023.

United Nations. (n.d.). Convention on Biological Diversity, key international instrument for sustainable development ("Convention"). https://www.un.org/en/observances/biological-diversity-day/convention#:~:text=The%20Convention%20on%20Biological%20Diversity,been%20ratified%20by%20196%20nations. Accessed 31 Jan 2023.

United Nations, Climate Action. (n.d.). Loss and damage: A moral imperative to act [interview with A Thomas]. https://www.un.org/en/climatechange/adelle-thomas-loss-and-damage. Accessed 31 Jan 2023.

United Nations, Climate Change. (n.d.). The Paris agreement ("Paris"). https://unf ccc.int/process-and-meetings/the-paris-agreement/the-paris-agreement. Accessed 31 Jan 2023.

United Nations Human Settlements Program (UN-HABITAT). (2020). World cities report 2022: Envisaging the future of cities. https://unhabitat.org/sites/def ault/files/2022/06/wcr_2022.pdf. Accessed 31 Jan 2023.

United Nations Population Fund. (2022). Urbanization. https://www.unfpa.org/ urbanization#:~:text=The%20world%20is%20undergoing%20the,swell%20to% 20about%205%20billion. Accessed 31 Jan 2023.

United Nations, Department of Economic and Social Affairs. (n.d.). The 17 goals ("SDGs"). https://sdgs.un.org/goals. Accessed 26 Jan 2023.

United Nations, Environment Programme. (2022a, November 22). COP27 ends with announcement of historic loss and damage fund ("COP27"). https://www. unep.org/news-and-stories/story/cop27-ends-announcement-historic-loss-and-damage-fund. Accessed 31 Jan 2023.

United Nations, Environment Programme. (2022b, October 27). Emissions gap report 2022b—The closing window: Climate crisis calls for rapid transformation of societies ("Emissions"). https://www.unep.org/resources/emissions-gap-report-2022b. Accessed 31 Jan 2023.

United Nations, Environment Programme. (n.d.). Facts about the climate emergency. https://www.unep.org/facts-about-climate-emergency. Accessed 31 Jan 2023c.

United Nations, Food and Agriculture Organization. (2021). The state of food security and nutrition in the world 2021: The world is at a critical juncture. https:// www.fao.org/state-of-food-security-nutrition/2021/en/. Accessed 31 Jan 2023.

United Nations, Global Compact. (n.d.). Business ambition for 1.5C. https://www. unglobalcompact.org/take-action/events/climate-action-summit-2019/business-ambition. Accessed 31 Jan 2023.

United Nations, Human Rights. (2022, July 12). Climate change exacerbates violence against women and girls. https://www.ohchr.org/en/stories/2022/07/ climate-change-exacerbates-violence-against-women-and-girls. Accessed 31 Jan 2023.

Werrell, C. E., & Femia, F. (Eds.). (2013, February). The Arab spring and climate change. Center for American Progress. https://www.americanprogress.org/wp-con tent/uploads/2013/02/ClimateChangeArabSpring.pdf. Accessed 31 Jan 2023.

Weston, P., & Greenfield, P. (2022, December 17). The US touts support for biodiversity—But at COP15, it remains on the sideline. *The Guardian*. https://www. theguardian.com/environment/2022/dec/17/cop15-us-biodiversity-cbd. Accessed 31 Jan 2023.

World Bank. (2022, October 6). Urban development: Overview. https://www. worldbank.org/en/topic/urbandevelopment/overview#:~:text=Today%2C% 20some%2056%25%20of%20the,people%20will%20live%20in%20cities. Accessed 31 Jan 2023.

World Bank Group. (2020). Reversals of fortune. https://openknowledge.worldb ank.org/bitstream/handle/10986/34496/9781464816024.pdf. Accessed 31 Jan 2023.

World Bank Group. (2021). The economic case for nature: A global Earth-economy model to assess development policy pathways. https://openknowledge.worldb ank.org/bitstream/handle/10986/35882/A-Global-Earth-Economy-Model-to-Ass ess-Development-Policy-Pathways.pdf?sequence=1&isAllowed=y. Accessed 31 Jan 2023.

World Economic Forum. (2022, May 24). One more reason to act fast on climate: Economics. https://www.weforum.org/agenda/2022/05/one-more-reason-for-rapid-climate-action-economics/. Accessed 31 Jan 2023.

World Economic Forum. (2023, January). The global risks report 2023. https://www3.weforum.org/docs/WEF_Global_Risks_Report_2023.pdf. Accessed 31 Jan 2023.

World Food Programme. (n.d.). Conflict and peace. https://www.wfp.org/conflict-and-peace. Accessed 31 Jan 2023.

World Health Organization (WHO). (2021, July 1). Billions of people will lack access to safe water, sanitation and hygiene in 2030 unless progress quadruples—Warn WHO, UNICEF. https://www.who.int/news/item/01-07-2021-bil lions-of-people-will-lack-access-to-safe-water-sanitation-and-hygiene-in-2030-unless-progress-quadruples-warn-who-unicef. Accessed 31 Jan 2023.

World Meteorological Organization. (2022a). Environment ("Environment"). https://public.wmo.int/en/our-mandate/focus-areas/environment. Accessed 31 Jan 2023.

World Meteorological Organization. (2022b). United in science ("Science") 2022b. https://library.wmo.int/doc_num.php?explnum_id=11308. Accessed 31 Jan 2023.

Worldometer. (2023). World population. https://www.worldometers.info/world-population/#growthrate. Accessed 31 Jan 2023.

WWF. (n.d.). 8 things to know about palm oil. https://www.wwf.org.uk/updates/8-things-know-about-palm-oil. Accessed 31 Jan 2023.

WWF. (2020). Knowledge hub. https://wwf.panda.org/discover/knowledge_hub/all_publications/living_planet_report_timeline/lpr_2012/demands_on_our_pla net/overshoot/. Accessed 31 Jan 2023.

WWF. (2022, November). Our climate's secret ally: Uncovering the story of nature in the IPCC Sixth Assessment Report. https://wwfint.awsassets.panda.org/dow nloads/wwf_our_climates_secret_ally_uncovering_the_story_of_nature_in_the_ ipcc_ar6.pdf. Accessed 31 Jan 2023.

3

Economic Development

*A human being is born into this world fully equipped not only to take care of him
or herself, but also to contribute to enlarging the well being of the world as a whole.
Let us join hands to give every human being a fair chance to unleash their energy
and creativity.*

Muhammad Yunus (2006)

THERE HAD BEEN STEADY PROGRESS IN REDUCING POVERTY DURING THE
PAST three decades, with particular gains in China and India. At the time
that the original edition of this book was being published, worldwide poverty
had dropped from 52% of the developing world's population in 1981, to
43% in 1990, to 22% in 2008. "The growth rates of the world's emerging
and developing economies have surged... Since 1980, over one billion people
around the world have ascended from poverty" (CSIS, 2013). That meant
that the developing world had achieved, five years ahead of the goal, the
United Nation's ambitions to cut the 1990 extreme poverty rate in half by
2015.

Unfortunately, however, there is a stunning reversal in the trajectory of
poverty due to the COVID-19 pandemic. The number of people living in
extreme poverty is growing for the first time in three decades. Rising inflation and the effects of the Russian invasion of Ukraine likely will exacerbate
the poverty crisis (United Nations "SDGs"). Between 657 and 676 million
people are projected to live in extreme poverty in 2022, compared to the
pre-pandemic estimate of 581 million (IISD, 2022).

© The Author(s), under exclusive license to Springer Nature
Switzerland AG 2023
A. Korngold, *A Better World, Inc.*,
https://doi.org/10.1007/978-3-031-31553-4_3

In addition to the growing number of people living in extreme poverty, there are 3.4 billion people, of the world's population of 8 billion, who are not considered extremely poor but who are recognized as being "vulnerable." They are people who have been seriously affected by recessions caused by COVID-19, price increases, and food and fuel shortages. Although many might have had opportunities to rise to the middle class under different global circumstances, they are at serious risk of being driven back financially as a result of a health, economic, or conflict shock. In a blog series originally launched by the Brookings Institution and the World Bank, economists recommend that governments pay attention to what they refer to as the forgotten 3 billion, "based on country-by-country risks characteristics to build more resilient populations" (Fengler et al., 2022).

Climate change is also driving increases in poverty, food insecurity, lost incomes, and poor health. "Tens of millions will be impoverished, leading to widespread displacement and hunger," according to Philip Alston, the UN Special Rapporteur on extreme poverty and human rights. "Climate change threatens to undo the last 50 years of progress in development, global health, and poverty reduction" (United Nations, Human Rights, 2019).

Furthermore, any advances have been grossly uneven in terms of countries, communities within countries, and particular groups of people. In spite of gains in China and India, for example, predictions are less promising elsewhere in Asia. Additionally, Afghanistan, Papua New Guinea, and North Korea are unlikely to end extreme poverty by the newly established 2030 timeframe (Kharas & Dooley, 2022). In Latin America, poverty rates have actually increased since 2015, in spite of more hopeful trends earlier in the twenty-first century (Ibid.). In Africa, poverty has continued to climb as a result of population growth, stagnant economic growth, and the pandemic. It is predicted that in the next decade, poverty will be concentrated in fragile and conflict-affected states primarily in sub-Saharan Africa (Ibid.). For women and girls worldwide, extreme poverty is projected to deepen (Korngold, 2014).

The United Nations established eight Millennium Development Goals (MDGs) following the UN Millennium Summit in 2000. Approved by the UN's member states and global institutions, the MDGs ranged from halving extreme poverty to halting the spread of HIV/AIDS and providing universal primary education, all by the target date of 2015.

In 2015, when the MDGs expired, all United Nations Member States established a new set of goals, referred to as the Sustainable Development Goals (SDGs). Described as a "shared blueprint for peace and prosperity for people and the planet, now and into the future," there are 17 SDGs designed to be achieved by 2030. This new 2030 Agenda includes 17 goals aimed to end poverty, together with improving health and education, reducing inequality, and stimulating economic growth, while also tackling climate change and working to conserve our oceans and forests (United Nations "SDGs").

Global Trends Present Threats as Well as Opportunities for Business

Companies Benefit by Investing in Economic Development

The private sector has played a pivotal role in promoting progress. According to a 2013 report by the Center for Strategic and International Studies, a nonprofit chaired by former US Senator Sam Nunn, the private sector, rather than US foreign assistance or philanthropy had become the key driver in advancing global prosperity. "At no other time in history has US foreign aid made up such a small share of global capital flows. In 1960, public capital accounted for 71% of financial flows to the developing world. As of 2013, it stood at only 9%. This aid and US leadership make a tremendous difference in international relations; the private sector, through its flows of capital, technology, and knowledge, has become a vital force in development" (CSIS, 2013).

By 2019, private sector finance had driven a steady increase in financial flows to developing countries. Private finance rose by 10% a year while public finance grew by only 2% a year. So that although public finance represented 64% of total financial flows to developing countries in 2010, public and private flows became almost equal by 2019 (Nishio & Tata, 2021).

For companies, alleviating poverty presents business opportunities, while simultaneously addressing a pernicious social issue. By helping to advance people from extreme poverty to the middle class, businesses anticipate achieving long-term strategic growth through access to new markets, workforce development, product innovation, and product distribution (Potter, 2012). In Africa, Asia, Latin America, and formerly Communist countries, businesses have been teaming up with NGOs, governments, and each other to foster employment, training and education, supply chain linkages, new products and services, business development, and regional capacity-building to strengthen economies (Korngold, 2014). Companies recognize that these locales will provide vast and growing market opportunities as wealth increases and consumers seek to increase their quality of life.

Dr. Allan Pamba, Executive Vice President, Diagnotics, Roche Africa, describes the scope of the opportunity for companies to invest in human capital development in Africa.

> Africa's greatest asset is not its mineral wealth -invisible under the ground, but rather its people who are very visible above ground! With a population of 1.4B people, average age 20 years, Africa is silently the envy of Europe, the US & Japan, big economies with ageing & even declining populations. Prioritizing Investments in Health, Education & Agriculture will elevate the quality of Africa's human Capital and certainly bring to life this huge Demographic dividend. Investment prioritization in Africa today is largely driven by short term political agendas and external parochial interests. These interests prioritize enabling infrastructure to extract its mineral resources. Local people are often outrightly ignored or moved around as pawns on a chessboard. For virtually all countries in Sub Sahara Africa, GDP allocation to Health sits below 10% and often is closer to the 3% mark. Africa will only truly accelerate development when she starts to take charge of her agenda and put her people first, nobody else is coming to do this. (Pamba, 2023)

Olufunmilayo Arewa describes the opportunity to invest in countries in Africa, as well as historic obstacles.

> The median age in Africa is under 20 years old. As we look to the future, African countries could be a potentially important source of future opportunities, growth, and prosperity, including for the majority of people within African countries. For Africans to benefit from and participate in such future opportunities, past patterns of doing business must be disrupted, including those that reflect colonial hangover. "Colonial Overhang" (or, "Colonial Hangover") has significant implications for digital-era participation, particularly because digital economy policies and laws relating to business, entrepreneurship, and innovation in many countries in Africa may lag behind other areas of the world and reflect norms of African marginalization. (Arewa, 2023)

Arewa's term, "Colonial Overhang," is defined in her book, *Disrupting Africa: Technology, Law, and Development* (Arewa, 2021). "Colonial overhang reflects continuing patterns of external determination and cut and paste borrowing that are far too often not sufficiently scrutinized."

Income Inequality Poses a Threat

Fifty-two percent of global income goes to the richest 10% of the global population, while only 8.5% is earned by the poorest half. A discrepancy that is even starker is the wealth gap. While 76% of all wealth is owned by the richest 10%, only 2% is owned by the poorest half of the people of the world (World Inequality Report, 2022). On the rise in most countries since the 1980s, inequality is highest in MENA, and has risen significantly in the United States, Russia, and India. East Asia and Latin America also see wide gaps. Europe has the lowest inequality levels. Economists point to these variations as evidence that inequality is a political choice, rather than an inevitability (Ibid.).

Particularly concerning is that wealth in rich countries is in private hands, while the share of wealth held by governments is close to zero. Without resources, states will not have the capacities to address major challenges of the century, from inequality itself to climate change (Ibid.).

Rising income and wealth inequality threaten economic development and the quality of life for entire societies. Income disparities drive health and social problems in countries worldwide and among states in the United States. Wealth inequality is a predictor of higher rates of crime and incarceration, threatening lives, degrading community resources, and contributing to social unrest (Sapolsky, 2018). A UN report cautions that rising inequality undermines trust in democracies and instead foments the rise of authoritarian and nativist movements (United Nations "UNDESA", 2020).

Global poverty threatens all of society, not only those who are marginalized. According to the International Monetary Fund, rising inequality in world income distribution can lead to "a large mass of unemployed and angry young people, mostly males, to whom the new information technologies have given the means to threaten the stability of the societies they live in, and even threaten social stability in countries of the wealthy zone" (Wade, 2001).

Gender and Racial Inequities Exacerbate Income Inequality

Gender inequalities continue to be high, with women earning only 35% of labor income, only a small improvement over 1990 when it was 30% (World Inequality Report, 2022). According to Oxfam, women are in the lowest paid jobs, earning 24% less than men; 700 million fewer women than men are in paid work; 75% of women in developing countries are in the informal economy, where they are less likely to have legal rights, social protections, or wages that are sufficient to rise out of poverty; and women do unpaid work that is valued at nearly eleven trillion dollars. Furthermore, Oxfam estimates that the economic costs to women in developing countries amounts to nine trillion dollars annually. Gender equality would not only be fair to women and good for families, but it would elevate entire economies (Oxfam Internet, n.d.).

Racial inequities continue to be driven by entrenched systemic barriers. In an article entitled "The [B]lack-white economic divide is as wide as it was in 1968," The Washington Post reports that while the median wealth of white households has tripled since the 1960s, the wealth of Black households has barely increased (Long & Van Dam, 2020). A New York Times article, entitled "A vast wealth gap, driven by segregation, redlining, evictions and exclusion separates Black and white America," shows how today's racial wealth gap is a legacy of American slavery and "the violent dispossession that followed." Without access to mortgages, Black families were systematically denied opportunities to grow wealth through home ownership (Lee, 2019). The Council on Foreign Relations cites both articles, showing that the unemployment rate for Black Americans has been twice that of white Americans for decades, and that Black Americans are vastly underrepresented in high paying professions, including in company c-suites (Siripurapu, 2022).

Impediments and threats to success include not only the pandemic, climate change, and corrupt governance, but also the lack of healthcare and education, and to a very great extent, negative attitudes toward girls and women. According to the UK's Department for International Development (DFID), girls and women bear a disproportionate burden of poverty in developing countries. Yet, it is possible to take effective, practical action that enables girls and women to fulfill their potential. Moreover, the benefits of investing in girls and women are transformational—for their own lives and for their families, communities, societies, and economies. Empowering girls and women has multiplier effects for economic growth. If we reach girls early enough in their lives, we can transform their life chances. Giving girls greater choice and control over decisions that affect them helps break the cycle of poverty between one generation and the next. This would enable us to stop poverty before it starts" (United Kingdom, 2011). DFID describes four pillars for action: delaying first pregnancy and supporting safe childbirth; channeling economic assets directly to girls and women; getting girls through secondary school; and preventing violence (Ibid.).

Poverty Threatens Business and Society

The vast majority of the world is poor, with almost four billion people out of a total world population of about eight billion, live on less than $6.70 a day (Roser, 2021). There are many reasons to care about the world's poorer citizens. Ethics, morality, and justice are motivating forces. Wealth inequality may also pose geo-political threats. "Global poverty is not solely a humanitarian concern. Over the long term, it can also threaten US national security," according to the results of an investigation conducted by Brookings (Rice, 2006). "In the twenty-first century, poverty is an important driver of transnational threats... With the advent of globalization and the rapid international movement of people, goods, funds, and information, transnational security threats can arise from and spread with dangerous speed to any part of the planet. They can emerge from remote regions and poor, weak states, turning them into potentially high-risk zones that may eventually, often indirectly, pose significant risks to distant peoples" (Rice, 2010). The report gives examples including deadly flu viruses, terrorist cell attacks on US navy vessels, the theft of biological or nuclear materials from poorly secured facilities in any of 40 countries, narcotics traffickers and crime syndicates, and flooding and other effects of climate change that can lead to millions of deaths.

In an article about Syria, "Without Water, Revolution," *New York Times* columnist Thomas Friedman asserted in 2013 that drought drove masses of farmers from their land to the cities, where there were insufficient jobs and infrastructure, and a lack of government response. The ensuing poverty ultimately led to frustration and civil war. "Young people and farmers starved for jobs—and land starved for water—were a prescription for revolution" (Friedman, 2013).

As shown in the chapter on climate change and energy, a special report by the Council on Foreign Relations as early as 2007 (Busby, 2007) brings attention to the destabilizing effects of storms, droughts, and floods. The threat arises from damage caused domestically from extreme weather, in addition to the disruption of "US interests in strategically important countries" (Busby, 2007). The Computer Network Assurance Corporation, a think tank funded by the US Navy, also released a report on climate change and national security prepared by a panel of retired US generals and admirals. The Council for Foreign Relations Special Report concluded that "declining food production, extreme weather events, and drought from climate change could further inflame tensions in Africa, weaken governance and economic growth, and contribute to massive migration and possibly state failure, leaving 'ungoverned spaces' where terrorists can organize."

It is in our power to create a better world where all people will have food, shelter, healthcare, an education, and the opportunity to work. There are three routes that must be pursued concurrently. First, the economies of regions where there has been extreme poverty must be transformed. Second, girls and women, as well as boys and men, must be empowered and provided access to education, healthcare, and the opportunity to earn a living. Third, in the United States, we must confront the legacy of slavery and the extreme discrimination and hardships the nation continues to inflict on Black Americans (Mineo, 2017). This vision of economic development and individual empowerment is possible when businesses, NGOs, and governments work in partnership. What is required is the regional infrastructure to promote and support education, healthcare, financial services, business development, regional capacity-building, open markets and free trade, and equal opportunity.

Marissa Shorenstein, who has held leadership positions at companies, in federal, state, and city government, and as an officer on multiple nonprofit boards, observes that:

> The business community has the power to shift not just global trends and markets—but to also shift economic power to a broader, more diverse, and more inclusive workforce that will ultimately lead to greater innovation, collaboration, and economic prosperity for all. While government and advocacy organizations play an important role in society's evolution to a more fair and equitable economy, global business has the market power and scale to more quickly move the needle and shift the paradigm. (Shorenstein, 2023)

Marissa Shorenstein is the Immediate Past Board Chair of Girls Who Code, a global NGO that is discussed in the Education chapter. She is also the former President of AT&T, Northern Region.

Corporations are realizing financial and strategic opportunities by investing in human, social, and economic capital in emerging markets and marginalized communities. This chapter shows examples of businesses serving as a powerful force in economic development and individual empowerment in some of the poorest regions of the world. By building stronger and more vibrant communities in previously impoverished areas, businesses, working in partnership with NGOs and governments, benefit by advancing all people toward prosperity. The cases in this chapter were selected for their innovation, variety, and impact, as well as for the capacity of the parties to accomplish their goals. Importantly, they show that the most effective approaches address challenges systemically, inclusively, and equitably.

Increasing Global Migration Affects Economies

Global migration has a powerful effect on economic development. Floods, droughts, storms, heat waves, fires, and sea level rise drive migration. So too do civil conflict, violence, human rights violations and persecution, and political unrest, often related to fierce competition for energy resources and land, as well as agricultural failure, rapid urbanization, failed government responses, and repressive regimes.

One hundred million people worldwide were forced to flee their homes in 2022 (United Nations "Displaced", 2022c). This is more than double the 42.7 million who remained forcibly displaced a decade ago, over three times the estimated number in 1970, and the most since World War II. "One hundred million is a stark figure—sobering and alarming in equal measure. It's a record that should never have been set," said UN High Commissioner for Refugees, Filippo Grandi (United Nations "UNHCR", 2022c). Conflicts and violence in Ethiopia, Burkina Faso, Syria, and Myanmar (Ibid.) drove the high numbers in addition to Russia's invasion of Ukraine.

The United States has been the main destination for international migrants since 1970. Since then, the number of foreign-born residents in the United States has quadrupled to 51 million, (Natarajan et al., 2022) in a national population of nearly 332 million.

While migration of large numbers of people can cause disruptions, it also represents a valuable opportunity, particularly to countries with declining demographics. In order to maintain current living standards and social support systems, the United States will require at least 35 million more workers by 2030. The EU will require an additional 80 million workers by 2050, and Japan will require another 17 million.

Peel away historic misconceptions and biases about migrants, immigrants, and asylum seekers, (Nowrasteh, 2021) and what remains is a powerful case for the value of migration to boost worldwide economies and innovation. This is in addition to the fundamental case for humanity. Welcoming strangers in a new land is an imperative in most teachings of ethics as well as religions.

Myriad studies show that immigrants generate wealth. This includes low-skilled workers as well as highly sought professionals with advanced degrees. Economist Michael Clemens demonstrates that workers in poor countries are underutilized, so that worldwide freedom of movement would in fact "increase the gross world product by between fifty and a hundred and fifty per cent" (Poll, 2020). Clemens points out that immigrants not only invest their own human capital by selling their labor, but they are also consumers of the products of other people's labor. As such, immigrants enrich communities (Pethokoukis, 2020). Consider the value of childcare workers, farm workers who harvest produce by hand, taxi drivers, and people who stock shelves in local markets, as well as Silicon Valley engineers, and high-profile stars such as entrepreneur Sergey Brin, authors Isabel Allende and Min Jin Lee, and the majority of players on the World Cup winning French soccer team (Onukwue & Shendruk, 2022).

Georgetown economist Anna Maria Mayda published a study in the National Bureau of Economic Research showing that for every H-1B worker that a company loses, the company hires 2.3 fewer US workers (Mayda et al., 2017). The H-1B visa allows employers to petition for highly educated foreign professionals to work in "specialty occupations," which are often positions in science, technology, engineering, and math. Clemens concludes that "extending equality means uncaging human potential," and that the world needs vision to recognize migration as the opportunity that it presents (Michael Clemens, n.d.).

McKinsey makes similar recommendations regarding the value of global migration.

> Moving more labor to higher-productivity settings boosts global GDP. Migrants of all skill levels contribute to this effect, whether through innovation and entrepreneurship or through freeing up natives for higher-value work. In fact, migrants make up just 3.4% of the world's population, but MGI's research finds that they contribute nearly 10% of global GDP. They contributed roughly $6.7 trillion to global GDP in 2015—some $3 trillion more than they would have produced in their origin countries. Developed nations realize more than 90% of this effect. (Woetzel et al., 2016)

Not only do migrants contribute to their new home countries, but they also enrich the countries they have left. In *Nomad Century: How Climate Migration Will Reshape Our World*, author Gaia Vince shows that "migrants also improve livelihoods, housing, education and opportunities in countries they physically leave behind because they remain economically linked to them" (Vince, 2022).

The World Bank reports that remittance flows remained resilient in 2020, despite COVID-19, showing a smaller decline than anticipated. Officially recorded remittance flows to low- and middle-income countries reached $540 billion in 2020, just 1.6% below the 2019 total of $548 billion. The shift in flows from cash to digital (see more in the next section) contributed to the steady flow (World Bank, 2021).

Many multinational companies recognize the strategic and financial opportunities presented by the growth in global migration. As demonstrated in the next case study, some businesses are benefiting themselves by investing in human capital development and employment of immigrants. They are advancing the vision of all people stimulating and sharing in global prosperity.

Companies and Nonprofits Partner to Invest in Human Capital

"Once a refugee gets a job, that's the moment they stop being a refugee," (TENT "Ulukaya", 2023) according to Hamdi Ulukaya, Owner, Founder, and Chairman of Chobani. Ulukaya himself immigrated to the United States from a small village in eastern Turkey. Five years after launching his company in 2007, Chobani became a billion-dollar brand. Today, it is the #1 selling yogurt in the United States. While further expanding the company and its food products, Ulukaya also established the Tent Partnership for Refugees (Tent) in 2016.

"We mobilize the business community to improve the lives and livelihoods of over. 36 million refugees forcibly displaced from their home countries," declares Tent (TENT, 2023). The partnership is comprised of over 300 multinational companies worldwide committed to including refugees. TENT provides research and assistance resources and services to advocate for and support companies in hiring, training, and mentoring refugees. Member companies represent a variety of industries, including technology and consumer goods, and financial and professional services firms.

"We focus on persuading and helping companies to integrate refugees for the long-term value to the company," explains Gideon Maltz, TENT's CEO, who has provided leadership to the nonprofit from the outset (Maltz, 2022). TENT shows that refugees have higher retention rates and are more willing to relocate for work. "It's their superpower," says Maltz. An additional benefit is strong consumer support for companies that include refugees, especially among young consumers, women, and people of color. Tent studies are conducted in partnership with global research institutions and NGOs. Materials include research papers, such as "Unlocking the Hidden Value: How Investing in Immigrant Talent Benefits Your Bottom Line," published by the nonprofit, Jobs for the Future, (Roberts, 2020) and guidebooks, such as "Guidance for European Countries Hiring Ukrainian Refugees," written by Tent in partnership with the law firm DLA Piper (TENT, 2022).

A study conducted by German economic consulting firm DIW Econ and sponsored by the Tent Partnership shows how effectively and sustainably companies were able to integrate refugees into their workforces while gaining loyal and talented employees. The study, based on the experiences of a hundred medium and large German companies, is particularly relevant given that Germany is a major destination for refugees, second only to the United States (United Nations UNHCR "2021 Report"). Results show that companies that hired refugees realized greater creativity, higher productivity, increased employee retention, and better marketing opportunities. Furthermore, 88% of the companies indicated plans to hire additional refugees in 2022 (DIW Econ, 2022).

The evidence supports the case for companies hiring refugees in the United States as well. Hiring refugees can benefit companies through higher retention rates (Dyssegaard & Roldan, 2018). Supporting refugees improves the perception of a brand among US consumers and increases sales, especially to younger consumers, women, and people of color. (Erdem et al., n.d.) Furthermore, immigrants and refugees are highly entrepreneurial. There are more than 3.2 million immigrant entrepreneurs, with a total business income of $88.5 billion, of which nearly 186,000 are refugees, with a total business income of $5 billion. Additionally, while they represent only 13.6% of the US population, immigrants account for 21.7% of business owners (New American Economy, n.d.).

Lilian Rauld, Head of Diversity, Equity, and Inclusion (DEI) for Sodexo and a big booster for Tent, did not need convincing of the case for hiring refugees (Rauld). Originally from Chile, now based in Sao Paulo, Brazil, Rauld herself researched the topic for her MBA thesis paper in 2014. At that time, refugees were arriving in Brazil from Syria, Congo, and Angola. Within a couple of years, while working at Sodexo, Rauld convinced the Vice President of Human Resources to hire its first refugee employee in their offices in Brazil. The number soon grew to 300. Then, making a commitment to Tent in 2018, Sodexo expanded its refugee hiring program to 1600 worldwide, including in the United States, Canada, and France. Refugee employees came from Haiti after each of the earthquakes, from Venezuela in 2018, and today from Pakistan and Afghanistan, among other countries.

Sodexo is a French food services and facilities management company, with over 400,000 employees, operating in 55 countries, and serving over 100 million customers daily. "Our company feeds employees and their customers, from public entertainment sites, museums, and zoos, to faculty and students in cafeterias at companies and universities worldwide," explains Rauld. She notes particular appreciation among university students who enjoy seeing Sodexo's food service employees from their own countries.

Having turned her MBA thesis into a book on the benefits to employers who employ refugees, Rauld soon became a useful resource to Tent and other corporations, including addressing a meeting of member companies in New York City in 2019. She speaks to the value of sharing research and ideas among Tent members.

Importantly, Sodexo recognizes the value of hiring and engaging people from a variety of backgrounds, including members of the LGBTQ+ community, people with disabilities, and people who were formerly incarcerated. "Our workforce must be reflective of the communities we serve." Gloria Puentes, Director, DEI External Strategic Partnerships at Sodexo, and Co-Lead, ONEsodexo, attests to higher retention rates, as well as personal and professional development among the broader employee community. "Retention rates are higher where people feel included."

While Tent provides the research and guidance to companies for hiring, supporting, and mentoring refugees, the organization relies on nonprofit partners to connect businesses with job candidates from the refugee community. Both Puentes at Sodexo and Maltz at Tent speak to the value of HIAS, the international Jewish humanitarian organization that provides vital services to refugees and asylum seekers and other forcibly displaced people in more than twenty countries. Originally established in the 1880s to aid Jewish refugees, today HIAS has offices throughout the United States, Europe, Africa, the Middle East, Latin America, and the Caribbean, to serve refugees of all backgrounds. Their tagline is "Welcome the stranger. Protect the refugee" (HIAS website).

With local partners on the ground in cities worldwide, HIAS helps refugees and asylum seekers find homes and connect with language learning centers and community colleges, as well as employment. Not only does HIAS assist companies that Tent has persuaded to hire refugees, but HIAS also provides information and support to Tent in advocating for better wages and benefits for refugees and asylum seekers. "Our interest is to help refugees and asylum seekers to become financially self-sufficient," explains Jessica Reese, Vice President of Institutional Development at HIAS (Reese, 2022). "Not only matching refugees and asylum seekers to jobs for their immediate financial well-being, but also to help refugees and asylum seekers pursue longer term career paths."

Reese at HIAS and Maltz at Tent also discuss the Airbnb Foundation's important role. As an independent nonprofit, the foundation's mission is to "unlock the power of sharing space, resources, and support in times of need."

For more than eight years, the foundation has assisted refugees with the Open Homes Initiative. Drawing on a variety of resources, from Airbnb company funding, private donations, and the generosity of hosts, Airbnb.org arranges housing for refugees free or at a discount. The foundation assists refugees coming from countries worldwide, including Afghanistan and Ukraine; they are provided with homes for up to thirty days in host communities worldwide. Housing is also arranged for people who flee from fires in California and hurricanes in the United States. "HIAS has been one of our oldest partners," explains Kemah George-Hertzog, who heads up Partnerships at Airbnb.org (George-Hertzos, 2022).

Maltz, Rauld, Puentes, Reese, and George-Hertzog appreciate the effectiveness of their partnerships. "HIAS is a powerhouse in this space, their reach is global, they are able to be flexible, and they have a tremendous impact worldwide," explains George-Hertzog from Airbnb.org. She also appreciates the trust and confidence that she and Reese share. For her part, Reese at HIAS comments that "we have to prove ourselves as valuable partners. We are interested in building long term relationships with corporate partners." Reese also observes that the COVID-19 crisis, along with wars in Ukraine and Afghanistan, have changed the way companies are engaging. "People at companies are giving thought to their values and aligning with issues that matter to them." Rauld at Sodexo talks about the synergy of purpose and mission, and the effectiveness of the partner. "Tent is always checking in, following up, seeing how they can be of further assistance. And, they can assist our company worldwide."

"Tent's role is to be the trusted intermediary between companies and nonprofits," explains Maltz at Tent. "We get companies excited about engaging. So we need nonprofit partners we can count on to effectively prepare and match people to jobs, often in multiple locations."

Together, companies are working together with nonprofits to ensure better lives for people who are escaping violence, poverty, and climate disasters, while investing in human capital to build better companies. This is vision.

Mobile Money Drives Systemic Change for an Inclusive Economy

Mobile money was a new technology innovation that made it possible for the first time for unbanked people living in poverty to participate in the economy by exchanging money for goods and services. Drawing in these previously excluded and ignored people ultimately became a financial boost for companies seeking to expand their presence and customer base in emerging markets.

The number of registered mobile money accounts in Kenya reached 67.9 million as of February 2022, (Statistica.com, n.d.) thereby surpassing the country's entire population of nearly 55 million people. (World Bank, n.d.). Launched in 2007 by Vodafone's Kenyan associate, Safaricom, M-PESA was the first mobile money service and fintech platform offered in Africa. M-PESA has since expanded to Tanzania, Mozambique, DRC, Lesotho, Ghana, Egypt, Afghanistan, and South Africa (Vodafone ,website). Mobile money is particularly prevalent in regions where the majority of people are too poor to have bank accounts, because fees and requirements are prohibitively expensive. Today, M-PESA's customers are making over $315 billion in transactions a year (McKinsey, 2022).

"Over the past ten years, mobile money has expanded from a niche offering in a handful of markets, to a global financial service connecting over a billion people to the formal economy, offering diverse services and improving lives and financial security" (GSMA, n.d.). Mobile money drives economic growth "by allowing easier access to larger amounts of trade credit." Additionally, "mobile money allows firms higher production, with important macroeconomic repercussions" (Beck, 2015). Mobile money has increased consumption expenditures, mitigated the effects of negative shocks, increased food security, and reduced extreme poverty. Furthermore, "mobile money impacted labor outcomes by allowing workers to shift into more productive occupations and firms to invest in fixed assets" (Bill & Melinda Gates Foundation, 2021). Mobile money drives systemic and inclusive progress in addressing poverty.

Vodafone and Safaricom Launched M-PESA in 2007

M-PESA is an electronic payment system accessible from ordinary mobile phones. It was developed by Vodafone, (Vodafone, website) a British multinational telecommunications company, and launched commercially by the company's Kenyan affiliate, Safaricom (Safaricom, website). With an M-PESA account, customers can use their phones to transfer funds to M-PESA users and non-users, pay bills, and purchase mobile airtime credit for a small, flat, per-transaction fee. The affordability of the service has provided access to formal financial services for impoverished people in Kenya. Pesa means "cash" in Swahili, so M-PESA means "mobile money."

Within just a few years, data showed strong evidence of M-PESA's market penetration with a previously ignored demographic. "Among the population outside Nairobi, during a period of four years when the prevalence of bank accounts remained relatively flat, the share of the unbanked who used M-PESA rose from about 21% in 2008 to 75% in 2011," according to *Slate* (Suri & Jack, 2012). "Similarly," the *Slate* article continued, "the share of non-Nairobi households with very low incomes who use M-PESA has also risen over time. According to our data, in 2008 fewer than 20% of the population outside the capital living on less than $1.25 per day used M-PESA, but by 2011, this share had steadily expanded to 72%."

Michael Joseph, who was managing director for Mobile Money for Vodafone and CEO of Safaricom in Kenya at the time of a 2013 interview, explained the origins of M-PESA (Joseph, 2013). Joseph recalled the period prior to 2007 when "there was a request for proposals (RFP) from the UK Department for International Development (DFID) to deepen the financial access of the unbanked people living in poverty." At that time, DFID led the UK government's fight against world poverty by implementing long-term projects "to help stop the underlying causes of poverty and respond to humanitarian emergencies" (Korngold, 2014). Joseph explained that "Nick Hughes, who was at Vodafone, came across this RFP and thought of using cell phones for the disbursement and repayment of microfinance loans. DFID awarded Vodafone £1 million which the company had to match. Hughes then approached a software company in Cambridge to write the original software program and build the hardware platform." By late 2006, Joseph said, Vodafone piloted the project in the town of Thika, just north of Nairobi, through his company Safaricom, in partnership with a microfinance provider, a bank, and other partners (Joseph, 2013).

Joseph explained that they soon observed that the participants used the phone for its ability to send money from one person to another, even though this was not the original intention of the project. So at Joseph's request, Hughes built a bigger and better platform to accommodate the interests of customers. "You see, many people leave their families to find work," Joseph said. "The challenge had been to find ways to send money home. You'd either have to travel home yourself, give the money to a bus driver, or not send it at all and leave them destitute" (Ibid.). In expanding the mobile phone service to provide banking services, Vodafone worked with the telecoms' regulator and the Central Bank of Kenya, the banking regulator. With the blessing of these two regulators to launch the mobile money products in March 2007, "the rest is history" (Ibid.).

"We pushed it hard. Added functionalities. Signed up a million subscribers in the first nine months. People could take money out of an ATM with their mobile phones, pay water and electricity bills, and buy air time," explained

Joseph. "This was not designed to be profitable, but rather to break even at best. And although this was a tremendous economic and social value for the community, this was not designed as a corporate social responsibility project. The business case was to build customer loyalty" (Joseph, 2013).

Joseph elaborated by explaining that at that time, there were four mobile phone operators in Kenya; it was a highly competitive market. Furthermore, the investment in software and hardware was very costly, and had been through many iterations. So it took a number of years and many mobile transactions for particular mobile services to become profitable. "This was about customer retention in a highly competitive market, and Safaricom was premium-priced. We wanted to keep subscribers in our network. That was the original intention." (Ibid.)

M-PESA soon became available in Tanzania, South Africa, and India. Joseph observed that there were many companies seeking to replicate M-PESA, but few were successful. He described M-PESA's unique success factors: "There's a lot of investment in making it work: in cash, dedication of effort, passion, and determination. It's a financial service that we are selling to poor people at the bottom of the pyramid. Not many companies have made that investment. Secondly, it's truly a social revolutionary product. It changes the lives of people enormously. People in emerging markets have no access to financial services in rural Africa. If you wanted to start a small business, you had to go to the city. M-PESA brought financial services to people's phones. And that enabled them to participate in the economy and conduct business. People are operating new businesses and feeling more secure." (Ibid.)

Joseph pointed out that by 2013, there were sixty to seventy thousand M-PESA agents throughout the country, so down the road they would be available for people throughout the country.

The M-PESA venture by Vodafone and Safaricom that originated in Kenya was designed to serve the companies' strategy of maintaining customer loyalty in order to build the bottom line over the long term. Ultimately, however, these pioneering companies achieved far more. They built their company revenues while empowering millions of people and entrepreneurs into a better life.

The Mobile Money Industry Is Growing in an Era of Economic Disruption

Economic disruptions stemming from the pandemic, climate change, and the Russian invasion of Ukraine are expected to hinder economic growth in the African continent in the coming year. These crises are also likely to drive an increase in the number of people who will fall into extreme poverty, climbing by more than two million additional people (African Development Bank Group, n.d.). In sub-Saharan Africa, the International Monetary Fund (IMF) predicts slow economic growth, given global financial conditions, rising food and energy process, public debt, and inflation (International Monetary Fund, 2022).

In this context, mobile money will be all the more important, particularly for low-income households (Ibid.). The value of mobile money transactions reached $1 trillion in 2021, the number of registered mobile money accounts worldwide has grown by tenfold, from 134 million in 2012 to over 1.35 in 2021 (GSMA, 2022). The number of mobile money providers doubled to 67 in the past decade.

New customer uptake and higher activity rates are driving growth, including for P2P (person to person), cash deposited, cash withdrawn, bulk disbursements for by employers for payrolls, merchant payments, bill payments, airtime, and international remittances. For P2P alone, the volume and frequency has jumped to 1.5 million transactions every hour. This is 22 times more than in 2012.

Africa dominates the world's mobile money transactions with seventy percent of its one trillion dollar value. Transaction values grew most significantly in the Middle East and North Africa (49%), sub-Saharan Africa (40%), and Latin America and the Caribbean (39%) (Onyango, 2022). The Global System for Mobile Communications (GSMA), an industry organization that represents the interests of mobile network operators worldwide, predicts further growth in existing markets in addition to newer markets in South Asia, and African counties, such as Nigeria, Ethiopia, and Angola.

As the mobile money pioneer, M-PESA continues to grow, with 51 million active customers across Kenya, Tanzania, the Democratic Republic of Congo, Mozambique, Lesotho, Ghana, and Egypt. Kenya accounts for more than 30 million customers (Safaricom, 2022b). The future looks promising according to M-PESA Africa's managing director Sitoyo Lopokoiyit:

[Most exciting are] the next 15 years, with the advent of the smartphone and the tech architecture, in terms of cloud services, microservices, active-active architecture, Always On architecture, cybersecurity advancements. And then more importantly is the youthful population that's available. Today over 50% of the population of the continent of Africa is below the age of 18.

When we launched M-PESA, it was about loyalty for GSM [Global System for Mobile Communications]. But today, I can count almost ten products that are loyalty for M-PESA: the lending, the savings program, the wealth management solutions, international remittances. (McKinsey, 2022)

According to the International Finance Corporation (IFC), success factors for M-PESA's growth include its anchor products, including national remittances, airtime purchases, bill payment, ATM withdrawal, and purchase of goods and services; market penetration; high literacy levels in Kenya; the regulatory environment, with the Central Bank of Kenya actively involved in the regulation of mobile money services; the ecosystem, which involves an extensive agent network; and limited competition (International Finance Corporation, n.d.).

Other mobile money market providers in Africa include Bank Zero in South Africa, First Mobile and Branch in Nigeria, and M-Shwari in Kenya. M-Farm and Twiga will be connecting urban customers with rural farmers using digital platforms, Iumia and Takealot are introducing e-commerce for local ride hailing, Hello Tractor and Trotro Tractor in Nigeria and Ghana respectively, and Lynk to connect households with carpenters, plumbers, and electricians (Lashitew, 2022).

A partnership driven transactional ecosystem has led to additional new service offerings in the past decade. For example, cash and vouchers from UN agencies and the World Food Program for global humanitarian assistance can be delivered more quickly, and with greater choice and dignity for recipients and local markets. Utility bill payments for off-grid energy, clean water, and sanitation are another example, although utility service providers must find ways to serve low income populations with affordable and reliable services. Additionally, bulk payments, such as salaries by employers and funds from development organizations and charities, are often transferred to recipients via digital payments. Insurance, including for life and funerals, health and hospitals, and agriculture weather, is now mobile-enabled. Furthermore, mobile-enabled remittances to LMICs grew faster than expected but there is still room for growth (GSMA, 2022).

The mobile money market has advanced agriculture solutions for smallholder farmers in Low and Middle Income Countries (LMICs), especially in South and Southeast Asia and sub-Saharan Africa. Smallholder farmers are farmers who produce crops and livestock on two hectares of land or less. They produce a third of the world's food.

Mobile money advancements for smallholder farmers include digitizing payments in agricultural value chains, funds to strengthen climate resilience from the UK Foreign, Commonwealth and Development Office and the Australian Department of Foreign Affairs and Trade. Nonetheless, while money-enabled digital financial services for famers is significant, less than a third of the demand for credit from smallholders in LMICs is being met. Additional support for financial inclusion and climate resilience for farmers will necessitate partnerships among multiple organizations and clear benefits for all sectors that participate (Ibid.).

In addition to partnerships, another enabler of mobile money markets is the system of money market agents. There are now three million agents in Africa who load and unload cash for customers (Economist, 2022).

Innovations that have advanced the mobile money market include the app that Safaricom introduced in 2021, which has the added feature of Discover, a new function for users to search for and access third-party products and services. Interoperability between banks and mobile money providers has also increased the value of transactions. Interoperability between Airtel Kenya, Safaricom (M-PESA), and Telkom Kenya was launched by the Central Bank of Kenya just this year (Central Bank of Kenya, 2022). This is an important step in driving greater efficiencies and reducing costs. Finally, more fully developed policies and regulations have driven investment, facilitated the rollout of new services, reduced costs, and mitigated risks for customers. Importantly, anti-money laundering and countering the financing of terrorism has reduced risks, while further enabling financial inclusion (GSMA, 2022).

While opportunities abound for the mobile money market to grow, there are barriers. For example, tax authorities are aware of the financial opportunity to build their revenues, but could make mobile money less affordable and discourage investment. In addition, there are gender disparities in the uptake of mobile money services. Barriers for women include the lack of perceived relevance, lack of knowledge and skills, unaffordable transaction fees, and social norms and the lack of family approval particularly in Bangladesh, Guatemala, Indonesia, and Pakistan (Ibid.).

Mobile Money Advances the UN Sustainable Development Goals (SDGs)

"An unintended consequence of the ubiquitous use of M-PESA in Kenya is that people have developed digital literacy even without any formal training whatsoever. Powered by free data bundles given out by Safaricom, families are buying and selling via WhatsApp and paying by using M-PESA. This has become part and parcel of everyday life," explains Caleb Ndaka, Co-Founder and Programs Lead at an education tech start up, Kids Comp Camp in Nairobi, and a Research Associate at The London School of Economics and Politics (Ndaka, 2022).

As shown in the section above, mobile money markets play a vital role in advancing SDG1: No poverty; SDG2: Zero hunger; SDG3: Good health and well-being; SDG5: Gender Equality; SDG6: Clean Water and Sanitation; SDG7: Affordable and Clean Energy; SDG12: Responsible Consumption and Production; SDG8: Decent Work and Economic Growth; SDG9: Industry, Innovation, and Infrastructure; SDG10: Reduced Inequalities; and SDG17: Partnerships for the Goals. There are tremendous opportunities to further advance these and other SDGs as mobile money is expands its services and its geography. Mobile money makes it more possible to achieve the vision of economic development and individual empowerment when businesses, NGOs, and governments work together to find and implement further solutions (United Nations Development Programme, n.d.).

Michael Joseph sums up the impact of mobile money:

> Mobile Money in its various forms has, since its original launch in Kenya in 2007, changed the lives of individuals and small businesses across the developing world. In addition, it has allowed businesses, corporations, governments, institutions and many other organisations to change the way they do business, increased transparency and reduced corruption due to the digital payments mechanism. No other product has done so much in such a short period (less than two decades) has had such a profound effect on the economies of developing countries. It continues to grow and be used more and more for all payments, remittances, fees and, in particular, where there is the need and desire to introduce a digital economy. (Joseph, 2023)

Inclusive Employment Benefits Business and Society

By expanding access to people with a wide variety of skill sets, qualities, and backgrounds, inclusive employment makes companies more innovative, competitive, and profitable in the global marketplace, in addition to increasing the consumption of market products and services. Companies that build truly diverse, inclusive, and equitable cultures are at an advantage by engaging the best workforces from the greatest pool of talent, and fostering positive, productive work environments.

Systemic racism is global and pernicious, degrading humanity, society, and economies worldwide. Addressing racism is a moral imperative. It also presents a powerful opportunity to unleash the economic potential of vast human capital resources. In France, by reducing racial and gender gaps in access to employment, the GDP would increase €150 billion over the next 20 years (Venturi, 2016). Brazil could grow consumption and investment by advancing educational and job opportunities to marginalized communities (Pereira, 2016). In Australia, racial discrimination has cost the nation's economy an estimated $44.9 billion, or 3.6% of GDP, every year in the decade from 2001 to 2011 (Deakin University, 2016). Extreme racism in China is well documented by Human Rights Watch, (Wang, 2021) undermining China's extensive investment interests in Africa. In the United States, the wealth gap between American whites and Blacks is projected to cost the economy between $1 trillion and $1.5 trillion in lost consumption and investment between 2019 and 2028. This translates to a projected GDP penalty of 4 to 6% in 2028 (Losavio, 2020; McKinsey, 2019).

Women continue to experience gender wage gaps worldwide due to differences in educational opportunity and attainment, gender segregation in jobs, discrimination, bias, lack of pay transparency, and caregiving responsibilities that fall disproportionately on women. The gender wage gap among OECD countries was 12% in 2021; it was 16.9 percent in the United States (Catalyst, 2022; OECD, 2022).

Race and gender equity in employment could boost economic growth and power innovation (Cook, 2021). Yet, hiring discrimination, based on gender, racial, and ethnic stereotypes, continue to limit job opportunities, income security, and wealth accumulation for many Americans (DiStasio & Larsen, 2020).

In the United States, Black Americans face systemic obstacles to getting good jobs (Weller, 2019). With the highest unemployment rates of any race/gender group, and weak earnings outcomes, Black men experience less upward and more downward mobility over time, relative to their parents, compared to any other race/gender group in the United States (Holzer, 2021). The gap in economic opportunity between Black and white households has widened during the pandemic, as Black Americans have faced more financial emergencies with fewer economic resources (Weller & Figueroa, 2021).

The recent jobs report reveals a growing racial employment gap, especially for Black women (Broady & Barr, 2022). Although women are making modest gains in the workplace, women of color still lag behind. Black women are hindered in a variety of occupations through limited leadership opportunities, the persistence of sexual harassment, and biases regarding competence, intelligence, and skill that are unrelated to actual performance (Wingfield, 2020).

Racial bias in hiring contributes to an increasing Black-White wealth gap. Even before sending off a single application, women and people of color tend to be channeled toward careers in low-paying industries, or in industries that hire women and people of color in primarily low-paying roles (National Fund for Workforce Solutions, 2022).

Algorithmic hiring systems, now used by 55% of human resources leaders in the United States, further exacerbate systemic discrimination, in spite of attempts by some to reduce prejudice (Engler, 2021). Methods of analyzing language in resumes and interviews have revealed biases against women and people with disabilities. Speech recognition models have shown biases against African Americans. Commercial AI facial analysis shows preferences based on skin color and is likely to discriminate against people with disabilities as well. Algorithms to promote job postings can result in biased outcomes against young women for STEM jobs and ageism against older candidates (Ibid.).

The United States's excessive and highly biased incarceration rates (Sawyer, 2020; Widra & Herring, 2021) further destroy opportunities for many Black Americans for education, jobs, financial security, housing, transportation, and wealth accumulation (Weller et al., 2022). Systemic racism is evident at every stage of the system, from policing to prosecutorial decisions, pretrial release processes, sentencing, correctional discipline, and even reentry. The racism inherent in mass incarceration affects children as well as adults and is often especially punishing for people of color who are also marginalized along other lines, such as gender and class (Balko, 2020; Gross et al., 2022; Sawyer, 2020). Formerly incarcerated people face major obstacles in finding stable employment, which further widens the racial wealth gap (Wang & Bertram, 2022; Weller et al., 2022). The economic cost of this systemic injustice is staggering. For the 14 million formerly incarcerated Americans, the impact to the United States in lost output is $65 billion (Center for Workforce Inclusion, n.d.).

LGBTQ+ employees also face discrimination and hostility in the workplace. In the European Union, one in five (21%) of LGBT people experienced discrimination at work in 2019. Transgender employees reported higher proportions of discrimination (36%) (E.U.F.R.A., 2020). In the United States, over 8 million workers in the United States identify as LGBT. (Sears et al., 2021) Just over 45% of LGBT workers have experienced unfair treatment at work, including harassment, being fired, or facing hiring discrimination based on their LGBT status (Human Rights Campaign, n.d.). This adverse treatment negatively affects their health and wellbeing and reduces their job commitment and satisfaction (Sears et al., 2021). Just over one-third of LGBT employees said that they have left a job because of how they were treated by their employer based on their sexual orientation or gender identity (Ibid.).

People with disabilities constitute yet another worldwide demographic that face stigma and discrimination (World Health Organization, 2022). One billion people (15% of the world's population) experience some form of disability. Disability can increase the risk of poverty, through lack of employment and education opportunities, lower wages, and increased cost of living.

There are 61 million adults with disabilities in the United States alone; that is 26% of adults (Centers for Disease Control and Prevention, 2022). The number will grow as more people develop Long COVID, which is now recognized as a Disability Under the ADA, Section. 504, and Section 1557 (U.S.H.H.S., 2021). The percentage of disabled people employed is just over 38%, compared to close to 76% for non-disabled people in 2020 (University of New Hampshire, 2021). This makes any unconscious biases against people with disabilities an economic problem that will only grow worse as Long COVID prevails and the US population ages.

Some companies recognize the opportunity to hire people with disabilities, in addition to designing goods and services to tap that market. As members of the nonprofit Disability:IN, four hundred United States- based companies recognize the imperative and benefits of disability inclusion and equality. The organization also partners with the Employer Assistance Network on Disability Inclusion to promote hiring of veterans with disabilities (EARN, website).

Microsoft, the American-based multinational technology company, has distinguished itself in its leadership in promoting inclusive hiring for people with disabilities. Hiring people with disabilities is "a skills play. A talent play," explains Neil Barnett, Director of Inclusive Hiring and Accessibility at Microsoft (Barnett, 2022). Barnett leads the Neurodiversity @ Work Roundtable at Disability: In, a nonprofit that empowers business to achieve disability inclusion and equality. The Roundtable, started and led by Microsoft, includes employers who pioneer and scale neurodiversity-focused hiring initiatives in a variety of industries including, but not limited to tech, biotech, financial services, consulting, manufacturing, retail, customer service, consumer packaged goods, and entertainment. In addition to promoting workforce inclusion and diversity, the group is launching the Neurodiversity Career Connector, a job search portal to connect neurodivergent job seekers with job opportunities at inclusive companies across industries. Microsoft prides itself for its leadership in building an inclusive culture. "Accessibility is an opportunity. Inclusive organizations that embrace best practices for employing and supporting persons with disabilities in the workplace outperform their peers. They also attract and keep top talent. Millennials, who will be 75% of the global workforce by 2020, choose employers who reflect their values. Diversity and inclusion top the list" (Microsoft "Start Your Journey").

Microsoft also recognizes the market advantage of inclusive technology design (Microsoft webpage). In 2015, Neil Barnett and Jenny Lay-Flurrie, who today is Microsoft's Chief Accessibility Officer, piloted and soon thereafter scaled the company's neurodiversity hiring program. They recognized that many autistic people are not only quite capable of meeting serious intellectual demands, but they also often have qualities that may be particularly suited for tech jobs, such as being detail-oriented and methodical (Vara, 2016). Microsoft also launched annual hackathons bringing together employees from across the company to hack solutions to the world's biggest challenges. The Ability Hack challenges employees to build opportunities that empower people with disabilities through technology (Lay-Flurrie, 2018). A few technology examples as a result of the ability hacks include Windows Eye Control, Learning Tools, and Seeing AI (Barnett, 2023).

HP, the American multinational technology company, also recognizes the market opportunity to ensure that its products and services are usable by as many people as possible. The company engages with members of the disability community worldwide for product testing and feedback, in addition to collaborating with nonprofit partners and subject matter experts. "We're learning from nonprofit partners and consumers," says Jordan Ragan, Global Outreach, HP who heeds the disability community's expectation: "Nothing about us without us" (HP, 2023).

Investing in Supportive Housing Is a Business Opportunity in the United States

Supportive housing is a well-documented, long-term solution to homelessness (National Alliance to End Homelessness, 2021). Residents in supportive housing receive comprehensive services that are voluntary and address the needs of each resident. Services can include employment education and training, mental and physical healthcare, and substance abuse disorder services. Supportive housing strengthens communities by improving healthcare and neighborhood safety, in addition to beautifying city blocks. The result is that property values are increased or stabilized over time. Supportive housing is also a cost-effective approach to improve the lives of people with multiple, chronic, and complex needs, who would otherwise draw heavily on more expensive community services such as homeless shelters, hospitals, emergency rooms, jails, and prisons (Corporation for Supportive Housing "101", 2022b). Investment capital for nonprofit supportive housing agencies can come from various sources including from private sector entities, federal, state, and local governments, nonprofit funders, and philanthropy. For private sector investors, these partnerships yield sufficient returns while achieving the benefits of supportive housing to residents and the community.

Corporation for Supportive Housing (CSH) is the national nonprofit leader in providing supportive housing, a proven model that prioritizes affordable housing paired with services focusing on person-centered growth, recovery, and success that contributes to the health and well-being of the entire community (Corporation for Supportive Housing website, 2022c). CSH recently celebrated their thirtieth anniversary of working with funders, investors, developers, service providers, and policy makers who collaborate with them to build housing solutions that "recognize the value and dignity of every human life" (Corporation for Supportive Housing "30 years", 2022d). Its impact is formidable (Corporation for Supportive Housing "Performance", 2022a) in:

- Providing loans, grants, project assistance, and advocacy to create access to 385,000 homes for people who need housing and important services to achieve stability and transform their lives.
- Making more than $1.5 billion in loans and grants.
- Helping communities create supportive housing through federal, state, and local public policy reforms.
- Working in 48 states, over 300 communities, across three regions of the United States.
- Presenting more than 1000 training events in the past few years through its Supportive Housing Training Center.

An important new initiative established by CSH in 2021 is Redesigning Access by Centering Equity (RACE Initiative). CSH was aware of the dichotomy: the overrepresentation of Black, Indigenous, People of Color (BIPOC) in the homeless system and institutional settings, along with the significant underrepresentation of BIPOC developers in the affordable and supportive housing sectors. To address this discrepancy, CSH established the RACE Initiative to expand BIPOC developers' access to capital and resources. The organization committed $200 million in lending and will steadily increase the funding in the next several years.

Importantly, the CSH model is designed to address systemic problems, not only in housing, but also in investments in BIPOC companies. The approach is collaborative with multiple sectors including companies, grass-roots communities, government, and nonprofits. CSH attests to its growing understanding that (Corporation for Supportive Housing, 2021).

[t]he root of the problems we were working to solve lay beyond failures in public policy and rather in the perpetual, systemic and structural racism built into the fabric of this country. It shows up particularly strongly in our work, given our country's long and intentional history of housing-related discrimination. To this day and across generations, the impacts of racially based housing discrimination have resulted in lower rates of homeownership, higher education, and wealth among BIPOC and elevated rates of homelessness and environmental-related health conditions, to name a few.

We cannot build thriving communities centered on housing aligned with services without focusing on equity and addressing fundamentally racist policies, practices, and institutions. To do our work effectively and equitably, CSH committed to the process to disentangle the grip of racism from national, state, and local systems and institutions.

We believe supportive housing can be a lasting and equalizing force that recognizes structural racism and addresses systemic policies that maintain these disparities. Operating from a racial equity framework demands that CSH must also turn the lens inward. Deep introspection requires examining our work and partnerships, making uncomfortable topics and conversations the norm, bringing marginalized voices and perspectives to the table, and ensuring that BIPOC employees, people, businesses, and communities have a real stake in charting the path forward.

One CSH employee observed that "if we can do this work right, it's part of the long term sustained impact shifting power from institutions to people" (Ibid.).

In its efforts to bring capital to BIPOC developers, CSH involves companies, foundations, and federally funded Community Development Financial Institutions (CDFIs). According to Deborah De Santis, CSH's CEO for more than sixteen years, "Fundamental to the success of the RACE Initiative is bringing big capital to BIPOC-led organizations" (De Santis, 2022). This requires changes in regulatory restrictions that have limited funding to BIPOC developers, so CSH is working with states to focus on racial equity and with syndicators, who are investors and developers.

Banks are essential partners. Bank of America made a $60 million investment in loans and equity financing for BIPOC leaders developing multi-family, affordable and supportive housing across the country. This commitment by the bank is part of their "$1.25 billion, five-year commitment to advance racial equality and economic opportunity in Black, Hispanic-Latino, and Asian communities with a focus on affordable housing, health and healthcare, jobs/reskilling, and small business" (Bank of America, 2021). "Profit with a purpose," is how Maurice Coleman describes these company investments. Coleman, previously a board member at CSH, is a Market Executive for Commercial Real Estate—Community Development Banking at Bank of America Merrill Lynch. "We're the bank of *all* Americans, improving their lives and well-being. We have all the tools to make this possible. Our goal is to make sure you have all the tools for you to become successful" (Ibid.).

Investments in People Will Advance the World's Economic Potential

It is detrimental for society to continue to exclude large swaths of the population from employment, housing, and access to goods and services. Some businesses recognize the opportunities inherent in increasing their markets to previously excluded and marginalized people. Moreover, it is time to call out and eliminate historic ignorance and bias that stubbornly obstruct attempts to build a flourishing world. Change requires systemic, innovative, and ground-breaking approaches. There is a plethora of partnership possibilities between companies, nonprofits, and governments to advance a vision of an inclusive, sustainable, and prosperous world for all. It is time to move forward together.

References

African Development Bank Group. (n.d.). African Economic Outlook 2022. https://www.afdb.org/en/knowledge/publications/african-economic-outlook. Accessed 28 Jan 2023.

Arewa, O. (2021). Disrupting Africa: Technology, law, and development. Cambridge University Press.

Arewa, O. (2023, January 20). Email to Alice Korngold.

Balko, R. (2020, June 10). There's overwhelming evidence that the criminal justice system is racist. Here's the proof. *Washington Post*. https://www.washingtonpost.com/graphics/2020/opinions/systemic-racism-police-evidence-criminal-justice-system/. Accessed 29 Jan 2023.

Bank of America. (2021, April 28). Press release—Bank of America providing $60 million fund for BIPOC affordable housing developers. https://newsroom.ban kofamerica.com/content/newsroom/press-releases/2021/04/bank-of-america-pro viding--60-million-fund-for-bipoc-affordable-.html. Accessed 30 Jan 2023.

Barnett, N. (2022, December 23). Interview with Alice Korngold.

Barnett, N. (2023, January 3). Email to Alice Korngold.

Beck, T. (2015, September 15). How mobile money is driving economic growth. World Economic Forum. https://www.weforum.org/agenda/2015/09/how-mob ile-money-is-driving-economic-growth/. Accessed 28 Jan 2023.

Bill & Melinda Gates Foundation. (2021, April). The impact of mobile money on poverty. https://docs.gatesfoundation.org/Documents/ImpactofMobileMone yonPoverty_ResearchBrief.pdf. Accessed 28 Jan 2023.

Broady, K., & Barr, A. (2022, January 11). December's jobs report reveals a growing racial employment gap, especially for Black women. Brookings. https:// www.brookings.edu/blog/the-avenue/2022/01/11/decembers-jobs-report-reveals- a-growing-racial-employment-gap-especially-for-black-women/. Accessed 29 Jan 2023.

Busby, J. W. (2007). Climate change and national security: An agenda for action. Council of Foreign Relations Press. https://www.cfr.org/report/climate-change- and-national-security. Accessed 28 Jan 2023.

Catalyst. (2022, March 11) .Women's earnings: The pay gap (quick take).. https:// www.catalyst.org/research/womens-earnings-the-pay-gap/. Accessed 29 Jan 2023.

Center for Strategic and International Studies ("CSIS"). (2013). Our shared opportunity: A vision for global prosperity. https://csis-website-prod.s3.amazon aws.com/s3fs-public/legacy_files/files/publication/130304_Nesseth_DevCouncil Report_Web.pdf. Accessed 28 Jan 2023.

Center for Workforce Inclusion. (n.d.). Formerly incarcerated job seekers: getting "back to business." https://www.centerforworkforceinclusion.org/our-work/for merly-incarcerated/. Accessed 29 Jan 2023.

Centers for Disease Control and Prevention. (2022, October 28). Disability impacts all of us. https://www.cdc.gov/ncbddd/disabilityandhealth/infographic-disability- impacts-all.html. Accessed 30 Jan 2023.

Central Bank of Kenya. (2022, April 8). Press release—Launch of mobile money merchant interoperability. https://www.centralbank.go.ke/uploads/press_releases/ 1691854698_Press%20Release%20-Mobile%20Money%20Merchant%20Inte roperability.pdf. Accessed 28 Jan 2023.

Clemens, M. (n.d.) Michael Clemens on inequality and migration. Ford Foun dation. https://www.fordfoundation.org/news-and-stories/big-ideas/inequalityis/ michael-clemens-on-inequality-and-migration/. Accessed 28 Jan 2023.

Coleman, M. (2022, September 12). Interview with Alice Korngold.

Cook, L. (2021, January 14). Addressing gender and racial disparities in the U.S. labor market to boost wages and power innovation. Washington Center

for Equitable Growth. https://equitablegrowth.org/addressing-gender-and-rac
ial-disparities-in-the-u-s-labor-market-to-boost-wages-and-power-innovation/.
Accessed 29 Jan 2023.

Corporation for Supportive Housing. (2021). Bending the arc toward equity.
https://www.csh.org/wp-content/uploads/2021/11/CSH-Race-Equity-Framew
ork-Report-2021-FINAL.pdf. Accessed 30 Jan 2023.

Corporation for Supportive Housing. (2022a). Performance ("Performance").
https://www.csh.org/about-csh/performance/. Accessed 30 Jan 2023.

Corporation for Supportive Housing. (2022b). Supportive housing 101 ("101").
https://www.csh.org/supportive-housing-101/. Accessed 30 Jan 2023.

Corporation for Supportive Housing website. (2022c). https://www.csh.org/.
Accessed 30 Jan 2023.

Corporation for Supportive Housing website. (2022d). 30 years of supportive
housing solutions ("30 years"). https://www.csh.org/about-csh/30-years-of-sup
portive-housing-solutions/. Accessed 30 Jan 2023.

Data Commons. (n.d.). United States of America. https://datacommons.org/place/
country/USA?utm_medium=explore&mprop=count&popt=Person&hl=en.
Accessed 28 Jan 2023.

Deakin University. (2016, April 6). Press release—counting the billion dollar cost of
racism in Australia. https://www.deakin.edu.au/about-deakin/news-and-media-
releases/articles/counting-the-billion-dollar-cost-of-racism-in-australia. Accessed
28 Jan 2023.

De Santis, D. (2022, September 9). Interview with Alice Korngold.

Disabilityin website. (n.d.). https://disabilityin.org/. Accessed 30 Jan 2023.

DiStasio, V., & Larsen, E. N. (2020). The racialized and gendered workplace:
Applying an intersectional lens to a field experiment on hiring discrimination
in five European labor arkets. *Social Psychology Quarterly, 83*, 229–250. https://
doi.org/10.1177/0190272520902994

DIW Econ. (2022, May). From refugee crisis to job engine: An analysis
of German businesses' experience in refugee integration. Tent Partnership
for Refugees. https://www.tent.org/resources/from-refugee-crisis-to-job-engine-
germany/. Accessed 28 Jan 2023.

Dyssegaard K. D., & Roldan, C. (2018). Refugees as employees: Good retention,
strong recruitment. https://www.tent.org/wp-content/uploads/2018/05/TENT_
FPI-Refugees-as-Employees-Report.pdf. Accessed 28 Jan 2023.

EARN website. (n.d.). Disabled veterans. https://askearn.org/page/disabled-vet
erans. Accessed 30 Jan 2023.

Economist. (2022, July 30). Africa's mobile money agents face an uncertain future. https://www.economist.com/middle-east-and-africa/2022/06/30/afr
icas-mobile-money-agents-face-an-uncertain-future. Accessed 28 Jan 2023.

Engler, A. (2021, March 12). Auditing employment algorithms for discrimination. Brookings. https://www.brookings.edu/research/auditing-employment-
algorithms-for-discrimination/. Accessed 29 Jan 2023.

European Union Agency for Fundamental Rights ("E.U.F.R.A.). (2020). A long way to go for LGBTI equality. https://fra.europa.eu/sites/default/files/fra_uploads/fra-2020-lgbti-equality-1_en.pdf. Accessed 29 Jan 2023.

Fengler, W., Kharas, H., & Caballero, J. (2022, Oct 21). The forgotten 3 billion. Brookings. https://www.brookings.edu/blog/future-development/2022/10/21/the-forgotten-3-billion/. Accessed 28 Jan 2023.

Friedman, T. (2013, May 18). Without water, revolution. *New York Times*. https://www.nytimes.com/2013/05/19/opinion/sunday/friedman-without-water-revolution.html?pagewanted=1&_r=3&hpw%20(June%209,%202013. Accessed 28 Jan 2023.

George-Hertzog, K. (2022, December 15). Interview with Alice Korngold.

Gross, S. R., Possley, M., Otterbourg, K., Stephens, K., Weinstock Paredes, J., & O'Brien, B. (2022). Race and wrongful convictions in the United States 2022. https://www.law.umich.edu/special/exoneration/Documents/Race%20Report%20Preview.pdf. Accessed 29 Jan 2023.

GSMA. (n.d.). Accelerating the mobile money ecosystem for the underserved, https://www.gsma.com/mobilefordevelopment/mobile-money/. Accessed 28 Jan 2023.

GSMA. (2022). State of the industry report on mobile money—2021. https://www.gsma.com/sotir/wp-content/uploads/2022/03/GSMA_State_of_the_Industry_2022_English.pdf. Accessed 28 Jan 2023.

HIAS website. (n.d.). https://hias.org/. Accessed 29 Jan 2023.

Holzer, H. (2021, March 1). Why are employment rates so low among Black men? Brookings. https://www.brookings.edu/research/why-are-employment-rates-so-low-among-black-men/. Accessed 29 Jan 2023.

Human Rights Campaign. (n.d.). The wage gap among LGBTQ+ wprlers om the Imoted States. https://www.hrc.org/resources/the-wage-gap-among-lgbtq-workers-in-the-united-states. Accessed 29 Jan 2023.

HP. (2023). HP spectrum success program. https://www.hp.com/us-en/hp-information/about-hp/diversity/spectrum-success.html. Accessed 30 Jan 2023.

International Finance Corporation. (n.d.). M-money channel distribution case—Kenya.

International Institute for Sustainable Development ("IISD"). (2022, July 13). SDGs report 2022 delivers "reality check" on reversal of progress. https://sdg.iisd.org/news/sdgs-report-2022-delivers-reality-check-on-reversal-of-progress/. Accessed 28 Jan 2023.

International Monetary Fund. (2022, October). Regional economic outlook for Sub-Saharan African. https://www.imf.org/en/Publications/REO/SSA/Issues/2022/10/14/regional-economic-outlook-for-sub-saharan-africa-october-2022. Accessed 28 Jan 2023.

Joseph, M. (2013, May 21). Interview with Alice Korngold.

Joseph, M. (2023, January 2). Email to Alice Korngold.

Kharas, H., Dooley, M. (2022, Febuary 2). The evolution of global poverty, 1990–2030. Brookings., https://www.brookings.edu/research/the-evolution-of-global-poverty-1990-2030/. Accessed 28 Jan 2023.

King, Jr. Rev. M. L. (1967). A Christmas sermon on peace. https://www.beaconbroadside.com/broadside/2017/12/martin-luther-king-jrs-christmas-sermon-peace-still-prophetic-50-years-later.html. Accessed 28 Jan 2023.

Korngold, A. (2014). A better world, inc.: how companies profit by solving global problems where governments cannot. Palgrave Macmillan.

Lashitew, A. (2022, November 21). Digital technologies open vast business opportunities in Africa. Brookings. https://www.brookings.edu/opinions/digital-technologies-open-vast-business-opportunities-in-africa/. Accessed 28 Jan 2023.

Lay-Flurrie, J. (2018, July 23). The ability hacks: The story of two hackathon teams embracing the transformative power of technology. https://blogs.microsoft.com/on-the-issues/2018/07/23/the-ability-hacks-the-story-of-two-hackathon-teams-embracing-the-transformative-power-of-technology/. Accessed 30 Jan 2023.

Lee, T. (2019, August 14). A vast wealth gap, driven by segregation, redlining, evictions and exclusion, separates black and white Americans. *New York Times*. https://www.nytimes.com/interactive/2019/08/14/magazine/racial-wealth-gap.html. Accessed 28 Jan 2023.

Long, H., Van Dam, A. (2020, June 4). The black-white economic divide is as wide as it was in 1968. *Washington Post*. https://www.washingtonpost.com/business/2020/06/04/economic-divide-black-households/. Accessed 28 Jan 2023.

Losavio, J. (2020, September). What racism costs us all. International Monetary Fund. https://www.imf.org/en/Publications/fandd/issues/2020/09/the-economic-cost-of-racism-losavio. Accessed 28 Jan 2023.

Maltz, G. (2022, October 26). Interview with Alice Korngold.

Mayda, A. M., & Ortega, F., Peri, G., Shih, K., & Sparber, C. (2017, October). The effect of the HB-1 quota on employment and selection of foreign-born labor. National Bureau of Economic Research (Working paper No. 23902). https://www.nber.org/papers/w23902. Accessed 28 Jan 2023.

McKinsey. (2019, August 13). The economic impact of closing the racial wealth gap. https://www.mckinsey.com/industries/public-and-social-sector/our-insights/the-economic-impact-of-closing-the-racial-wealth-gap. Accessed 28 Jan 2023.

McKinsey. (2022, June 29). Driven by purpose: 15 years of M-Pesa's evolution (podcast). https://www.mckinsey.com/industries/financial-services/our-insights/driven-by-purpose-15-years-of-m-pesas-evolution. Accessed 28 Jan 2023.

Microsoft. (n.d.). Start your journey. https://query.prod.cms.rt.microsoft.com/cms/api/am/binary/RE4wNu4. Accessed 30 Jan 2023.

Microsoft webpage. (n.d.). Accessibility help and learning. https://support.microsoft.com/en-us/accessibility. Accessed 30 Jan 2023.

Mineo, L. (2017, December 7). The need to talk about race. Harvard Gazette. https://news.harvard.edu/gazette/story/2017/12/bryan-stevenson-seeks-national-conversation-about-slaverys-legacy/. Accessed 28 Jan 2023.

Natarajan, A., Moslimani, M., & Lopez, M. H. (2022). Key facts in recent trends in global migration.

National Alliance to End Homelessness. (2021, March). Permanent supportive housing. https://endhomelessness.org/ending-homelessness/solutions/permanent-supportive-housing/. Accessed 30 Jan 2023.

National Fund for Workforce Solutions. (2022, March 11). Racial bias in hiring widens Black-White wealth disparity. https://nationalfund.org/racial-bias-in-hiring-practices-widens-the-black-white-wealth-disparity/. Accessed 29 Jan 2023.

Ndaka, C. (2022, November 23). Interview with Alice Korngold.

New American Economy. (n.d.). Entrepreneurship. https://www.newamericaneconomy.org/issues/entrepreneurship/. Accessed 28 Jan 2023.

Nishio, A., & Tata, G. (2021, November 3). How the structure of global aid and development finance is changing. Brookings. https://www.brookings.edu/blog/future-development/2021/11/03/how-the-structure-of-global-aid-and-development-finance-is-changing/. Accessed 28 Jan 2023.

Nowrasteh, A. (2021). The most common arguments against immigration and why they are wrong. Cato Institute. https://www.libertarianism.org/sites/libertarianism.org/files/2021-04/The%20Most%20Common%20Arguments%20Against%20Immigration%20and%20Why%20They%27re%20Wrong.pdf?hsCtaTracking=5b590920-b88a-4641-ba7b-5fdc41e9a266%7Cba17362a-c667-46dd-9170-b112363474e3. Accessed 28 Jan 2023.

Onukwue, A., & Shendruk, A. (2022, December 2). The immigrants' World Cup: see all the players who crossed border to play football. Quartz. https://qz.com/the-immigrants-world-cup-see-all-the-players-who-cros-1849840305. Accessed 28 Jan 2023.

Onyango, S. (2022, May 4). Africa accounts for 70% of the world's $1 trillion mobile money market. Quartz. https://qz.com/africa/2161960/gsma-70-per cent-of-the-worlds-1-trillion-mobile-money-market-is-in-africa. Accessed 28 Jan 2023.

Organization for Economic Cooperation and Development ("OECD"). (2022). Data: Gender wage gap. https://data.oecd.org/earnwage/gender-wage-gap.htm. Accessed 29 Jan 2023.

Oxfam International. (n.d.). Why the majority of the world's poor are women. https://www.oxfam.org/en/why-majority-worlds-poor-are-women. Accessed 28 Jan 2023.

Pamba, A. (2023, February 10). Interview with Alice Korngold.

Pereira, C. (2016). Ethno-racial poverty and income inequality in Brazil. Commitment to equity (Working Paper Series. 60) Tulane University, Department of Economics. https://ideas.repec.org/p/tul/ceqwps/60.html. Accessed 28 Jan 2023.

Pethokoukis, J. (2020, December 1). The economics of expanding immigration: My long-read Q & A with Michael Clemens. American Enterprise Institute. https://www.aei.org/economics/the-economics-of-expanding-immigration-my-long-read-qa-with-michael-clemens/. Accessed 28 Jan 2023.

Pew Research Center, 16 Dec. https://www.pewresearch.org/fact-tank/2022/12/16/key-facts-about-recent-trends-in-global-migration/#:~:text=The%20United%20States%20has%20more,measure%20by%20a%20wide%20margin. Accessed 28 Jan 2023.

Poll, Z. (2020, February 20). The case for open borders. *New Yorker.* https://www.newyorker.com/culture/annals-of-inquiry/the-case-for-open-borders. Accessed 28 Jan 2023.

Potter, J. (2012, July 26). The power of business-driven development. Business Fights Poverty. https://businessfightspoverty.org/the-power-of-business-driven-development/. Accessed 28 Jan 2023.

Rauld, L. (2022, November 9). Interview with Alice Korngold.

Reese, J. (2022, November 7). Interview with Alice Korngold.

Rice, S. E. (2006, March 1). The threat of global poverty. Brookings. https://www.brookings.edu/articles/the-threat-of-global-poverty/. Accessed 28 Jan 2023.

Rice, S. E. (2010). Poverty and state weakness. In: S. E. Rice, C. Graff, C. Pascual (Eds.), *Confronting poverty: Weak states and U.S. national security.* Brookings.

Roberts, L. (2020, May). Unlocking hidden value: how investing in immigrant talent benefits your bottom line. Jobs For the Future. https://jfforg-prod-new.s3.amazonaws.com/media/documents/Immigrant_Talent_Report-050520-final.pdf. Accessed 28 Jan 2023.

Roser, M. (2021, Dec 9). Global economic inequality: What matters most for most for your living conditions is not who you are, but where you are. Our World In Data. https://ourworldindata.org/global-economic-inequality-introduction. Accessed 28 Jan 2023.

Safaricom. (2022a). M-PESA https://www.ifc.org/wps/wcm/connect/e0d2a9bd-16b9-4a36-8498-0b2650b9af8b/Tool%2B6.7.%2BCase%2BStudy%2B-%2BM-PESA%2BKenya%2B.pdf?MOD=AJPERES&CVID=jkCVy-n. Accessed 28 Jan 2023.

Safaricom. (2022b, Mar). Safaricom crosses 30 million monthly active M-PESA customers. https://www.safaricom.co.ke/personal/m-pesa/m-pesa-journey. Accessed 28 Jan 2023.

Safaricom website. (n.d.). https://www.safaricom.co.ke/. Accessed 28 Jan 2023.

Sapolsky, M. (2018, November 1). How economic inequality inflicts real biological harm. Scientific American. https://www.scientificamerican.com/article/how-economic-inequality-inflicts-real-biological-harm/#:~:text=Basically%2C%20more%20unequal%20societies%20have,homicide%2C%20and%20higher%20incarceration%20rates. Accessed 28 Jan 2023.

Sawyer, W. (2020,July 27). Visualizing the racial disparities in mass incarceration. Prison Policy Initiative. https://www.prisonpolicy.org/blog/2020/07/27/disparities/. Accessed 29 Jan 2023.

Sears, B., Mallory, C., Flores, A., & Conron. (2021, September). LGBT people's experience of workplace discrimination and harassment. UCLA School of Law, Williams Institute. https://williamsinstitute.law.ucla.edu/publications/lgbt-workplace-discrimination/. Accessed 29 Jan 2023.

Shorenstein, M. (2023, January 27). Interview with Alice Korngold.

Siripurapu, A. (2022, April 20). The U.S. inequality debate. Council of Foreign Relations. https://www.cfr.org/backgrounder/us-inequality-debate. Accessed 28 Jan 2023.

Statistica.com. (n.d.). Total registered mobile money accounts in Kenya from September 2019 to February 2022. https://www.statista.com/statistics/1188510/registered-mobile-money-accounts-in-kenya/. Accessed 28 Jan 2023.

Suri, T., & Jack, B. (2012, February 27). Reaching the poor: mobile banking and financial inclusion. Slate. https://slate.com/technology/2012/02/m-pesa-ict4d-and-mobile-banking-for-the-poor.html. Accessed 28 Jan 2023.

TENT. (2022, December). Guidance for European companies hiring refugees from Ukraine. https://www.tent.org/resources/guidance-for-european-companies-on-hiring-refugees-from-ukraine/. Accessed 28 Jan 2023.

TENT website. (2023). https://www.tent.org/. Accessed 28 Jan 2023.

TENT website ("Ulukaya"). (2023). Hamdi Ulukaya. https://www.tent.org/hamdi-ulukaya/. Accessed 28 Jan 2023.

United Kingdom, Department for International Development. (2011). A new strategic vision for girls and women: stopping poverty before it starts. https://assets.publishing.service.gov.uk/government/uploads/system/uploads/attachment_data/file/67582/strategic-vision-girls-women.pdf. Accessed 28 Jan 2023.

United Nations. (2022a). Progress on the sustainable development goals: the gender snapshot 2022 ("Gender"). https://unstats.un.org/sdgs/gender-snapshot/2022/GenderSnapshot.pdf. Accessed 28 Jan 2023.

United Nations. (2022b). The sustainable development goals report 2022. https://unstats.un.org/sdgs/report/2022/. Accessed 26 Jan 2023.

United Nations, UN News. (2022c, December 26). 2022c year in review: 100 million displaced, "a record that should never have been set" ("Displaced"). https://news.un.org/en/story/2022c/12/1131957. Accessed 28 Jan 2023.

United Nations, UN News. (2022d, May 23). UNHCR: A record 100 million people forcibly displaced worldwide ("UNHCR"). https://news.un.org/en/story/2022d/05/1118772. Accessed 28 Jan 2023.

United Nations, UNHCR. (2022e). Global trends: forced displacement in 2021 ("2021 Report"). https://www.unhcr.org/62a9d1494/global-trends-report-2021. Accessed 28 Jan 2023.

United Nations, Department of Economic and Social Affairs ("UNDESA"). (2020). UNDESA World Social Report 2020. https://www.un.org/development/desa/dspd/world-social-report/2020-2.html. Accessed 28 Jan 2023.

United Nations, Human Rights. (2019, June 25). Press release—UN expert condemns failure to address impact of climate change on poverty. https://www.ohchr.org/en/press-releases/2019/06/un-expert-condemns-failure-address-impact-climate-change-poverty. Accessed 28 Jan 2023.

United Nations, Department of Economic and Social Affairs. (n.d.). The 17 goals ("SDGs"). https://sdgs.un.org/goals. Accessed 26 Jan 2023.

United Nations, Development Programme. (n.d.). The SDGs in action. https://www.undp.org/sustainable-development-goals?utm_source=EN&utm_medium=GSR&utm_content=US_UNDP_PaidSearch_Brand_English&utm_campaign=CENTRAL&c_src=CENTRAL&c_src2=GSR&gclid=Cj0KCQiAm5ycBhCXARIsAPldzoWAHpy8Gw8kYuESM0rtxIy0R7QkRjaQa1-7Xbes0hZgbFu8JaeDG PgaAmAwEALw_wcB. Accessed 28 Jan 2023.

United States Department of Health and Human Service ("U.S.H.H.S."). (2021, July 26). Guidance on "Long COVID" as a disability under the ADA section 504, and section 1557. https://www.hhs.gov/civil-rights/for-providers/civil-rights-covid19/guidance-long-covid-disability/index.html. Accessed 30 Jan 2023.

University of New Hampshire, Institute on Disability. (2021). Annual report on people with disabilities in America. https://disabilitycompendium.org/sites/default/files/user-uploads/Events/2022ReleaseYear/Annual%20Report%20---%202021%20---%20WEB.pdf. Accessed 30 Jan 2023.

Vara, V. (2016, June 9). Microsoft wants autistic coders; can it find them and keep them? Fast Company. https://www.fastcompany.com/3062835/microsoft-autism-hiring. Accessed 30 Jan 2023.

Venturi, R. (2016) The economic cost of workplace discrimination in France: billions of euros in lost potential. https://www.strategie.gouv.fr/sites/strategie.gouv.fr/files/atoms/files/dp-anglais-discrimination.pdf. Accessed 28 Jan 2023.

Vince, G. (2022). Nomad century: how climate migration will reshape our world. Flatiron.

Vodaphone website. (n.d.). https://www.vodafone.com/about-vodafone/what-we-do/consumer-products-and-services/m-pesa. Accessed 28 Jan 2023.

Wade, R. H. (2001, December). The rising inequality of world income distribution. International Monetary Fund, Finance and Development. https://www.imf.org/external/pubs/ft/fandd/2001/12/wade.htm. Accessed 28 Jan 2023.

Wang, Y. (2021, February 18). From Covid to blackface on TV, China's racism problem runs deep. Human Rights Watch. https://www.hrw.org/news/2021/02/18/covid-blackface-tv-chinas-racism-problem-runs-deep/. Accessed 28 Jan 2023.

Wang, L., & Bertram, W. (2022, February 9). New data on formerly incarcerated people's employment reveal labor market injustices. Prison Policy Initiative. https://www.prisonpolicy.org/blog/2022/02/08/employment/. Accessed 28 Jan 2023.

Weller, C. (2019, December 5). African Americans face systematic obstacles to getting good jobs. Center for American Progress. https://www.americanprogress.org/article/african-americans-face-systematic-obstacles-getting-good-jobs/. Accessed 29 Jan 2023.

Weller, C., Amaning, A., & Vallas, R. (2022, December 13) America's broken criminal legal system contributes to wealth inequality. Center for

American Progress. https://www.americanprogress.org/article/americas-broken-criminal-legal-system-contributes-to-wealth-inequality/. Accessed 29 Jan 2023.

Weller, C., & Figueroa. (2021, July 28). Wealth matters: The black-white wealth gap before and during the pandemic. Center for American Progress. https://www.americanprogress.org/article/wealth-matters-black-white-wealth-gap-pandemic/. Accessed 29 Jan 2023.

Widra, E., & Herring, T. (2021, September). States of incarceration: The global context 2021. Prison Policy Initiative. https://www.prisonpolicy.org/global/2021.html. Jan 29 2023.

Wingfield, A. H. (2020, October). Women are advancing in the workplace, but women of color still lag behind. Brookings. https://www.brookings.edu/essay/women-are-advancing-in-the-workplace-but-women-of-color-still-lag-behind/. Accessed 29 Jan 2023.

Woetzel, J., Madgavkar, A., Rifa, K., Mattern, F., Bughin, J., Manyika, J., Elmsary, T., diLodovico, A., & Hasyagar, A. (2016, November 30). Global migration's impact and opportunity, McKinsey Global Institute. https://www.mckinsey.com/featured-insights/employment-and-growth/global-migrations-impact-and-opportunity. Accessed 28 Jan 2023.

World Bank. (n.d.). Population, total—Kenya. https://data.worldbank.org/indicator/SP.POP.TOTL?locations=KE. Accessed 28 Jan 2023.

World Bank. (2021, May 12). Press release—Defying predictions, remittance flows remain strong during COVID-19 crisis. https://www.worldbank.org/en/news/press-release/2021/05/12/defying-predictions-remittance-flows-remain-strong-during-covid-19-crisis. Accessed 28 Jan 2023.

World Health Organization. (2022, December 2). Fact sheet: Disability. https://www.who.int/news-room/fact-sheets/detail/disability-and-health. Accessed 30 Jan 2023.

World Inequality Report. (2022). Executive summary. https://wir2022.wid.world/executive-summary/. Accessed 28 Jan 2023.

Yunus, M. (2006, December 10). Nobel lecture upon being awarded the Nobel Peace Prize. https://www.nobelprize.org/prizes/peace/2006/yunus/facts/

4

Education

It is our duty to stand up for humanity. Step in and correct things that are wrong.

Leymah Gbowee (2011)

Seventy percent of ten-year olds in low- and middle-income countries are unable to read or understand a simple text. Referred to as the learning poverty rate, COVID increased this indicator to 70%, up from 53% pre-pandemic (Meinck et al., 2022; UNICEF, 2022). COVID reduced educational achievement in the United States as well. Average reading scores for nine-year olds declined five points during the pandemic, the largest drop in three decades. Mathematics scores fell by seven points, the largest drop in the five decades since scores were tracked (The Nation's Report Card, n.d.).

The potential learning losses that have accrued for today's young generation, and for human capital development, are extreme. Worldwide, the United Nations estimates that from 2020 to 2021, 147 million children missed more than half of their in-class instruction. This could result in their losing $17 trillion in lifetime earnings in present value. Nearly 405 million schoolchildren live in 23 countries that are yet to fully open schools, and many schoolchildren are at risk of dropping out altogether (UNICEF "Data", n.d.).

Racial and gender inequities heighten learning loss. Girls, children from disadvantaged backgrounds, children in rural areas, children living with disabilities, and children from ethnic minorities have been most severely disadvantaged by school closings during COVID (United Nations "SDG4"). Disruptions to education systems due to COVID exacerbated learning inequalities for vulnerable groups of girls and young women.

Intersectionality can create further educational disparities. Girls fall behind when they face challenges of discrimination based on race, ethnicity, religion, migration status, and/or disability. In 42 countries, children with disabilities had less access to early childhood education than children without disabilities. Girls with disabilities fared even worse (United Nations "Gender", 2022).

In the United States, during COVID, historically underserved racial communities fell the furthest behind (Sustainable Development Solutions Network, 2021). The pandemic has inflicted the greatest toll on students for these groups who lack access to computers and laptops, a quiet place to work, and teacher support (The Nation's Report Card Sec II, n.d.). As a result, the white–Black score gap worsened, growing from 25 points in 2020 to 33 points in 2022 in mathematics.

The rise in migration has limited access to education for children and families who are fleeing human rights abuses, violence and conflicts, climate-related disasters, and untenable economic and political conditions. World-wide, there are 100 million displaced people (United Nations, UN News, 2022). Nearly half of all refugee children are unable to attend school (United Nations, UNHCR, 2022). Refugee girls are further deprived with even less access to education (United Nations, IOM, 2022).

The lack of a decent education is human tragedy for these children, denying them a bright future that meets their aspirations and allows them to be autonomous, productive, and contributing citizens. Society's role is to provide all its children with an education to lead fulfilling lives.

Businesses Can Play an Important Role in Advancing Education

Neglecting the educational needs of children from underserved communities has a detrimental effect on the economy. "Unless the pandemic's impact on student learning can be mitigated and students can be supported to catch up on missed learning, the global economy could experience lower GDP growth over the lifetime of this generation. In fact, by 2040, incomplete education related to COVID-19 could translate to annual losses of $1.6 trillion to the global economy, or 0.9 per cent of predicted total GDP" (McKinsey, 2022).

Instead, by investing in opportunities for underserved children, we can establish the conditions for economic vitality, as well as social stability, peace, and security (World Bank, 2022).

Education is an existential matter for business. For companies, a well-educated workforce is essential to be competitive in the global marketplace. Skilled talent is necessary to develop new technology, products, and services to meet the needs and demands of developed and emerging regions. Future generations who are educated in science, technology, engineering, and math (STEM) will be valuable to businesses in advancing solutions to vital global issues such as climate change and energy, food supply and agriculture, healthcare, and ecosystems. STEM education is not only necessary to prepare students for obvious careers in technology, but also for jobs in manufacturing and construction, recycling and waste management, fashion and architecture, and healthcare.

Not only do corporations have a deep and fundamental interest in our developing a highly qualified workforce, but they also bring powerful resources to the table. Financial resources are just part of the equation. Most significantly, businesses bring people with experience and expertise, along with their passion, commitment, and technological assets to create and drive change. Furthermore, unlike governments, companies have a broader global mandate; corporations cross borders, languages, and cultures to accomplish their purposes. When it comes to educating the world's workforce, businesses are not limited by geographic boundaries.

Education is so central to business that it would be difficult to find a major company that does not contribute in some way to addressing the education crisis, either through philanthropy, employee volunteering, executive involvement on nonprofit boards, or a combination. Companies do so, not only for the reasons discussed in this chapter, but also for education's appeal to employees and consumers.

Fortunately, there is a plethora of outstanding global and national nonprofits that excel at engaging companies to improve education and help students. For example, involving businesspeople in classrooms, mentoring, volunteering, and philanthropy. Junior Achievement, and Teach for America are outstanding examples of such organizations that have a global presence, as well as City Year, Year Up, and Braven, that focus on the United States. These nonprofits and many more galvanize hundreds of the world's major corporations in service and funding to improve schools, keep students engaged and in school, make education more affordable, and help young people to gain access to higher education and jobs.

Successful partnerships must manage tricky issues. First, some from the corporate sector might demand top-down instant results, while educators might seek more research-oriented, consensus-driven, longer-term approaches. To further complicate matters, leaders with limited terms— including politicians—require short-term solutions in order to show results to their constituents, whereas improving the education system requires longer-term problem solving. Additionally, there is the difficult and sensitive issue of outcome determination and measurement: Are these initiatives truly addressing systemic problems? Can achievement be documented? Can successful initiatives be replicated and scaled?

As shown in this chapter, there are solutions that can provide children with the education they need to flourish. Furthermore, corporate investments and partnerships are catalytic and essential in advancing new models to remedy educational, racial, and social gaps. Collaboration between business, nonprofits, and government can provide breakthroughs. By scaling corporate engagement in programs that work, the vision of education and opportunity for all our children can become a reality.

Experience demonstrates that there are several fundamental principles that are essential for the success of educational initiatives worldwide. This chapter describes specific corporate initiatives that promote systemic change in education that is equitable and inclusive. Effective models are not cookie cutter. Instead, they are centered on the needs and interests of students in particular regions. The best programs are often home grown by people who themselves emerged from communities that have been deeply deprived of resources and opportunity. One of the most significant lessons is the imperative to create and implement programs that are hybrids, drawing on successful models from a variety of regions, but adapted with deep respect and understanding of local communities. Companies have the vast resources—human, financial, and technological, global footprints, and market incentives to continue to advance progress.

Inequities in Education Inhibit Economic Mobility

Inequities in Higher Education Limit Opportunities

In the past two decades, the United States dropped from 2nd to 16th among OECD countries in bachelor's degree attainment among people ages 25 to 34 (Calahan et al., 2021). Extreme wealth disparities, particularly by race and ethnicity is an important factor, given that federal financial aid has not kept pace with the increase in tuition expenses and financing for postsecondary education has shifted from public funding to students and their families. Significantly, 66% of higher education expenses in OECD countries were covered by public sources; in the United States, only 36% were funded by the government. As a result, in 2020, the college graduation rate among students from families in the highest income quartile was four times higher than for students from families in the lowest income quartile. Furthermore, students of color bear the burden of long-lasting debt.

Lifetime earnings are determined by one's level of education. Because of the link between family wealth and educational attainment, the likelihood of absolute mobility is limited; students from low-income families are less likely to advance to higher socioeconomic levels. In the United States, the median lifetime earnings for people with high school degrees is $1.6 million, compared to $2.8 for college graduates. For professional degree holders, the median is $4.7 million. Moreover, racial inequity takes its toll. The medians are lower for Black and Hispanic/Latino Americans: $1.4 million for high school graduates; $2.3 million for college graduates; and $3.7 million for professional degree holders (Carnevale et al., 2021).

Furthermore, learning loss due to COVID-19 could result in earning losses totaling $28 trillion over the rest of this century (Chapman & Belkin, 2022). If learning loss isn't reversed, it would equate to a 1.6% drop in lifetime earnings for the average K-12 student. Learning loss brings about lower high school graduation rates and college enrollment, higher teen motherhood, and arrests and incarceration(Kane et al., 2022).

Labor market discrimination further exacerbates racial, ethnic, and gender inequities for young workers, ages 25–35. Given equal levels of education, women are less likely to be employed in "good jobs" that pay at least $35,000 annually and $57,000 at the median. The share of white men with good jobs is 62%. White women 50%. Black men 39%. Black women 35% (Georgetown, 2023).

These data points run counter to the notion of "the American Dream," popularized by James Truslow Adams in his 1931 book *The Epic of America* (Adams, 1931).

> The American dream, that dream of a land in which life should be better and richer and fuller for every man, with opportunity for each according to his ability or achievement. It is a difficult dream for the European upper classes to interpret adequately, and too many of us ourselves have grown weary and mistrustful of it. It is not a dream of motor cars and high wages merely, but a dream of social order in which each man and each woman shall be able to

attain to the fullest stature of which they are innately capable, and be recognized by others for what they are, regardless of the fortuitous circumstances of birth or position.

Also referred to as "intergenerational mobility," this cherished principle maintains that education advances children beyond the limitations of their parents' economic status. Unfortunately, however, this American Dream appears to be idealized. Intergenerational income mobility has in fact declined in the United States since 1980, especially for Black families (Mazumder, 2022). In addition to variations in mobility along racial lines, there are also regional variations in mobility. "Areas with high mobility have less residential segregation, lower income inequality, better primary schools, higher levels of social capital, and greater family stability" (Ibid.).

The failure of the American Dream is particularly disappointing given that educational mobility is higher in other high-income countries. Countries in Western Europe, Canada, South America, parts of the Middle East, and South Africa have higher rates of mobility, for example, compared to low- and middle-income countries. Importantly, "countries with higher rates of mobility have (i) higher tax revenues and rates of government expenditures, especially on education; (ii) better child health indicators (less stunting and lower infant mortality); (iii) higher school quality (more teachers per pupil and fewer school dropouts); and (iv) less residential segregation" (van der Weide et al., 2021).

When privileges of birth determine one's access to education and related job opportunities, then individuals, families, and entire communities are unfairly deprived. This in turn diminishes a country's economic development, peace, and security. It is in the public interest for governments to ensure that all people have opportunities to achieve their greatest potential to become contributing members of society.

Given the power of higher education to influence one's likelihood of employment, compensation level, and socioeconomic status, the trend away from public funding for higher education is concerning. Previous generations of students attended colleges supported by state funds, which were funded by broad-based taxes on older generations. Now, students and their families increasingly pay their own way, given the more recently prevailing view that education is a private investment, rather than a public good. Individuals may not be able to finance this high-return investment in higher education on their own; the economy-wide benefits of higher education suggest that a purely private financing market will lead to under-investment in education (Mitchell et al., 2018).

A poorly educated citizenry undermines national security, by threatening economic growth and competitiveness, physical safety, intellectual property, US global awareness, and US unity and cohesion. Too many young people are not employable in an increasingly high-skilled and global economy, and too many are not qualified to join the military because they are physically unfit, have criminal records, or have an inadequate level of education (Eberstadt & Abramsky, 2022).

Globally, the education crisis is front and center on the intergovernmental agenda. The United Nations has been so committed to the primacy of education that "Quality Education" was established as Sustainable Development Goal (SDG) 4. The 17 SDGs are a universal call to action to end poverty, protect the planet, and improve the lives and prospects of everyone, everywhere. In 2015, all UN Member States adopted a 15-year plan to achieve the 17 Goals by 2030 (United Nations "Agenda", n.d.). "Experts put the funding needs in the trillions, and we've so far been working in billions. The irony of the situation is that while the world has been awash in savings—so much so that real interest rates have been falling for several decades—we have not been able to find the capital needed for investments in education, health care, and infrastructure" (Sachs et al., 2022).

Companies like the ones featured in this chapter recognize the impact they can have and the value to business and society by working in partnership with local experts and partners. These are investments in the workforce and on the ground leaders in regions worldwide.

Inequities in STEM Education Further Limit Opportunities

Employment in computer and information technology occupations is projected to grow faster than the average for all occupations in the next decade; salaries in this sector are particularly robust. In the United States, the median annual wage for computer and information technology occupations was twice the median annual wage for all occupations. Median salaries for computer network architects with a bachelor's degree were $120,520, and over $100,000 for information security analysts, quality assurance analysts, testers, and software developers (BLS, 2022).

Yet Blacks Americans, Hispanics/Latinos, and American Indians or Alaska Natives continue to be underrepresented among science and engineering (S&E) degree recipients relative to their representation in the overall population (National Center for Sciences and Engineering Statistics, 2021). Girls and women are discouraged from science and math throughout their education, thereby reducing their preparation and opportunities for careers as adults. Men vastly outnumber women majoring in most STEM fields in college. Women comprise only 28% of STEM positions. Even fewer women are employed in some of the highest-paid and fastest growing jobs, like computer science and engineering (AAUW, n.d.).

The imperative to educate children and young adults is not only a matter for the United States but throughout the world. In Africa, for example, according to the Brookings Institute, "Africa's youths can help solve the global tech shortage" (Mansson, 2022). Governments alone have not been able to achieve society's interests, nor meet the needs of employers, in preparing people for the workforce of today and tomorrow. Worldwide, only 35% of students in STEM education are women, and only three percent in information and communication technology studies. According to the 2022 SDG Progress Report, "girls are systematically steered away from science and math careers" (Sachs et al., 2022; United Nations "Gender", 2022).

Success in educating young people in STEM translates into opportunities for employment and self-sufficiency for families and better economies everywhere. Worldwide, STEM education and research are fundamental to national development and productivity, economic competitiveness, and societal wellbeing (Freeman et al., 2019).

Some businesses are a vital force, especially when they partner with on the ground educators, NGOs/nonprofits, and local ministries to find new solutions to improve education. Together, they are finding ways to provide the education that students require to be successful, fulfilled, and effective contributors in the world.

Hybrid Models Are Uniquely Suited to Drive Solutions in Local Communities

Advocates and successful models demonstrate the effectiveness of problem-solving initiatives that are created by—and often led by—people in the community being served. This concept is contrary to the more traditional approach whereby, as some claim, solutions are parachuted in from the Global North who believe they know what is best. The best interventions are more likely to be developed, and implemented, by people who know and understand the local culture and needs. Some companies and foundations are beginning to recognize and support this approach.

A Vision of the Hybrid Model

Olufunmilayo Arewa explains the colonial origins of the more traditional approach. She recommends instead using "more flexible frameworks to harness creativity and innovation that are modified as needed based on local needs and priorities" (Arewa "Remarks", 2022).

Arewa holds up the example of Francis Kéré, who won the 2022 Pritzker Prize, architecture's highest honor. Born in Burkina Faso, now living in Germany, Kéré is the first Black architect and first architect from Africa to win the Pritzker Prize. Kéré's approach steps outside of the shadow of what Arewa refers to as "colonial overhang," featuring instead "a much-needed model that can inspire us and show us an important avenue for potential future paths" (Ibid.).

Arewa is a business and law professor at Temple University, with advanced degrees in economics, law, and anthropology. "I am a daughter of two diasporas from Africa. The first, an involuntary one of enslaved people, brought by my mother's ancestors to the New World. My father was born in Nigeria in present-day Ondo state. He came to the United States around the time of Nigeria's independence in 1960" (Arewa, 2021). Arewa has lived in countries worldwide, including Germany and Nigeria.

As Arewa describes in her book, *Disrupting Africa: Technology, Law, and Development*, (Arewa, 2021) colonialism served external interests primarily European governments and commercial interests. In discussions with NGO and business leaders, she explains.

> Colonial overhang reflects continuing patterns of external determination and cut and paste borrowing that are far too often not sufficiently scrutinized. Old and borrowed models, policies, and laws with past histories, contexts, assumptions, disputes, and accommodations are inflexible, rarely keep up with changes in source of laws and policies. Colonial overhang casts a long shadow in mindsets, systems, infrastructures, global and local power frameworks, legal and policy structures, and operating cultures.
>
> Instead, we need better, more flexible frameworks to harness creativity and innovation that are modified as needed based on local needs and priorities. Kéré designs buildings that serve the community he came from, by including using indigenous materials and local symbols. (Arewa "Remarks", 2022)

As an architecture school student at the Technical University of Berlin, to which Kéré won a scholarship, he raised money to build an elementary school in his hometown of Gando. By engaging local residents in construction, and "drawing blueprints for them in the sand," he builds structures for and with communities, incorporating their materials, their programs, and their unique characters. "They are tied to the ground on which they sit and to the people who sit within them. They have presence without pretense and an impact shaped by grace," said the Pritzker jury in its citation. "Kéré is pioneering architecture — sustainable to the earth and its inhabitants — in lands of extreme scarcity," said Tom Pritzker, chairman of the Hyatt Foundation, which sponsors the award (Pogrebin, 2022). Kéré's achievements remind us that educational initiatives come in many varieties—his in bricks and mortar—and not just curriculum.

"Working in impoverished areas demands skills beyond design," said Kéré. He stresses in particular the importance of patience. "You have power shortages, you have the Internet that is broken all the time — you have to be passionate and believe in the project," he said. "I make sure I don't get frustrated, to imagine doing architecture in a different way that is not very fast." Kéré's deep connection to his home community informs his practice, including his integrating local symbols like the baobab or palaver tree, as well as a traditional blue boubou garment he wore as a child. "[Kéré] not only wants the community to participate in the creation of architecture, Kéré said, but to connect with it and feel transported. 'They get more than a building,' Kéré added. 'They get inspiration'" (Ibid.).

At present, Kéré is involved in rebuilding Burkina Faso's parliament building. He has been discouraging the government from constructing a Western-style official building. "You have to understand that the economy, the social behavior, the traditions in Burkina Faso are completely different than those in Europe or the United States. The main meeting structure in Burkina Faso is the tree. Even in the city, that is where people meet, sitting under the shade, to discuss things. I want to create a structure that is also a kind of organic meeting point, where everyone can go, rather than an isolated structure with high walls and security and a fence to keep people out of it. Gathering spaces are almost nonexistent in the capital. Why couldn't we have one on top of the parliament, with a green roof that people could walk onto?" (Heyman, 2016).

An NGO in Kenya is a Model of Grassroots Organizing

Kennedy Odede is the Founder and CEO of Shining Hope for Communities (SHOFCO), the Kenya's largest grassroots organization, whose centerpiece programs are tuition-free schools and leadership academies for girls (Odede, 2015). Launched in Kibera, a neighborhood outside of Nairobi, and one of the world's poorest and largest slums, the organization is now in more than fifty communities nationwide.

Key to SHOFCO's success is its direct relevance to local needs and the community context, as well as Odede's deep personal connection to the communities served by SHOFCO. The concepts sound similar to what Arewa describes as hybrid models. The support and engagement from almost sixty global companies and foundations have helped SHOFCO to achieve so much.

Odede, the oldest of eight children, grew up in Kibera, a crowded slum teeming with violence, and without sewage systems, roads, running water, nor access to education or healthcare. As a young teenager, Odede was homeless, starving, and living in terror, "shivering under a bed," hiding from paramilitary police spraying bullets in one of their frequent neighborhood raids. Surrounded by despair, Odede had the courage and spirit to start a youth group, first playing soccer, and then performing street theater to discourage domestic violence. Eventually, with support and encouragement from an American student, Jessica Posner, Odede had the opportunity to go to the United States where he gained a scholarship to Wesleyan University. Upon graduating, he quickly returned, together with Posner, to transform his grassroots initiative into schools for girls, the most vulnerable members of the community (Odede & Posner, 2016).

Just ten years old, SHOFCO has served 2.4 million people in seventeen slums, educating girls and boys in tuition-free schools, and placing hundreds of young people in jobs and internships, in addition to distributing 2.5 million liters of water, providing healthcare in clinics, and promoting wealth accumulation through savings and loan organizations (SHOFCO, 2022).

Funding from nearly sixty multinational corporations and foundations has made it possible for SHOFCO to achieve so much. "Safaricom was the game-changer," says Odede. Safaricom is the largest telecommunications company in Kenya, and Robert Collymore was its CEO back in 2015. "Robert Collymore recognized the organization's greater potential from the beginning, when we walked through Kibera and he visited the schools. He understood the value to the community, as well as the importance to Kenyan based companies to invest in girls education, in addition to providing clean water and other valuable services. Safaricom has been a long term partner," explains Odede (Read more about Safaricom in the chapter on Economic Development.).

Based on his experience building SHOFCO, Odede speaks to the importance of "local and indigenous leaders creating the table and co-designing solutions. Low- and middle-income countries are home to a multitude of local, community-based organizations that are driving innovative and cost-effective solutions in their communities. Local organizations are nimble and can move quickly, which is crucial."

Odede addresses the need to shift funding and power, and with a basis in trust.

> If world leaders are as committed to progress as they say in their speeches and press conferences, they must face their internal biases and place trust in local community leaders. Trust requires recognizing the strength of local organizations and understanding that outsiders cannot always know what's best for communities. (Odede "Opinion", 2022)

> In Africa, white-led institutions have shaped the development and social entrepreneurship landscape, deciding who succeeds and who fails. Only recently has there been a growing recognition of these imperialist dynamics, which uplift foreign-led practitioners more than local ones. There is a growing consensus that the future should and must be created and led by Africans, because real progress requires it to be on our own terms. And yet, this is just talk until funders shift resources and power, at scale, towards local solutions. (Ibid.)

Odede discusses this perspective from his personal experience.

> In my 10-year journey as co-founder of SHOFCO, working in Kenya's urban slums, I have experienced the racial barriers that many Africans face. Addressing these systemic disparities begins with soul-searching and public declarations from funders, but it can't stop there. Closing the race gap in philanthropy demands radical candor. Only when funders are open about identifying racial bias and holding the philanthropic community accountable, will emerging Black leaders have equal chances for success. Real transformation in African development means shifting power, moving away from traditional aid dependence. Perhaps my own imagination would have been cut down by the reality of short, restricted funding cycles that defined my early years, if not for my optimism.

> As a black community organizer who has achieved some success in navigating the business of philanthropy, Odede feels an obligation to open the door for the next generation of Africans beginning their journeys as leaders and grassroots organisers.

> I'm hopeful about what I'm seeing in the world at this moment, and what this time of reckoning might teach us about race and philanthropy if we are brave enough to face it.

We must not let this opportunity pass without progress. All I ask are three things of funders: challenge the belief that "local solutions cannot scale" and do the hard work of creating supportive ecosystems that develop solutions that scale; as you fund and award white founders working in communities of colour (at home and abroad), ensure you apply the same level of recognition and support to leaders of colour who possess the same or greater skills and knowledge of their environment; and lastly, mandate diversity within the teams that allocate resources and make investment decisions. (Ibid.)

Caleb Ndaka has a similar perspective on the value of local leadership.

The biggest challenge we have to devolving technology to rural and low-income communities in Africa, where over 70% of Africans live, is not technology - that is devices and connections - it is people. It is empowering local communities to leverage technology to solve their own problems and not the other way round. It is people first, then technology. Local leaders play a critical role of mobilizing local communities to embrace and use technology. (Ndaka, 2022)

Caleb is the Co-Founder and Program Lead of Kids Comp Camp in Kenya and Rwanda, and Research Associate at the London School of Economics and Political Science. Kids Comp Camp is a grassroots education technology initiative that helps children in rural communities to develop skills that are competitive for them to thrive in today's digital driven society. In the first 5 years, Kids Comp Camp had already had an impact on over 10,000 beneficiaries. It has been recognized by a number of leadership groups, including the Internet Governance Forum (IGF) 2016 that awarded them with the Funds for Internet Research and Education (FIRE) award (Funds for Internet Research and Education website, n.d.). To accomplish these milestones, Kids Comp Camp works in partnerships with leading organizations including Microsoft, Google, and General Electric (GE), and M-PESA Foundation and over 1000 community trainers (Ndaka, 2022).

Sean Rafter is also convinced that the most effective partnerships are with locally run organizations on the ground. Rafter, whose work with VillageReach is discussed in the Healthcare chapter, is Managing Director, Humanitarian and Emergency Health Logistics (HELP). He describes the expense, resource drain, and bureaucracy involved with working with large philanthropic institutional partners and multi-lateral organizations. "We like working with leaders on the ground. They are diligent with the project charter. The approach is more ethical, more impactful." Rafter observes that the traditional humanitarian business model needs to change. "There are more private philanthropists who want to see funds made available directly to organizations on the ground" (Rafter, 2022).

HP's Ambitious Goal to Accelerate Digital Equity Worldwide

While there are a vast number of corporate initiatives to improve education, HP Inc.'s approach stands out for its scope, innovation, and deep engagement with local communities. Headquartered in Palo Alto, California, HP is a multinational technology company with a product and service portfolio of personal systems, printers, and 3D printing solutions. With over $63 billion in annual revenues and 51,000 employees, HP has operations in more than 186 countries.

HP set a goal of accelerating digital equity for 150 million people by 2030. Among the company's initiatives is the Digital Equity Accelerator, which helps scale digital equity for women and girls worldwide, elderly people, educators, people with disabilities, and historically marginalized persons. By providing all people with the tools and digital literacy to use technology to their full potential, HP aims to broaden opportunities for everyone to participate in the digital economy (HP, 2023).

HP's model is noteworthy because it seeks to advance systemic change, equity, and inclusion. Additionally, the company's approach is to meet the specific needs of each community by working in partnership with local educators, nonprofits, and ministries.

HP's Successful Approach to Investing in NGO Partnerships

For guidance in choosing the countries and NGOs for the Digital Equity Accelerator, HP looked to an intermediary that had expertise, credibility, and relationships with effective organizations worldwide. The company chose Aspen Digital as its partner, an NGO that "empowers policy-makers, civic organizations, companies, and the public to be responsible stewards of technology and media in the service of an informed, just, and equitable world" (Aspen Institute, 2023).

"We sought Aspen Digital's guidance in choosing organizations that effectively serve aging populations, girls and women, immigrants and refugees, BIPOC, and people with disabilities," explained Michele Malejki, Global Head, Social Impact, HP. Ultimately, seven NGOs were invited to participate, including three from the US, two from India, and two from Morocco (Malejki, 2022).

The focus of each of the seven organizations varied from providing the elderly with telehealth services, bringing internet access to rural villages, and introducing young women to STEM careers. The common purpose was to facilitate access to healthcare, education, and economic opportunity for marginalized people.

In addition to the Accelerator program, HP leverages strategic partnerships and programs to make progress toward its digital equity goal. One such strategic partner is Girl Rising, an NGO that works for a world where all girls can learn, thrive, and rise (Girl Rising website, n.d.). Originally created to produce the 2013 award winning feature documentary, Girl Rising, (Girl Rising "Documentary", n.d.-b) the organization was subsequently transformed to advance regional educational initiatives worldwide. Today, the nonprofit reaches ten million adolescents in twelve countries together with over 110 partners, including local organizations. Girl Rising works with educators, schools, nonprofits, communities, governments, and businesses, to provide education for girls, while also fostering confidence and positive gender attitudes to advance equity. "We work with organizations around the world to support locally led change that accelerates and strengthens quality education and greater opportunity for girls" (Girl Rising website, n.d.). Eighty percent of Girl Rising's "target population fall under the low-income bracket, with some communities falling below the poverty line earning less than US$1.90 a day" (Girl Rising "About", n.d.-a).

HP initially provided funding to help create and distribute the film. Ultimately, the company became a multi-year partner to advance Girl Rising's educational mission. HP recognized that it and Girl Rising were strategically aligned for improving educational outcomes for 100 million learners particularly through the company's digital equity program. Financial funding has been only one aspect of HP's valuable support. Christina Lowery, CEO of Girl Rising, explains the myriad ways that the company has added value (Lowery, 2022). Most importantly, says Lowery, HP's Malejki constantly scans the landscape to find innovative ways to advance the nonprofit's mission and work. One example is HP engaging NABU, a children's book publisher, to collaborate on a book about gender equity in Kenya. Another example is HP creating events at the World Economic Forum in Davos to give Lowery a platform to share the organization's work and engage additional partners. Most importantly says Lowery, HP never "over engineered" programs and events, nor did HP overtly showcase their brand. "That was the secret sauce to the partnership—HP understanding that by putting Girl Rising first, the company would ultimately achieve its purposes of promoting digital literacy and gender equity."

Based on her experience with HP, Lowery explains that a truly meaningful and productive NGO–corporate partnership is based on honest, true, and deep mutual respect. The key factors for such success have included long term, multi-year partnerships to achieve sustainable impact; co-creating and iteratively enhancing systems to measure and evaluate impact, and track and communicate metrics; engaging company employees as volunteers to advance the nonprofit's work; and appreciating the value of global citizen storytelling.

Ongoing collaboration has been a game-changer, explains Lowery. HP was in touch, for example, to explore potential synergies as the company established new initiatives, such as teacher digital training in Nigeria. Similarly, the door was open for Girl Rising to be in touch with HP to explore ways they could work together to advance important educational programs in the face of obstacles presented by COVID. For example, with HP's help, Girl Rising was able to support Slam Out Loud in shifting its programming via WhatsApp to disseminate arts activities to nonprofit partners and ministries in India. Making its content accessible in various Indian languages, Slam Out Loud has reached 14.8 million youths across 23 Indian states and 19 countries "to find their voice through creative expression and build essential life skills to dream bigger."

Not only does HP recognize the value of an educated citizenry worldwide, but the company has invested complementary resources, including human capital, financial funding, and technology support, to advance effective programs for systemic change for society's marginalized groups. By identifying effective NGOs and establishing meaningful, measurable, long-term solutions, HP ensures that the company is leveraging partnerships for their expertise, credibility, and access to remote communities. These are solutions that work in advancing a vision of education for all children.

HP's Model to Accelerate Digital Equity for 150 Million People by 2030

HP has designed a methodical approach to accelerate digital equity for 150 million people in communities worldwide by 2030: Work in close partnership with local schools, nonprofits, and ministries to understand the scope of the digital literacy gap in countries facing the greatest challenges, identify barriers to access, work in close partnership with educators on the ground to develop and advance innovative solutions for digital equity, then scale solutions that work (HP, 2021). Importantly, this goal is timed for success in the near future, so that HP and its teams are accountable in our lifetimes. This is not a mythical aspiration to be achieved thirty years from now; rather, this is a timeframe for which today's leaders will be held responsible.

As described earlier in this chapter, COVID magnified the educational challenges facing communities in underserved nations. The pandemic precluded full time classroom learning. This presented a formidable barrier to access, particularly for regions that lacked computers and financial resources. HP's most successful initiative to advance digital equity despite school closings has been HP Innovation and Digital Education Academy (HP IDEA), which was launched in late 2020.

As a first step, HP engaged with ministries of education by listening to their challenges and helping to find solutions to advance their goals. HP approached ministries as advisors, not as salespersons, helping to create hybrid education programs free of charge for the first year. "You need to move the needle on things that matter to them," explained Mayank Dhingra, Senior Education Business Leader, Southern Europe, Middle East, and Africa, HP (Dhingra, 2022). Dhingra is the architect of HP IDEA as well as a suite of complementary programs. To further deepen their understanding of the challenges, HP convenes ministerial delegates in problem-solving roundtables, often along with other education-centric organizations such as UNESCO, T4 Education, and others.

With the support of ministries, HP engages high-performing teachers as HP IDEA Fellows in an eight-month immersive instructional leadership program. Most importantly, the program supports teachers in achieving their aspirations to learn digital skills, and for the teachers themselves to apply an innovation mindset to transform the pedagogical framework in their respective schools. With their newfound expertise, teachers lead the way in identifying challenges, finding solutions for their respective schools and communities, and effecting change at scale. Teachers graduate with a certificate of completion and granting of an HP IDEA Fellowship title. HP also wants to give graduating teachers public recognition for the roles they play in transforming education. Graduates in South Africa appreciated being recognized by the President of South Africa and the former Executive Director of UN Women.

In 2022, HP IDEA has graduated cohorts of teachers in Kenya, Nigeria, South Africa, UAE, Tanzania, Uganda, Oman, Rwanda, Ghana, and Kazakhstan. in addition to launching new cohorts in Zanzibar, Morocco, Turkey, Ukraine, Saudia Arabia, and The Gambia. By the start of 2023, HP will be working with fourteen ministries of education across seventeen countries, to involve over 30,000 teachers. HP IDEA is aligned with the UN Sustainable Development Goals (SDGs), (United Nations "SDG4", n.d.) the Organization for Economic Cooperation and Development (OECD), (OECD "Education", n.d.) and the Continental Educational Strategy of

Africa (CESA, 2016–2025) (African Union Commission, 2017) objectives. Coursework for teachers was developed in consultation with educators on the ground and includes coursework from Harvard University and the University of Michigan.

In addition, together with Intel and Microsoft, HP launched the Africa Education Medal to recognize and honor outstanding individuals who have demonstrated leadership, impact, and advocacy in the field of education (T4 Education "Medal", 2023a). The jury to select an annual winner is comprised of global luminaries in education. In 2022, the inaugural Medal was awarded to Professor Mamokgethi Phakeng, Vice Chancellor of the University of Cape Town, South Africa. Growing up in rural South Africa during Apartheid, Phakeng became the first Black female South African to earn a Ph.D. in Mathematics Education in 2002. She has published more than eighty research papers and five edited volumes that shape mathematics education in classrooms across Africa and beyond (T4 Education "Winner", 2023b).

Oprah Winfrey recognized and congratulated Professor Phakeng in a video that has been viewed worldwide (T4 Education, n.d.). The Africa Education Medal elevates the importance of advancing education while also showcasing HP's value in promoting digital equity.

Ukraine is among the countries where HP is implementing HP IDEA. The company is working together with Ed Camp Ukraine, a nonprofit that unites educators to help them develop professionally (EdCamp Ukraine, n.d.). Led by its chairman, Oleksandr Elkin, the organization is providing remote learning opportunities to tens of thousands of teachers. "Education is a key factor of society building, a guarantee of a successful Ukraine," says Elkin. "We are excited about the opportunity to work with HP IDEA. Already, there are three times more teacher applications for the first cohort to go through the program, so we will need to add more" (Elkin, 2022).

HP conducts rigorous outcomes measurements with quarterly reporting of social impact. The endeavor reflects an NGO ethos, but HP is confident that doing good for the world is also good for business and will support commercial growth in the long term. "This sends a message internally and externally that HP is committed to its role in closing the digital gap, and that means a great deal to both our customers and employees," explains Dhingra.

As of this writing, more than 74 million students and adults have benefited from HP-sponsored education initiatives since 2015 (HP, 2023). Importantly, HP understands that systemic, inclusive, and equitable solutions must be designed with local partners and experts in order to address the unique barriers to students, schools, and communities.

Additional Companies Invest in Nonprofits to Advance Education

Girls Who Code and its Corporate Partners are Building a Pipeline of Engineers

"Girls and women are systematically tracked away from science and math throughout their education, limiting their access, preparation, and opportunities to go into these fields as adults," according to the American Association of University Women (AAUW) (AAUW, n.d.). In fact, by the time they reach college, women are significantly underrepresented in science, technology, engineering, and math (STEM) majors—making up only 21% of engineering and 19% of computer and information science majors (Ibid.). Moreover, workplace discrimination is reported by half the women and people of color in STEM positions, according to the Pew Research Center (Pew Research Center, 2018).

Carol Juel, Executive Vice President and Chief Technology and Operating Officer, Synchrony, a consumer financial services company, has experienced these challenges first-hand. Discouraged from being a STEM major in college, she eventually found her way back to her childhood interest in STEM later in her professional career. "It's a disservice to girls and a disservice to employers that girls and women are discouraged from this path," says Juel (2023) This conviction drives Juel's passion for Girls Who Code (GWC), where she serves on the Board of Directors. "As a leader, you need to continue to adapt the workforce."

"The customer base is diverse, and that is the business case," explains Juel. "GWC is helping to build the pipeline. That may be noble, but it's also practical." In fact, over 71% of GWC's funding comes from companies. "This is not altruistic," says Reshma Saujani, the visionary who founded GWC (Girls Who Code "Team", n.d.). "Companies are doing what they need to do to find more tech employees, and diversity is good for business" (Saujani, 2023).

Together with its corporate partners, GWC is turning things around by building the world's largest pipeline of female engineers (Ibid.). Over the last 10 years, GWC has served over 500,000 students, more than half of whom are from diverse backgrounds. 115,000 of GWC alumni are now college and post-college aged. Its alumni go on to earn degrees in Computer Science and related fields at seven times the national average (Girls Who Code website, n.d.). "We're changing the culture of what a computer scientist looks like and working to build a tech industry that looks like the diverse communities we live in today" (Barrett, 2023).

Women's representation in computer jobs has declined since 1990, even while employment in computer jobs has more than quadrupled. Furthermore, the fastest growing and highest paying jobs, which are in engineering and computer science, remain heavily male dominated (Corbett & Hill, 2015). The discrepancies in employment and salaries matter. Women lose out on important opportunities, and companies miss out on valuable talent that is essential to reach and serve lucrative markets. "Giving women equal opportunities to pursue and thrive in STEM careers helps narrow the gender pay gap, enhances women's economic security, ensures a diverse and talented STEM workforce and prevents biases in these fields and the products and services they produce," according to AAUW (AAUW, n.d.).

Challenges facing women in STEM education and careers are well documented. STEM fields are often viewed as masculine, and teachers and parents often underestimate girls' math abilities starting as early as preschool. Furthermore, because fewer women study and work in STEM, these fields tend to perpetuate inflexible, exclusionary, male-dominated cultures that are not supportive of or attractive to women and minorities. Additionally, girls have fewer role models in STEM careers, including in media and popular culture; and even fewer role models who are women of color. All these impediments discourage girls early on, undermining their confidence and interfering with their ambitions (Girls Who Code website, n.d.).

GWC offers several programs to meet the interests of women, girls, and non-binary individuals, ranging from Clubs that serve students as young as the third grade, to summer programs for high school students, to Hiring Summits for college graduates entering the tech workforce. While most of the programs focus on participants in the US, GWC summer programs reach students in the United States, UK, India, Brazil, Egypt, Rwanda, the Philippines, and beyond. These include the Virtual Summer Immersion Program and the Self-Paced Program for high school students, in addition to Hiring Summits with corporate partners. Synchrony participates in Hiring Summits and is one of 50 + corporate partners that supports classroom learning in the Summer Immersion Programs.

"Our involvement with GWC benefits our company as much as the students. Many of them work in multiple jobs and have family caregiving responsibilities while they are attending school. They embody the very qualities employers want — fortitude and resilience," says Juel (2023) "Gender and racial diversity and equity is central to everything that GWC does. We want to make sure that students have the tools, resources, and access they need. And we want to create equitable and safe environments." Not only does Synchrony host Summer Immersion Program classrooms, which serve hundreds of students each year, but they also provide technology to students who need it; and recruit volunteers from across the company to serve on panels, lead virtual workshops, and provide feedback on student projects. Students get a real sense of what it means to work in tech at Synchrony. "It doesn't matter how smart you are or how hard you work," explains Juel, "if the workplace is not welcoming" (Ibid.).

"Girls Who Code Girls" is a particularly exciting and innovative new program at GWC. Today, 77% of video game developers are men, and only 20% of all characters are women. GWC's new initiative provides a desktop and mobile gaming experience empowering girls to create personalized video game characters with code. The platform aims to disrupt the dominance of male characters by inspiring users of all backgrounds to envision a gaming experience that's more reflective of themselves and their communities. As described on the website:

> *Girls Who Code Girls* was designed to celebrate the diversity of the GWC community while teaching computer science fundamentals. The experience provides infinite code-able combinations, from hair texture to skin specificity to body size, and coders will be able to code their avatars with unique and underrepresented attributes. The learnings from the experience will be collected and shared with the intention of impacting the future of female characters in games. The library of characters will also be licensable and offered to gaming companies to inform their game development. (Girls Who Code, 2022)

"Though almost half of all gamers are women, we don't see them represented in game development," explains said Tarika Barrett, CEO of Girls Who Code (Barrett, 2023). "That's why we created *Girls Who Code Girls*. By turning users into creators, we're empowering our community to use coding to upend the status quo and imagine a future where they can harness their passion and creativity into a career in tech. We want our students to know that they deserve to take up space in gaming and game development and can create characters that reflect the best parts of who they are" (Ibid.).

"GWC is changing the culture of the tech industry," says Juel. This is good for society and good for business (Juel, 2023).

Technovation and its Corporate Partners Inspire Girls to Be Leaders and Problem Solvers

Technovation is a global tech education nonprofit that inspires girls to be leaders and problem solvers in their lives and their community. Over the last fifteen years, the organization has trained 150,000 young women to be technology entrepreneurs and innovators. In aggregate, they have developed 10,000 solutions to community challenges, such as domestic violence, the opioid epidemic, e-waste, and including 1700 mobile apps addressing climate change, accessibility, bullying, and more. Importantly, Technovation focuses on building trust with local community leaders, who bring Technovation to their schools, organizations, and towns to share an understanding of their particular needs and goals. Technovation programs are intentionally flexible in order to adapt them to diverse community needs and engage with existing support networks.

Technovation students are supported by 19,000 volunteers, many from companies, who are trained as mentors and program facilitators. As a result of their participation in Technovation programs, girls and families understand computer science and AI better, and they are more confident leaders and problem solvers (Technovation, 2021). Founder and CEO Tara Chklovski appreciates the value of corporate partners, not only for funding but also for employee skill-based volunteering, mentoring, and hiring Technovation students for positions for paid internships. Chklovski highlights Shopify as an important partner, crediting them for their long-term involvement over the course of more than eight years, including supporting over 3,000 girls, hosting 180 Technovation-related events, helping to advance a thousand Technovation alumnae with professional development, and providing funding (Chklovski, 2022).

Technovation board member Gabriela Burian is passionate about supporting the organization. "Having had the opportunity to receive a graduate level education in agricultural engineering in my home country of Brazil, I understand the value of opportunities for women in STEM education and careers." Burian is Global Head of Multi-Stakeholder Partnerships, Stakeholder Affairs and Strategic Partnerships, Bayer.

> In my position at Bayer, I have the great honor to work with multi-stakeholder partnerships worldwide to find innovative solutions to food security and climate change, including in countries that suffer the most. As part of the Technovation community, I get to meet with girls and young women from Brazil and other Latin American countries to encourage and inspire them to find new solutions to community problems by building tech products that they themselves develop, and to advance into STEM career. (Burian, 2023)

Per Scholas and its Corporate Partners Prepare BIPOC Women and Men for Tech Careers

Per Scholas is a national US nonprofit that seeks to develop a "thriving workforce with equitable access to education" (Per Scholas, 2023). The organization's mission it to "advance economic equity through rigorous training for tech careers and to connect skilled talent to more than 850 employers nationwide." In more than 20 cities across America, Per Scholas provides "skills training and access to employer networks often excluded from tech careers." More than 17,000 graduates have advanced in successful careers in tech via the organization's tuition-free technical training.

The vast majority (85%) of Per Scholas learners are people of color. One in three are women. More than half have a high school diploma as their highest degree, and yet only a third of more than 200,0000 new tech jobs created annually require a college degree. Per Scholas helps to close the opportunity gap for working age adults who do not even earn a living wage to invest in the future. The organization's graduates earn four times their pre-training wage in their first job post-graduation (Ayala, 2022).

According to President and CEO Plinio Ayala, the organization's mission and vision is not only to prepare students for jobs, but also for longer term careers and to build wealth. Per Scholas is implementing a three-year plan to scale by enrolling ten thousand learners annually, a large share through remote learning, while measuring and improving the impacts of new and evolving strategies (Ibid.).

Per Scholas is supported by scores of companies and organizations such as Google, Nationwide, Infosys, BlackRock, Barclay's, and JPMorgan Chase, as well as the Bill & Melinda Gates Foundation and Ballmer Group, that recognize the imperative to develop an inclusive workforce for futures in tech. Ayala explains that an important value that these and other companies provide to the nonprofit and its students is the creation of customized, co-designed training programs, so that graduates are best prepared for positions and ultimately careers at each company (Ibid.).

"Talent is a differentiator," explains Jennie Sparandara, Managing Director at JPMorgan Chase. "This is why JPMorgan invests in skill building in communities. As a major employer, we know one of our chief assets is talent." Furthermore, Sparandara describes the growing need for tech talent at JPMorgan Chase and other global companies. "Tech talent is not just for tech companies. All our jobs are tech-enabled" (Sparandara, 2023).

Sparandara comments on the value of Per Scholas in anticipating the skills that companies will need and staying aligned, by building strong relationships with employers. She points out that Per Scholas built state of the art training facilities to prepare students for jobs in cybersecurity. "The organization keeps informed about the evolutions in the demand for talent, and they stay nimble."

Per Scholas also adds value in expanding the company's pipeline of candidates. "By creating opportunities for individuals from diverse backgrounds to develop their skills in areas like software engineering, Per Scholas is helping prospective employees and companies like us. When people from previously underserved communities are trained for the jobs of the future, everyone benefits."

For a company that recognizes the opportunity to build a more diverse workforce with employees who are well prepared for tech jobs of the future, Per Scholas is a valuable resource. Together, companies and nonprofits are bringing previously marginalized people directly into the pipeline—a pipeline of high demand jobs for today and the future.

Businesses: In Partnership with NGOs and Governments—Can Make the Education Vision Possible

International corporations seek to develop girls and boys, women and men to be well prepared, contributing members of the global workforce. First, companies need access to highly capable, well-prepared, and motivated individuals to be effective problem solvers in local communities throughout the world. Second, successful people who are earners become consumers for company goods and services. Third, companies and nonprofits are drawing into the talent pipeline people who have previously been marginalized. This is good for society and good for business.

Governments have the authority and responsibility to educate young people. Academic institutions, NGOs, and regional educators and experts are crucial partners for systemic, inclusive, and equitable change. Businesses have the resources, global reach, and self-interest to make success possible. This is an opportunity for companies, civil society, and governments to collaborate in advancing young people and adults to lead fulfilling lives and become productive citizens for an inclusive, sustainable, and prosperous future.

References

Adams, J. T. (1931). The epic of America. Little Brown and Company.

American Association of University Women (AAUW). (n.d.). The STEM gap: Women and girls in science, technology, engineering and mathematics. https://www.aauw.org/resources/research/the-stem-gap/. Accessed 31 Jan 2023.

African Union Commission. (2017). Implementation and monitoring of CESA 16–25. In: *CESA Journal*, *2*(Dec), 3. https://au.int/en/documents/20171217/continental-education-strategy-africa-2016-2025-cesa-16-25-vol-02-dec-2017. Accessed 31 Jan 2023.

Arewa, O. B. (2021). *Disrupting Africa: Technology, law, and development*. Cambridge University Press.

Arewa, O. B. (2022, March 22). Remarks in discussion with host Alice Korngold at Forum for NGO and business leaders ("Remarks").

Aspen Institute. (2023). *Aspen digital*. https://www.aspeninstitute.org/programs/aspendigital/. Accessed 31 Jan 2023.

Ayala, P. (2022, September 13). Interview with Alice Korngold.

Barrett, T. (2023, January 5). Interview with Alice Korngold.

Bureau of Labor Statistics (BLS). (2022, September 08). Computer and information technology occupations. https://www.bls.gov/ooh/computer-and-information-technology/home.htm. Accessed 31 Jan 2023.

Burian, G. (2023, January 3). Email to Alice Korngold.

Cahalan, M. W., Addison, M., Brunt, N., Pooja Patel, R., & Perna, L. W. (2021). *Indicators of higher education equity in the United States: 2021 historical trend report*. The Pell Institute. http://pellinstitute.org/downloads/publications-Indicators_of_Higher_Education_Equity_in_the_US_2021_Historical_Trend_Report.pdf. Accessed 31 Jan 2023.

Carnevale, A. P., Cheah, B., & Wenzinger. (2021). The college payoff: More education doesn't always mean more earnings. Georgetown University, Center on Education and the Workforce. https://cewgeorgetown.wpenginepowered.com/wp-content/uploads/cew-college_payoff_2021-fr.pdf. Accessed 31 Jan 2023.

Chapman, B., & Belkin, D. (2022). Pandemic learning loss could cost students $70,000 in lifetime earnings. *Wall Street Journal*, *27*(Dec). https://www.wsj.com/articles/pandemic-learning-loss-could-cost-students-70-000-in-lifetime-earnings-11672148505. Accessed 31 Jan 2023.

Chklovski, T. (2022, August 23). Interview with Alice Korngold.

Corbett, C., & Hill, C. (2015). Solving the equation: The variables for women's success in engineering and computing (pp. 7–13). AAUW. https://www.pewresearch.org/social-trends/2018/01/09/women-and-men-in-stem-often-at-odds-over-workplace-equity/. Accessed 31 Jan 2023.

Dhingra, M. (2022, October 11). Interview with Alice Korngold.

Eberstadt, N., & Abramsky, E. (2022, September 20). America's education crisis is a national security threat. *Foreign Affairs*. https://www.foreignaffairs.com/world/america-education-crisis-national-security-threat. Accessed 31 Jan 2023.

EdCamp Ukraine. (n.d.). *What we do*. https://www.edcamp.ua/en/main-page/. Accessed 31 Jan 2023.

Elkin, O. (2022, October 24). Interview with Alice Korngold.

Freeman, B., Marginson, S., & Tytler, R. (2019). An international view of STEM. In: A. Sahin, M. J. Mohr-Schroeder (Eds.), *STEM education 2.0, Brill, Leiden* (pp. 350–363). The Netherlands. https://www.researchgate.net/publication/335551705_An_international_view_of_STEM_education. Accessed 31 Jan 2023.

Funds for Internet Research and Education (FIRE) website. (n.d.). https://www.fireafrica.org/. Accessed 31 Jan 2023.

Gbowee, L. (2011). *Mighty be our powers: How sisterhood, prayer, and sex changed a nation at war*. Beast Books/Perseus Books Group.

Georgetown University, Center on Education and the Workforce ("Georgetown"). (n.d.). *The uncertain pathway from to a good job*. https://cew.georgetown.edu/cew-reports/pathway/. Accessed 31 Jan 2023.

Girl Rising. (n.d.-a). About us ("About"). https://girlrising.org/about-us. Accessed 31 Jan 2023.

Girl Rising. (n.d.-b). Watch the award-winning documentary *Girl Rising* ("Documentary"). https://girlrising.org/documentaries/girl-rising. Accessed 31 Jan 2023.

Girl Rising website. (n.d.). https://girlrising.org/. Accessed 31 Jan 2023.

Girls Who Code. (n.d.). Our team ("Team"). https://girlswhocode.com/about-us/team. Accessed 31 Jan 2023.

Girls Who Code. (2022, December 5). *Girls Who Code launches digital experience to change the future of women in gaming*. https://girlswhocode.com/news/girls-who-code-launches-digital-experience-to-change-the-future-of-women-in-gaming. Accessed 31 January 2023.

Girls Who Code website. (n.d.). https://girlswhocode.com/. Accessed 31 Jan 2023.

Heyman, S. (2016, November 16). In Burkina Faso, rebuilding with a local touch. *New York Times*. https://www.nytimes.com/2016/10/19/arts/design/in-burkina-faso-rebuilding-with-a-local-touch.html. Accessed 31 Jan 2023.

HP. (2021). *Sustainable impact report 2021*. https://www8.hp.com/h20195/v2/GetPDF.aspx/c08228880.pdf#page=85. Accessed 31 Jan 2023.

HP. (2023). *Digital equity transforms lives*. https://www.hp.com/us-en/hp-information/sustainable-impact/community.html. Accessed 31 Jan 2023.

Juel, C. (2023, January 5). Interview with Alice Korngold.

Kane, T. J., Doty, E., Patterson, T., & Staiger, D. O. (2022). What do changes in state test scores imply for later life outcomes? Center for Education Policy Research, Harvard University. https://educationrecoveryscorecard.org/wp-content/uploads/2022/10/Long-Term-Outcomes.pdf. Accessed 31 Jan 2023.

Lowery, C. (2022, October 19). Interview with Alice Korngold.

Malejki, M. (2022, September 7). Interview with Alice Korngold.

Mansson, C. V. (2022, November 8). Africa's youths can help solve the global tech challenge. Brookings. https://www.brookings.edu/blog/africa-in-focus/2022/11/08/africas-youths-can-help-solve-the-global-tech-talent-shortage/. Accessed 31 Jan 2023.

Mazumder, B. (2022, April). Intergenerational economic mobility in the United States. Federal Reserve Bank of Chicago. https://www.chicagofed.org/research/mobility/intergenerational-economic-mobility. Accessed 31 Jan 2023.

McKinsey. (2022, April 4). How COVID-19 caused a global learning crisis. https://www.mckinsey.com/industries/education/our-insights/how-covid-19-caused-a-global-learning-crisis. Accessed 31 Jan 2023.

Meinck, S., Fraillon, J., & Strietholt, R. (2022). The impact of the COVID-19 pandemic on education. UNESCO. https://unesdoc.unesco.org/ark:/48223/pf0000380398/PDF/380398eng.pdf.multi. Accessed 31 Jan 2023.

Mitchell, M., Leachman, M., Masterson, K., & Waxman, S. (2018, October 4). Unkept promises: State cuts to higher education threaten access and equity. Center on Budget and Policy Priorities. https://www.cbpp.org/research/state-budget-and-tax/unkept-promises-state-cuts-to-higher-education-threaten-access-and. Accessed 31 Jan 2023.

National Center for Science and Engineering Statistics. (2021, April 29). Women, minorities, and persons with disabilities in science and engineering. National Science Foundation. https://ncses.nsf.gov/pubs/nsf21321/report/executive-summary. Accessed 31 Jan 2023.

Ndaka, C. (2022, November 23). Email to Alice Korngold.

Odede, K. (2015, May 13). Interview with Alice Korngold.

Odede, K. (2020, September 7). Closing the race gap in philanthropy demands radical candor. *The Guardian*. https://www.theguardian.com/global-development/2020/sep/07/closing-the-race-gap-in-philanthropy-demands-radical-candour. Accessed 31 Jan 2023.

Odede, K. (2022, November 25). Opinion: COP 27 left out Africans, but climate progress still possible ("Opinion"). Devex. https://www.devex.com/news/opinion-cop-27-left-out-africans-but-climate-progress-still-possible-104483. Accessed 31 Jan 2023.

Odede, K., & Posner, J. (2016). Find me unafraid: Love, loss, and hope in an African slum. Ecco/Harper Collins.

Organization for Economic Cooperation and Development (OECD). (n.d.). Education. https://www.oecd.org/education/. Accessed 31 Jan 2023.

Per Scholas. (2023). About. https://perscholas.org/about-per-scholas/. Accessed 31 Jan 2023.

Pew Research Center. (2018, January 9). Women and men in STEM often at odds over workplace equity. https://www.pewresearch.org/social-trends/2018/01/09/women-and-men-in-stem-often-at-odds-over-workplace-equity/. Accessed 31 Jan 2023.

Pogrebin, R. (2022, March 15). Pritzker prize goes to architect from West Africa. *New York Times*. https://www.nytimes.com/2022/03/15/arts/design/pritzker-prize-francis-kere.html. Accessed 31 Jan 2023.

Rafter, S. (2022, November 7). Interview with Alice Korngold.

Sachs, J., Lafortune, G., Kroll, C., Fuller, G., & Woelm, F. (2022). *Sustainable development report 2022*. https://s3.amazonaws.com/sustainabledevelopment.report/2022/2022-sustainable-development-report.pdf. Accessed 31 Jan 2023.

Saujani, R. (2023, Jan 3). Interview with Alice Korngold.

Shining Hope for Communities (SHOFCO). (2022). 2021 Impact. https://www.shofco.org/our-impacts/. Accessed 31 Jan 2023.

Sparandara, J. (2023, January 13). Interview with Alice Korngold.

Sustainable Development Solutions Network. (2021, May 5). In the red: The US failure to deliver on a promise of racial equality. https://www.sustainabledevelopment.report/reports/in-the-red-the-us-failure-to-deliver-on-a-promise-of-racial-equality/. Accessed 31 Jan 2023.

Technovation webpage. (2021). https://www.technovation.org/. Accessed 31 Jan 2023.

The Nation's Report Card. (n.d.). Reading and mathematics scores decline during COVID-19 pandemic. https://www.nationsreportcard.gov/highlights/ltt/2022/. Accessed 31 Jan 2023.

T4 Education. (n.d.). Oprah Winfrey congratulates Prof. Mamokgethi Phakeng on winning Arica education medal. https://www.youtube.com/watch?v=ZfmfgKRa8Fc. Accessed 31 Jan 2023.

T4 Education. (2023a). Africa education medal ("Medal"). https://t4.education/prizes/africa-education-medal/africa-education-medal-home. Accessed 31 Jan 2023.

T4 Education. (2023b). Professor Mamokgethi Phakeng: Africa education medal winner 2022 ("Winner"). https://t4.education/prizes/africa-education-medal/2022-winner. Accessed 31 Jan 2023.

UNICEF. (n.d.). COVID-19 and children: UNICEF data hub ("Data"). https://data.unicef.org/covid-19-and-children/. Accessed 31 Jan 2023.

UNICEF. (2022, Jan 23). Press release—COVID-19 scale of education loss "nearly insurmountable." warns UNICEF. https://www.unicef.org/press-releases/covid19-scale-education-loss-nearly-insurmountable-warns-unicef. Accessed 31 Jan 2023.

United Nations. (n.d.). The sustainable development agenda ("Agenda"). https://www.un.org/sustainabledevelopment/development-agenda/. Accessed 31 Jan 2023.

United Nations. (2022). Progress on the sustainable development goals: The gender snapshot 2022 ("Gender"). https://unstats.un.org/sdgs/gender-snapshot/2022/GenderSnapshot.pdf. Accessed 31 Jan 2023.

United Nations, IOM. (2022). World migration report 2022. https://publications.iom.int/books/world-migration-report-2022. Accessed 31 Jan 2023.

United Nations, UNHCR. (n.d.). What we do: Education ("What"). https://www.unrefugees.org/what-we-do/education/. Accessed 31 Jan 2023.

United Nations, UNHCR. (2022). Education. https://www.unhcr.org/en-us/educat ion.html?query=education. Accessed 31 Jan 2023.

United Nations, UN News. (2022, Jun 16). More than 100 million now forcibly displaced: UNHCR report. https://news.un.org/en/story/2022/06/112 0542. Accessed 31 Jan 2023.

United Nations, Department of Economic and Social Affairs. (n.d.). The 17 goals: SDG 4 ("SDG 4"). https://sdgs.un.org/goals/goal4. Accessed 31 Jan 2023.

van der Weide, R., Lakner, C., Mahler, D. G., Narayan, A., & Ramasubbaiah, R. (2021). *Intergenerational mobility around the world*. World Bank Group (Working Paper) https://openknowledge.worldbank.org/handle/10986/35827. Accessed 31 Jan 2023.

World Bank. (2022). The state of global learning poverty: 2202 update. https:// thedocs.worldbank.org/en/doc/e52f55322528903b27f1b7e61238e416-020002 2022/original/Learning-poverty-report-2022-06-21-final-V7-0-conferenceEd ition.pdf. Accessed 31 Jan 2023.

5

Health

*Building a broader sense of the commons—beyond nationality—will guarantee our
entire species a share of the fruits of scientific progress, regardless of where we happen
to be born or to fall ill.*

—Paul Farmer (2013)

LET'S START BY COUNTING THE DEAD. For children under five years old,
although the global mortality rate fell to 37 deaths per 1000 live births in
2020, children in sub-Saharan Africa continued to have the highest rates of
mortality in the world—fourteen times higher than the risk for children in
Europe and North America. Sub-Saharan Africa and southern Asia account
for more than 80% of the world's 5 million deaths of children under five
years old in 2020, even though these regions only account for 53% of the
global live births (World Health Organization "Child", 2022).

For children ages 5–14 years, 9.8 million will die between 2019 and 2030.
Almost 80% of these projected deaths will occur in sub-Saharan Africa (5.8
million) and Southern Asia (2 million). In January 2022, WHO reported
that the highest regional mortality rates for children aged 5–9 years and
10–14 years were in sub-Saharan Africa and South-East Asia (World Health
Organization "Older Children", 2022).

For adults as well as children, regional inequities are glaring. A woman
in sub-Saharan Africa has around a 130 times higher risk of dying from
causes relating to pregnancy or childbirth than a woman in Europe or North
America (World Health Organization "Backsliding", 2022).

© The Author(s), under exclusive license to Springer Nature
Switzerland AG 2023
A. Korngold, *A Better World, Inc.*,
https://doi.org/10.1007/978-3-031-31553-4_5

COVID-19 has exacerbated the mortality rate worldwide. A Lancet COVID-19 Commission report shows that in the past two years, "widespread, global failures at multiple levels in the COVID-19 response led to millions of preventable deaths and reversed progress made towards the UN Sustainable Development Goals (SDGs) in many countries."

> This staggering death toll is both a profound tragedy and a massive global failure at multiple levels. Too many governments have failed to adhere to basic norms of institutional rationality and transparency, too many people— often influenced by misinformation—have disrespected and protested against basic public health precautions, and the world's major powers have failed to collaborate to control the pandemic. (Sachs et al., 2022)

Hereagain, inequity rears its ugly head. As of the fall of 2022, only 24% of Africa's population had completed their primary vaccination series compared to of 64% at the global level (World Health Organization "Vaccination", 2022). "The end of the COVID-19 pandemic is within sight, but as long as Africa lags far behind the rest of the world in reaching widespread protection, there is a dangerous gap which the virus can exploit to come roaring back," said Dr. Matshidiso Moeti, WHO Regional Director for Africa (Ibid.).

"COVID-19 has created not only a health crisis [in Africa], but an economic contraction never experienced before with such speed," according to Brookings (Songwe, 2022). In addition, COVID increased unemployment, which is not only a grave threat to families and communities, but it also limits purchasing power. Brookings reports that, as of January 2022, there were over 300 million infected and 5.5 million dead as of January of 2022 worldwide—with 9.4 million confirmed infected and more than 220,000 confirmed dead in Africa alone (Pate, 2022).

Climate change is also exacerbating the mortality rate worldwide. In fact, the World Health Organization (WHO) reports that climate change is the single biggest health threat facing humanity (World Health Organization 2021). In Africa, climate-related health emergencies are on the rise, accounting for more than half of public health events recorded in the region over the past two decades. WHO's analysis found that of the 2121 public health events recorded in the African region between 2001 and 2021, 56% were climate related. The region is witnessing an increase in climate-linked emergencies, with 25% more climate-related events recorded between 2011 and 2021 compared with the previous decade (World Health Organization "Emergencies", 2022).

"It seems that poverty is the mother of inequality in health. The unequal distribution of resources has expanded due to climate change and increasing violence. Low- and middle-income countries experience worse health outcomes than high-income countries: the life expectancy is 34 years lower, the under-5 mortality around 100 times higher, deaths due to interpersonal violence and suicide are 30 times higher … We must urgently address the impact of poverty on health, life, and death," says Mohsen Naghavi, M.D., Ph.D., MPH, Professor of Health Metrics Sciences and Director of Subnational Burden of Disease Estimation at the Institute for Health Metrics and Evaluation (IHME) at the University of Washington (Institute for Health Metrics & Evaluation, 2022).

Understanding the causes of death in various regions is useful to improve how people live. "Measuring how many people die each year helps to assess the effectiveness of our health systems and direct resources to where they are needed most. For example, mortality data can help focus activities and resource allocation among sectors such as transportation, food and agriculture, and the environment as well as health," according to the World Health Organization (WHO) (World Health Organization, 2021). It shows that *how* people die also correlates with a country's economic status.

Non-communicable diseases (NCDs) not only dominate mortality figures at a global level, but also account for the majority of deaths in high-income countries (Ritchie et al., 2019). Examples include ischemic heart disease, or from stroke and other cerebrovascular disease, or lung, trachea, and bronchus cancers. In low- and middle-income countries, the most common causes of death are infectious disease, malnutrition, nutritional deficiencies, and neonatal and maternal deaths. In South Africa and Botswana, the leading cause of death is HIV/AIDS. In high-income countries, however, the share of deaths caused by infectious disease, poor nutrition, maternal deaths, and HIV/AIDS is very low (Ibid.). In children under 5 years, the leading causes of death are preterm birth complications, birth asphyxia/trauma, pneumonia, congenital anomalies, diarrhea, and malaria. These "can be prevented or treated with access to simple, affordable interventions including immunization, adequate nutrition, safe water and food and quality care by a trained health provider when needed," according to the WHO. Eighty percent of deaths among children under 5 years are in sub-Saharan Africa and southern Asia (World Health Organization 2020).

There are several health issues to watch in 2023 (Institute for Health Metrics & Evaluation, 2022), including Long COVID; mental health; the impact of climate change; cardiovascular disease, the leading causes of death globally; lower respiratory infections; poverty's role in health; health systems strengthening; diabetes; road injuries; dementia; and population aging (Ibid.). The prevalence and damage related to many of these health threats can be mitigated with better and more equitable access to care.

There are economic considerations related to poor health outcomes. For example, a recent Brookings report shows that in the US alone, Long COVID is keeping as many as four million people out of work, accounting for 15% of the nation's labor shortage. The annual cost of wages lot to long COVID is estimated between $170 to 230 billion dollars annually (Bach, 2022).

Healthcare Matters to Companies

Healthcare is a vital concern for companies. They require healthy employees to perform their jobs productively; businesses also seek to reduce their healthcare expenditures. Additionally, when families are healthy, employees can focus on their work rather than caretaking at home. Moreover, companies want to expand market opportunities to engage billions of new consumers. Healthy consumers of all ages, in all regions of the world, have the purchasing power and interest in acquiring goods and services necessary for robust markets. A well population and an efficient healthcare system provide a sound economy in which companies can operate and thrive. Furthermore, solving healthcare challenges provides commercial opportunities for companies, and especially to demonstrate their prowess for innovation and to partner with governments and NGOs who are key stakeholders.

Healthcare services, vaccinations, and medicines can reduce the death rate and improve the world's health. Access to these services by all people is key for moral, practical, and economic reasons. "Promoting and protecting health is essential to human welfare and sustained economic and social development. This was recognized more than 30 years ago by the Alma-Alta Declaration signatories, who noted that Health for All would contribute both to a better quality of life and also to global peace and security," according to WHO (World Health Organization, 2010). The Alma-Alta Declaration emerged from the International Conference on Primary Healthcare held in 1978. The Declaration expressed the need for urgent action by all governments, all health and development workers, and the world community to protect and promote the health of all the people of the world (World Health Organization, 1978).

The centrality of global health to peace and prosperity was recognized in the UN Millennium Goals (MDGs). In 2000, all UN Member States committed to help achieve eight goals, which included good health and well-being. These goals are also central to the and 2030 Sustainable Development Goals (SDGs), agreed upon by all UN Member States in 2015. The seventeen SDGs are designed to serve as a shared blueprint for peace and prosperity for people and the planet, now and into the future. Case studies below indicate how some companies are making meaningful contributions in advancing several related SDGs, including Good Health and Well-being (SDG3); Industry, Innovation, and Infrastructure (SDG9); Reduced Inequalities (SDG10); and Partnerships for the Goals (SDG17). As shown in The Lancet Commission on lessons for the future from the COVID-19 pandemic, "The deepening of socioeconomic inequities, coupled with economic and public health setbacks and growing social and political tensions, has jeopardised the 2030 SDG agenda" (Sachs et al., 2022).

The cases in this chapter show a variety of approaches that companies are taking in partnership with NGOs, academic institutions, and governments to address global healthcare challenges. In each case, companies are benefiting communities while also enhancing their own financial and strategic opportunities in emerging markets.

Companies Partner with NGOs to Improve Health in Some of the World's Poorest Communities

Companies in the case studies below have played pivotal roles at important inflection points for the development of highly successful interventions. In each case, businesses are providing infrastructure and logistics expertise, while the NGOs plan and implement healthcare solutions together with the communities and people they serve. Importantly, the companies themselves benefit by their involvement.

Companies Provide Technical Expertise in Logistics in Sub-Saharan Africa

In spite of progress in reducing child mortality rates worldwide, children in sub-Saharan Africa continue to have the highest rates of mortality in the world at 74 deaths for 1000 live births, 14 times higher than for children in Northern America and Europe (World Health Organization "GHO"). NGO VillageReach works with governments to increase access to essential healthcare services, medicines and vaccines to people in remote villages in Africa. "We build people-centered health solutions that improve equity and access to care. Radical collaboration with governments, partners and the private sector strengthens our ability to scale and sustain these solutions. Our work enables access to quality health care for 58 million people" (VillageReach website).

Technical expertise in logistics systems has been provided pro bono by UPS, a United States-based shipping and receiving and supply chain management company, and the Kühne Foundation.

For UPS, its involvement also served to advance the company's own innovation strategies (Ruiz Interview, 2022). "The work The UPS Foundation did engaging with drone companies Zipline and with Swoop Aero and Village reach provided UPS with experience and learnings on drone performance and capabilities that were instrumental in developing UPS's drone airline" (Ibid.). Receiving certification from the Federal Aviation Administration (FAA) in 2019, the new drone airline became the first commercial operator to perform a drone delivery for an actual paying customer outside of line of sight. UPS Flight Forward Inc. is a wholly owned subsidiary of UPS focused on drone delivery (Etherington, 2019).

Expertise from UPS and Kühne made it possible for VillageReach to address vital healthcare challenges more quickly and with more impact. In Africa, infectious diseases, including pneumonia, diarrhea, and malaria, along with pre-term birth complications, birth asphyxia and trauma and congenital anomalies, remain the leading causes of death for children under five. COVID-19 too has had a direct impact on child mortality. Furthermore, there are systemic challenges, including strained and under-resourced health systems and limitations on care-seeking and preventative measures like vaccination and nutrition systems (World Health Organization "GHO").

Consider the Democratic Republic of Congo (DRC), which is geographically the largest country in sub-Saharan Africa, roughly the size of Western Europe. The DRC is abundantly rich in natural resources, such as tantalum, which is used in most electronic items, as well as gold and coltran. The DRC, however, is the poorest country in the world in terms of personal income. Most of the country's 100 million residents live on less than $1.60 a day.

A fundamental challenge in providing essential healthcare services in the DRC is the predominance of remote communities that have little access to resources in urban and tertiary care centers. Further exacerbating the health crisis, 43% of children are malnourished, and only 23% of rural areas have access to drinking water (Lendahand, undated). The roots of the bleak conditions in the DRC can be traced to colonization, which was particularly brutal, leaving a legacy of violence, corruption, and extreme poverty, as well as a lack of infrastructure to provide access to education and healthcare (Britannica, 2023).

Just a few years ago, the only way to provide essential healthcare services and vaccines people in the DRC's Equateur Province required healthcare workers to travel as far as 71 miles, involving two three-hour boat trips and six hours by foot (VillageReach "DRC", undated). Through mud, trees, and deep rivers with no bridges, medical providers journeyed to reach a population comprised of over 2.6 million people across eighteen health districts. Today, the NGO VillageReach partners with dozens of community organizations, including ministries of health, to increase access to quality healthcare for 58 million people across twenty countries in sub-Saharan Africa. The NGO supports 380,000 local health workers who deliver products and services to the most underserved families and provide health products to 250,000 health facilities.

Crucial to VillageReach's success are its partners, including multinational corporations and foundations. Companies provide valuable logistics and supply chain expertise to the NGO to help increase access to medicines and vaccines, improve the capacity of the health workforce, and enable better decision-making for patients, health workers, and policymakers. Their involvement is not only humanitarian but benefits the companies as well.

UPS Helps Solve Last Mile Logistics for Access to Life Sustaining Care

Expert in getting items from point A to point B, UPS has played a pivotal role in helping to connect twenty hospitals with thousands of clinics to provide medicines and vaccines and pick up and deliver lab samples. In partnership with VillageReach, the American multinational shipping and receiving and supply chain management company created a bi-direction infrastructure to support on-demand access to healthcare items. The model was further enhanced in 2020 with the introduction of drones to transport essential items.

With support from The UPS Foundation, UPS Healthcare, and UPS Flight Forward, VillageReach helped scale Drones for Health. "Drones have been a game changer, increasing access to lifesaving vaccines and medicines," says Emily Bancroft, President of VillageReach (Bancroft 14 Oct, 2022). Drones save time and create cost efficiencies, particularly in areas where travel is geographically challenging for cars, motorcycles, and boats.

"UPS contributes essential financial, technical, and human capital to help advance our organization's work," explains Bancroft. VillageReach contracts with Swoop Aero and Zipline for drone services. Bancroft, who has led VillageReach through a period of substantial growth since 2010, is expert in in-country supply chain, health workforce development, and digital health technologies.

Since March 2021, UPS has delivered 1.5 billion vaccines to people with the lowest vaccination rates, in countries of greatest need across Africa. Some of these include Ghana Malawi, Nigeria, Zambia, Cameroon, and Ethiopia, to name a few (Ruiz Interview, 2022). Additionally, the company helps to train health ministries and healthcare workers to establish and maintain a cold chain, which is a low temperature-controlled supply chain network. To ensure the efficacy of vaccines, the network must be an unbroken, uninterrupted series of refrigerated production, storage, and distribution activities, along with the necessary equipment and logistics. Partnering with the Global Alliance for Vaccines and Immunization (GAVI) in Geneva, along with USAID, and ministries of health, UPS created a training program called Strategic Training for Immunization Supply Chain Managers (STEP). UPS Humanitarian Experts on Mission provided ongoing mentoring and facilitating after conducting the training workshops. GAVI is public–private global health partnership, established in 2000, to improve access to vaccines for children living in the world's poorest countries (GAVI, undated).

"The UPS Foundation's Health and Humanitarian Relief Program was originally created in the aftermath of the devastation of Hurricane Katrina in New Orleans and surrounding areas," explains Joe Ruiz, Vice President of Social Impact and The UPS Foundation.

> At that time of crisis, we were at the crossroads. The immense scale of the disaster and the number of requests for support called for a more strategic approach to UPS's response. As a result, we created a network of humanitarian partners whom we assembled to address mitigation, preparedness, disaster response and recovery, and we began to leverage UPS's logistics superpowers—our skilled volunteers. (Ruiz Interview, 2022)

Building on its work in helping communities struck by disasters in the United States, UPS and the UPS Foundation expanded its humanitarian work globally. "Solving the last mile logistics is key to addressing Sustainable Development Goal (SDG) 3: Ensuring healthy lives and promoting well-being for all ages," says Ruiz. The Logistics Emergency Team (LET) is a public–private partnership that brings together leading logistics companies to provide humanitarian capacity in the aftermath of large natural disasters. Since 2008, UPS has engaged in more than 20 humanitarian missions with the U.N Global Logistics Cluster (Logistics Cluster, 2014). The LET was established at the World Economic Forum in 2005.

UPS also partners with the UN and leading US and international agencies, including the Red Cross, The Salvation Army and Good360. Good360 is a philanthropic twenty UN agencies, the International Committee of the Red

Cross, and Good360. Good360 is a philanthropic NGO that collaborates with companies to source highly needed goods and distribute them through a network of diverse nonprofits that support people in need (Good360 website).

Ruiz explains the benefits of providing global health and humanitarian services in partnership with VillageReach and other NGOs. First, "our work in providing global humanitarian services fosters innovation. For example, exploring opportunities for VillageReach to deploy drones to serve remote communities was a case study for us, ultimately helping our company to assess the reliability and performance of drones for expanded use in our business," says Ruiz

> In addition to all the people we have helped with our drone projects, our first mover investments in humanitarian drone projects helped make it possible for UPS to become the first private sector company to receive FAA certification and the first company to provide commercial drone service. I think that's a great example of how our work can be strategic catalysts aligning business goals and humanitarian impact. (Ruiz "Email" 20 Nov)

"Second, our employees love it," says Ruiz. "By volunteering on the Logistics Emergency Team or as a UPS Humanitarian Expert on Mission helping to build the capacities of NGOs, assisting in countries worldwide, employees have a sense of purpose. This helps build loyalty to UPS."

Ruiz also talks about UPS's encouragement and support for people serving on nonprofit boards. Board experience, he explains, is a way for employees to engage productively in advancing missions that are personally meaningful, while also fostering personal, professional, and leadership development (See Korngold, 2005).

Bancroft speaks to the value of the collaboration with UPS. "What makes UPS a great partner is that they leverage a number of assets to help us advance our mission. Not only funding, but also expertise for innovation and capacity building. This is a long-term, multifaceted relationship" (Bancroft, 23 Nov).

Kuhne Foundation Models Supply Chain Logistics for Humanitarian Aid

Another important partner for VillageReach is the Kühne Foundation (Bancroft 23 Nov). "The value we bring is modeling and analyzing to transfer supply chain and logistics knowledge that will improve lives, opportunities, and the potential of people, communities, and economies around the world.

Working with a range of government, academic, professional, and NGO institutions, we identify vulnerabilities and bottlenecks in supply chains that benefit humanity, and explore scenarios to create long term systemic solutions," explains Sean Rafter (Rafter, 2022). Managing Director of HELP Logistics, (HELP website) established in 2014 as an NGO subsidiary of the Kühne Foundation (Kühne Foundation website). Foundation has regional offices serving Asia, the Middle East, East Africa, and West Africa.

Klaus-Michael Kühne, then Chief Executive Officer and later Chairman of the Board of Directors of Kuehne + Nagel, together with his parents, established the Kühne Foundation. The "key priority of the Kühne Foundation is the support for training, further education, as well as research and science in the area of logistics" (Kühne Foundation website).

The Kühne Foundation supports projects with a focus on education and training, research, and science in the fields of transportation and logistics, as well as other areas of science, particularly medicine. It also contributes funding for humanitarian and charitable issues as well as for cultural projects.

Rafter explains the factors that make the foundation's partnership with VillageReach so effective. The ideal organization, he says, is a last mile primary healthcare delivery organization like VillageReach. "Working directly with the local NGO is best. Such a relationship lends itself to accountability, ethics, impact, and efficiencies, strategically and financially" (Rafter, 2022). With an on-the-ground provider, there can be clarity about the scope, deliverables, expectations, and funding.

According to Rafter, an alignment of vision and values with an NGO partner is essential, as well as a trusting relationship. "The best collaborators are between people, not organizations," he explains. The foundation's model is to help design systemic solutions, then elevate contextual logistics and learning for instructional design, and marry it with the European framework for academia. "Our interest is in providing content to lift the curriculum so that regional universities become more international in preparing students for the global marketplace."

Companies Help Advance Healthcare for Women and Children in Africa

Since 2001 when it was first founded in South Africa, mothers2mothers (m2m) has provided healthcare services to nearly 15 million people in ten countries in Africa. The organization's unique approach is its Mentor Mother Model. "m2m trains and employs local mothers living with HIV as peer-to-peer mentors who serve as community health workers in under-resourced clinics and communities," explains Frank Beadle de Palomo, President and Chief Executive Officer since 2012 (Beadle de Palomo "Interview", 2022). More than 1800 African women serve as "Mentor Mothers," helping patients while also creating well-being for themselves and their families.

A number of companies provided essential assistance in helping to establish the business model and structure to support the NGO's lifesaving work. Some companies play an important role today as well. They speak to the value to businesses as well, including supporting their employees' personal and professional development, fostering relationships and trust with regional ministries of health, and improving communities where there might be future market opportunities.

Company engagement is valuable in advancing community-centered, systemic change to improve healthcare delivery services in Africa. "By shifting power to communities, and training and employing women living with HIV as community health workers, we have seen grassroots female leadership transform the health and well-being of communities," explains Beadle de Palomo and Ilda Kuleba, Regional Director, Lusophone Countries (Beadle de Palomo & Kuleba, 2022). m2m knows that its model works. "We have virtually eliminated the transmission of HIV from mother-to-child for people enrolled in our services for eight consecutive years, and helped to keep over two million at-risk mothers and children alive" (mothers2mothers "Scale", 2022).

It is clear to us that the journey to 'Health for All' must be led by the people who know their communities best. Mentor Mothers use their lived experience and understanding of local realities to connect with their peers and provide the health services they need. They are trusted providers, including during COVID-19 when they provided continuous support to their communities after being designated as essential workers. (Beadle de Palomo & Kuleba, 2022)

Originally focusing specifically on mother-to-child transmission of HIV, today Mentor Mothers deliver integrated primary healthcare services to women, children ages 0–9, adolescents 10–24, and special populations, including internally displaced people (Beadle de Palomo "Interview", 2022b). Beadle de Palomo indicates that the one-stop service is essential to make it easier for people to access care.

Africa's healthcare systems are experiencing a shortage of 4.2 million health workers, thereby limiting access to vital, lifesaving care for women and families. Over half of Africans, around 615 million people, lack access to the healthcare they need. According to Africa Front Line First, the continent has an annual financing gap of $4.4 billion. So m2m's Mentor Mothers play an essential role. In 2021, the NGO enrolled 1,251,581 new clients, a 20% increase over the previous year, at 544 locations (mothers2mothers "Impact").

Companies Help Establish NGO's Infrastructure

According to Robin Smalley, m2m's co-founder and director in its early days, "this was about putting women front and center as the solution in keeping mothers alive. And children. Both. You can't separate the two. If the child is born healthy and the mother dies, the child won't reach its fifth birthday. It's not only humane, it's good sense, and it's good business" (Smalley, May 3, 2013).

While Smalley and Dr. Mitch Besser, founder and medical director, were building programs and delivering services, Smalley reports that they had no acumen for establishing the business and financial infrastructure for their rapidly growing enterprise. "Pfizer was a lifesaver," Smalley explained. "As soon as I got in touch, they deployed a Pfizer Global Health Fellow who worked with us for three months, full-time, to establish a financial records system. From then on, we had a series of Fellows, sometimes two at a time, for six months at a time, up until 2011.

"The Pfizer Fellows established a variety of systems to support our growing business, including human resources, payroll, communications, monitoring and evaluation, and so on. We didn't even need a chief financial officer until 2009. Each of the Fellows was outstanding, and each person rolled up their sleeves and jumped right in with great enthusiasm. I don't know how we would have done this."

HP provided essential services and expertise for m2m's development. ("HP" in this case refers to the Hewlett-Packard Company, prior to its separating into HP Inc. and Hewlett Packard Enterprises in 2015.) The company created a mobile technology and cloud solution for m2m. "HP is transforming m2m's operations from paper-based records to a digital system that will help the organization," according to HP's Senior Director, Sustainability and Social Innovation Programs at the time (Librie, 2013).

m2m's chief financial officer in 2013, explained the intake process for m2m patients in order to illustrate HP's contribution in saving lives (Heffernan, 2013). "We worked in clinics alongside state or privately employed health workers. The expectant mothers would wait outside in long lines for their neonatal visits. When a mother found out for the first time that she is HIV-positive, the health worker often had insufficient ability and limited time to provide a very complicated explanation about the medications and infant-feeding practices necessary to prevent transmission to the baby" (Ibid.).

At that point, the health workers referred the women to m2m in the neighboring trailer. The women usually arrived to us in shock and despair, said Heffernan. They were received by m2m's Mentor Mothers who had themselves been through this experience. m2m's Mentor Mothers were trained to talk with the expectant mothers and prepare them for what lay ahead. The mentor mothers admitted the new patients into a program and regime to help them stay on their medications, and follow the right feeding habits, so that they and their children could live healthy lives. "The key to success is in the follow up by the mentors. Our studies have shown that if the women return for three visits, transmission of HIV can be virtually eliminated," explained the m2m CFO. HP provided three important values to m2m, he explained. "First, for the Mentor Mothers. Until HP helped us shift to an electronic data system, the mentors kept notes on paper when they met with their new patients. Now, the mentors use mobile phones and text messaging, which makes it easier and more efficient for mentors to collect and automatically upload this data to help ensure that mothers return for their follow ups."

The second benefit was that HP helped m2m to establish a database system that "provided much richer analysis of the data in order for us to make decisions about the program and how to make it more effective. This was an immense value to look at outputs and impact."

HP's final contribution was to strengthen the organization's entire information technology infrastructure. "We had various databases, including financial, that weren't talking to one another. HP came up with architecture and design, so we could make more efficient use of data and share information across various applications and platforms."

In total, summarized the CFO, "at program and site levels, as well as from an IT infrastructure perspective, this was a fantastic relationship with HP" (Ibid.).

From the company's point of view, "the Mentor Mothers were limited by the need to document and keep paper records. We were able to create a cloud-based solution by using cell phones, which are ubiquitous. Texting enabled the mentor mothers to maintain records of their mentees and do their follow ups more efficiently. This also allowed the mentors to spend more time with the mothers" (Librie, 2013).

As to the challenges, HP wanted to ensure that the infrastructure was manageable and sustainable. "We wanted to know that it would be easy for the mentors to use, and that it could be maintained without difficulty: That it would truly be better from a user point of view."

According to HP, "we are fortunate to have worked with very talented and dedicated folks. They gave up their free time and spent countless hours far beyond the call of duty."

For HP, projects like the one with m2m provide the company with an opportunity to demonstrate the value of HP's technology and expertise in providing solutions for social impact. Additionally, "working with various projects in emerging markets facilitates HP's working relationships with ministries of health in emerging markets which often lead to commercial opportunities" (Ibid.).

Companies Help Advance NGO's Longer-Term Growth

"From my perspective, serving for decades in the public health sector, many corporations have a huge heart for the type of work mothers2mothers and other NGOs do on a daily basis around the world in solving so many vexing problems or addressing untold numbers of inequalities," explains Beadle de Palomo of m2m (Beadle de Palomo "Email", 2022). However, Beadle de Palomo believes that "the original model of financial funding only is changing. As social responsibility has moved from a 'nice to have' to a 'must have' in the past several years, companies want to do more by becoming true partners in helping NGOs solve problems and attain their mission objectives."

> So many corporations want to go deeper with us, participate in problem identification, devise mutually fulfilling solutions, and deploy innovative methodologies for achieving them. We're now putting our heads together more than ever at the front end of processes. That creates a much richer, more robust dynamic than a transactional relationship. We're tapping into deeper reservoirs of talent within our corporate donor audiences, and the resulting ideation is on a much higher scale than we could have ever achieved on our own as an NGO. This means we can tackle bigger challenges, go further, and reach more deserving clients faster than ever. (Ibid.)

Consider these two examples cited by the m2m CEO:

> Global pharmaceutical giant, Johnson & Johnson, has a secondment program in which mid- and senior-level executives provide their time, expertise, and counsel in helping NGOs like ours address specific challenges. In our case, we put our heads together to identify how J&J's program could help us think through and shape m2m's risk, governance, and compliance structure not only driven by our own organizational growth, but also given recent seismic shifts

in how bilateral and multilateral funders are now viewing issues like NGO localization in countries where they deliver services. J&J seconded a senior-level legal counsel to help us understand the legal environment and structure ourselves accordingly. (Ibid.)

And while not a corporation, but rather a venture philanthropy organization, Zurich-based LGT Venture Philanthropy has gone so much further beyond being one of m2m's long-time donors for the past ten years, to being a close thought partner in how we can scale and measure our operations and impact; we now meet quarterly to share results and thoughts. Further, their fellowship program has led to more than a dozen professionals joining us for a year to support us in such areas as resource mobilization, strategic planning, country operations, policy and advocacy, and finance. (Ibid.)

Companies have advanced their partnerships strategically to benefit the businesses as well as the nonprofits. As seen in the case studies in this chapter, companies are leveraging their involvement to foster personal and professional development for their employees, deepening connections and good will with clients and customers, fostering relationships with regional governments, engaging with communities that might become future markets, and joining together in promoting the UN Sustainable Development Goals (SDGs). In their work with m2m, companies are making meaningful contributions in advancing Good Health and Well-being (SDG3); Industry, Innovation, and Infrastructure (SDG9); Reduced Inequalities (SDG10); and Partnerships for the Goals (SDG17) (United Nations "SDGs").

Company Supports Partners in Health in Establishing Haiti's First Teaching Hospital

"As you seek to imagine or reimagine solutions to the greatest problems of our time, harness the power of partnership," advised Paul Farmer in a commencement speech entitled "Countering Failures of Imagination," published in *To Repair the World* (Farmer, 2013). Described as the man "who would cure the world" (Kidder, 2004). Farmer founded and led Partners in Health (PIH) from 1987 until his untimely death in 2022. PIH's work is based on the belief that "health care is a universal human right. Around the world, we fight injustice by providing care first to those who need it most" (Partners in Health website). True to its belief in long-term relationships with local organizations based in settings of poverty, PIH has been working in partnership with its sister organization, Zanmi Lasante (ZL), which is led and run by Haitians.

In the wake of the devastating 2010 earthquake, HP contributed its unique value and assets by helping PIH to establish rural Haiti's first teaching hospital, Hôpital Universitaire de Mirebalais (HUM). The hospital was designed to provide primary care services to 185,000 people in Mirebalais and two nearby communities, where people had limited access to quality healthcare. (Note: This was a program of Hewlett Packard Company prior to the separation into HP Inc. and Hewlett Packard Enterprises in 2015.)

As described by HP, the company provided "the information technology infrastructure to support all of the applications needed to run a modern hospital of this scale as well as critical communications systems. HUM was outfitted with a high-capacity server rack that provides connectivity across the campus … HP workstations are situated throughout the hospital, equipped with 27-inch monitors to enable teaching opportunities in the operating rooms and optimum radiology image viewing … In addition to providing technology and funding, HP employees around the world contributed their time and expertise to the design, build-out, and installation of the IT systems at HUM" (Korngold, 2014). PIH recognized HP's important contribution (Partners in Health, 2013). The Business and Human Rights Center shared the story as well.

HP's then Senior Director of Sustainability and Social Innovation Programs commented on the unique challenges of this project. It was essential for the grid to be resilient in the most challenging of environments, providing easy-to-use, fail-proof technology that can be operated with minimal training.

The HUM itself presented a difficult situation. One of the biggest issues was connectivity in a remote part of the country that had been severely damaged by the earthquake in 2010.

"Haiti was already one of the poorest countries in the world, when the devastating earthquake of 2010 damaged its infrastructure even further," explained the HP Senior Director. "When Paul Farmer said that Partners in Health (PIH) wanted to build a teaching hospital two hours north of Port-au-Prince, that would be a tremendous challenge."

HP's Senior Director described the vision: "We wanted to bring together the best people from our company and PIH to install the best technology to create an integrated system for the hospital. The backbone is HP technology, computing, networking, switches, and internet. This is a great demonstration project of a fully integrated solution in the most challenging conditions." HP contributed the technology and the expertise, demonstrating to potential customers its prowess in creating innovative, high-impact solutions to the most difficult problems in the most trying circumstances.

Additionally, said HP's Senior Director, "the systems had to be sustainable." For sustainability, HP needed to ensure that the hospital would have service contracts that met its needs, and that people would be properly trained to manage the system on an ongoing basis. "We had a great partner in PIH. This was a shared collaboration. We sat together and worked towards a shared objective" (Korngold, 2014).

Through its work with PIH in establishing the teaching hospital in Haiti, HP was contributing to the MDGs, the 2000–2015 healthcare goals agreed to by all United Nations Member States. Ultimately, in 2015, all UN Member States approved the 2030 Sustainable Development Goals (SDGs); these goals include Good Health and Well-being (SDG3); Industry, Innovation, and Infrastructure (SDG9); Reduced Inequalities (SDG10); and Partnerships for the Goals (SDG17). (United Nations "SDGs") HP had a clear business case for its engagement in pro bono projects such as its partnership with PIH in establishing the teaching hospital in Haiti, and working with m2m in Africa. For HP, these engagements provided an opportunity to bring technology and people together to have a positive social and environmental impact in developing markets.

"This is the theme that unifies all of our sustainability and social innovation programs in education, healthcare, and environment," the Senior Director explained. "These experiences enable us to demonstrate HP's technology and expertise in challenging circumstances. These opportunities also open the doors to new business relationships."

Farmer described a visit to Mirebalais Hospital in 2012. The hospital "sprawled across a small dell like a temple, gleaming white and girdled by [Black] Haitian ironwork" (Partners in Health website). By 2013, the new hospital opened its doors. A 205,000-square foot, 300-bed teaching facility, the institution offers advanced care across multiple specialties, including a full-service emergency department, critical care units, oncology, general, and orthopedic surgery, among others. It also provides digital imaging, an open-source electronic medical records system, and high-tech classrooms to train the next generation of Haitian doctors and nurses (Partners in Health "Haiti"). By 2019, University Hospital received international accreditation as a teaching institution, with six residency programs to prepare well-trained clinicians in Haiti.

For the past two years, Haiti has been facing local violence and conflicts, in addition to the repercussions of yet another earthquake in the summer of

2021. Nonetheless, ZL health workers say they will continue their work on behalf of patients, notably: (Partners in Health, 2022).

- In 2021, ZL nurses and doctors attended to 20,220 deliveries.
- Each month, the emergency department at University Hospital cares for an average of 700 patients for just maternal health-related reasons.
- In 2021, ZL provided care to 2083 mental health patients. One in five were 18 years old or younger.
- In 2021, ZL delivered treatment for malnutrition to over 2600 children.
- ZL has created 190 beds for COVID care, become one of the clinical groups in the country to save the lives of COVID patients, and been invited to advise other hospitals and the national response.
- Between July 2020 and June 2021, ZL diagnosed and treated 623 women for breast cancer.

As described by Farmer, the vision is to move people "from patient to provider, and from needy to donor," in order to help break the cycle of poverty and disease. "That's our sustainability model" (Farmer, 2013).

Businesses Benefit by Improving Access to Health Services

The corporate engagement initiatives described in this chapter have been instrumental in improving health and well-being in some of the poorest regions of the world, where the availability of healthcare services, vaccines, and medicines has been limited. In each case, the critical factor for success has been the effective collaboration between companies and NGOs on the ground, as well as mutual respect between the partners. mothers2mothers is particularly illustrative of the value of peer-to-peer, mother-to-mother service workers, that, at the same time, provide mentor mothers with employment.

Access to healthcare services for all people is vital for moral, practical, and economic reasons. Companies are recognizing that they will benefit by partnering with NGOs and governments in leveraging their expertise and assets—including technology, human capital, and financial investments—to help improve the health of people in underserved communities.

References

Bach, K. (2022, August 24). *New data shows long Covid is keeping as many as 4 million people out of work.* Brookings. https://www.brookings.edu/research/new-data-shows-long-covid-is-keeping-as-many-as-4-million-people-out-of-work/#:~:text=Using%20a%20longitudinal%20survey%2C%20it,author%20defined%20as%20long%20Covid. Accessed 26 Jan 2023.

Bancroft, E. (2022, October 14, November 23). *Interviews with Alice Korngold.*

Beadle de Palomo, F. (2022a, October 12). *Interview with Alice Korngold ("Email").*

Beadle de Palomo, F. (2022b, September 7). *Interview with Alice Korngold ("Interview").*

Beadle de Palomo, F., & Kuleba, I. (2022, September 9). Opinion: Prioritize community health workers to unlock health for all. *Devex.* https://www.devex.com/news/sponsored/opinion-prioritize-community-health-workers-to-unlock-health-for-all-103945. Accessed 26 Jan 2023.

Britannica. (2023). *Congo free state.* https://www.britannica.com/place/Congo-Free-State. Accessed 26 Jan 2023.

Etherington, D. (2019, October 1). UPS gets FAA approval to operate an entire drone delivery airline. *TechCrunch.* https://techcrunch.com/2019/10/01/ups-gets-faa-approval-to-operate-an-entire-drone-delivery-airline/. Accessed 26 Jan 2023.

Farmer, P. (2013). *Repair the world.* University of California Press.

GAVI. (undated). *About our alliance.* https://www.gavi.org/. Accessed 26 Jan 2023.

Good360 website. (undated). https://good360.org/

Heffernan, M. (2013, June 20). *Interview with Alice Korngold.*

HELP Logistics website. (undated). https://www.help-logistics.org/

Institute for Health Metrics and Evaluation. (2022, December 20). *11 global health issues to watch in 2023, according to IHME experts.* https://www.healthdata.org/acting-data/11-global-health-issues-watch-2023-according-ihme-experts. Accessed 26 Jan 2023.

Kidder, T. (2004). *Mountains beyond mountains.* Random House.

Korngold, A. (2005). *Leveraging good will: Strengthening nonprofits by engaging businesses.* Jossey-Bass, a division of Wiley.

Korngold, A. (2014). *A better world, inc.: How companies profit by solving global problems where governments cannot.* Palgrave Macmillan.

Kuhne Foundation website. (undated). https://www.kuehne-stiftung.org/foundation/mission. Accessed 26 Jan 2023.

Logistics Cluster. (2014, December 4). *UPS, the UPS Foundation and the Cologne Bonn airport jointly support the logistics cluster led by the UN Food Programme.* https://logcluster.org/blog/ups-ups-foundation-and-cologne-bonn-airport-jointly-support-logistics-cluster-led-un-world-food. Accessed 26 Jan 2023.

Lendahand. (undated). Poverty in the Democratic Republic of Congo. https://www.lendahand.com/en-EU/blog/755-poverty-in-the-democratic-republic-of-congo. Accessed 26 Jan 2023.

Librie, C. (2013, May 6). *Interview with Alice Korngold*.

Mothers2Mothers. (2022, July). *Increased scale and remarkable impact ("Scale")*. https://m2m.org/wp-content/uploads/2022/07/22-0726_APR_FINAL.pdf. Accessed 26 Jan 2023.

Mothers2Mothers. (undated). *Our impact ("Impact")*. https://m2m.org/our-impact/. Accessed 26 Jan 2023.

Partners in Health. (2013, April 26). *Press release—From vision to reality*. Hopital Universitaire de Mirebalais. https://www.pih.org/press/from-vision-to-reality-hopital-universitaire-de-mirebalais. Accessed 26 Jan 2023.

Partners in Health. (2022, October 4). *With instability in Haiti, doors remain open at PIH Facilities*. https://www.pih.org/article/instability-haiti-doors-remain-open-pih-facilities. Accessed 26 Jan 2023.

Partners in Health website. (undated). https://www.pih.org/. Accessed 26 Jan 2023.

Partners in Health website. (undated). *Haiti*. https://www.pih.org/country/haiti. Accessed 26 Jan 2023.

Pate, M. A. (2022). Public health: Ensuring equal access and self-sufficiency (chapter 2). In *Foresight Africa 2022*. Brookings. https://www.brookings.edu/essay/public-health-ensuring-equal-access-and-self-sufficiency/. Accessed 26 Jan 2023.

Rafter, S. (2022, November 7). *Interview with Alice Korngold*.

Ritchie, H., Spooner, F., & Roser, M. (2019, December). Causes of death. In *Our world in data*. https://ourworldindata.org/causes-of-death. Accessed 26 Jan 2023.

Ruiz, J. (2022a, November 20). *Email to Alice Korngold ("Email")*.

Ruiz, J. (2022b, October 25). *Interview with Alice Korngold ("Interview")*.

Sachs, J., Abdool Karim, S., Aknin, L., Allen, J., Brosbol, K., & Colombo, F. (2022). The *Lancet* commission on lessons for the future from the COVID-19 pandemic. *The Lancet 400*(10359), 1224–1280. https://www.thelancet.com/journals/lancet/article/PIIS0140-6736(22)01585-9/fulltext. Accessed 26 Jan 2023.

Smalley, R. (2013, May 3). *Interview with Alice Korngold*.

Songwe, V. (2022, February 3). *Strategies for financing Africa's health sector*. Brookings. https://www.brookings.edu/blog/africa-in-focus/2022/02/03/strategies-for-financing-africas-health-sector/. Accessed 26 Jan 2023.

United Nations, Department of Economic and Social Affairs. (undated). *The 17 goals ("SDGs")*. https://sdgs.un.org/goals. Accessed 26 Jan 2023.

VillageReach. (undated). *Our work in the DRC ("DRC")*. https://www.villagereach.org/where-we-work/drc/. Accessed 26 Jan 2023.

VillageReach website. (undated). https://www.villagereach.org/

World Health Organization. (1978). *Declaration of Alma-Alta*. https://cdn.who.int/media/docs/default-source/documents/almaata-declaration-en.pdf?sfvrsn=7b3c2167_2. Accessed 26 Jan 2023.

World Health Organization. (2010). *The world health report: health systems financing: the path to universal coverage.* https://apps.who.int/iris/handle/10665/44371. Accessed 1 June 2023.

World Health Organization. (2020, September 8). *Children: Improving survival and well-being.* https://www.who.int/news-room/fact-sheets/detail/children-reducing-mortality. Accessed 26 Jan 2023.

World Health Organization. (2021, October 30). *Climate change and health.* https://www.who.int/news-room/fact-sheets/detail/climate-change-and-health. Accessed 26 Jan 2023.

World Health Organization. (2022a, April 6). *Africa faces rising climate-linked health emergencies ("Emergencies").* https://www.afro.who.int/news/africa-faces-rising-climate-linked-health-emergencies. Accessed 26 Jan 2023.

World Health Organization. (2022b, January 28). *Child mortality (under 5 years) ("Child").* https://www.who.int/news-room/fact-sheets/detail/levels-and-trends-in-child-under-5-mortality-in-2020#:~:text=Since%201990%2C%20the%20global%20under,1%20in%2027%20in%202020. Accessed 26 Jan 2023.

World Health Organization. (2022c, October 20). *COVID-19 vaccination program roll-out stagnates in Africa ("Vaccination").* https://www.afro.who.int/news/covid-19-vaccination-roll-out-stagnates-africa. Accessed 26 Jan 2023.

World Health Organization. (2022d, January 28). *Older children and young adolescent mortality (5 to 14 years) ("Older Children").* https://www.who.int/news-room/fact-sheets/detail/older-children-and-young-adolescent-mortality-(5-to-14-years)#:~:text=Key%20facts,for%20children%20under%205%20years. Accessed 26 Jan 2023.

World Health Organization. (2022e, October 18). *Staggering backsliding across women's, children's and adolescents' health revealed in new UN analysis ("Backsliding").* https://www.who.int/news/item/18-10-2022e-staggering-backsliding-across-women-s--children-s-and-adolescents--health-revealed-in-new-un-analysis. Accessed 26 Jan 2023.

World Health Organization, The Global Health Observatory. (undated). *Child mortality and causes of death ("GHO").* https://www.who.int/data/gho/data/themes/topics/topic-details/GHO/child-mortality-and-causes-of-death. Accessed 26 Jan 2023.

6

Human Rights

The true measure of our character is how we treat the poor, the disfavored, the accused, the incarcerated, and the condemned. We are all implicated when we allow other people to be mistreated. An absence of compassion can corrupt the decency of a community, a state, a nation.

—Bryan Stevenson (2015)

NOT A DAY DOES GO BY WITHOUT NEWS OF HUMAN RIGHTS ABUSES. THESE might be perpetrated by governments denying basic civil liberties or equality treatment or failing to guarantee a humane rule of law. National governments might have shut off people's access to the Internet in dozens of countries in response to protest movements and military conflicts, as well as key national events (Greig, 2022; Keep It On, 2022). The horrors of human trafficking continue unabated in cities in which we live and work; trafficking is a multi-billion dollar criminal industry that denies freedom to 27.6 million people around the world. A vast amount of deeply personal and intimate information about people's lives is accumulated, purchased, and sold to serve commercial or government interests.

Moreover, the products and services that companies produce and that consumers use daily might be tainted by human rights abuses of workers in the supply chain. The clothes we wear might have been made in factories like the one in Bangladesh where more than a hundred garment workers perished in the Tazreen factory fire in 2012 (ILO, undated) or the one in a shabbily constructed multi-story building, like Rana Plaza, where more

A. Korngold, *A Better World, Inc.*, https://doi.org/10.1007/978-3-031-31553-4_6

than a thousand people were killed in 2013 when the structure collapsed. In fact, there were more than 150 factory fires and other safety episodes between 2012 and 2018, all connected to the country's garment industry. Over 1300 people died in those incidents, and more than 3800 people were injured (Hasnat & Schmall, 2021; United Nations, UN News, 2022). The International Labor Organization (ILO) reported that Bangladesh's regulatory framework and inspections "had not been able to keep pace with the development of the industry" (United Nations, UN News, 2020).

While human rights have been violated for as long as time, new media bring vivid images about victims directly onto the electronic devices in our very hands. Too often, elements of the corporate sector have been responsible for creating the human rights abuses and economic injustices that continue to plague the world today. With knowledge comes a growing discomfort with the pain and suffering of others. Consumers feel they are especially complicit with respect to the products they purchase, wear, and use (Gunther, 2013). Employees, customers, and investors are ready to be activated.

In an article about The Reverend Dr. Martin Luther King, Jr., *The New York Times* columnist Jamelle Bouie, explains it best. "To connect to laborers around the world, to see that their struggles relate to ours and ours relate to theirs, is to begin to forge the "network of mutuality" that we will need to tackle our global problems as well as to confront the obstacles to our collective liberation from domination and hierarchy" (Bouie, 2023).

Governments have not been particularly effective in addressing human rights abuses worldwide. In the case of freedom of expression and privacy on the Internet, for example, governments can even be central to the problem. As you will see in this chapter, however, some corporations working in partnership with NGOs are becoming potent players in addressing supply chain matters, human trafficking, freedom of expression and privacy on the Internet, and other human rights issues. Not only is this the right thing to do from a moral perspective, but it is also good business: it protects and builds brands, elevates employee morale and loyalty, and mitigates significant financial and regulatory risks. This serves the bottom line.

What does a better world look like when it comes to human rights? It seems quite simple. The ethic of reciprocity, best known as "the golden rule," says it best: "Do unto others as you would have them do unto you."

The golden rule has resonance in today's business world. Given contemporary social challenges, a number of business, academic, and civic leadership organizations are recognizing the importance of *empathy* for personal and professional success. In his commencement speech at MIT, Apple CEO Tim

Cook stated: "People will try to convince you that you should keep empathy out of your career. Don't accept this false premise" (Zaki, 2019).

Businesses that play leading roles in advancing human rights do not always act out of purely altruistic motives. Some companies do the right thing because they have been shamed in the media for a horrific scandal, and the public humiliation has damaged sales; other companies are proactive to mitigate risk. Additionally, businesses have learned that there can be tremendous financial costs associated with human rights abuses.

Case studies published by the World Resources Institute (WRI) show that resistance from communities and other stakeholders can delay permits, construction, operations, and revenues, cause conflicts with local labor markets, and increase costs for financing, insurance, and security, and reduce output. According to the WRI report, "Development Without Conflict: The Business Case for Community Consent," community resistance can arise at any point in a cycle. This can have negative impacts on the company far beyond the scope of the project in dispute, "including negative impacts on stock prices, brands, and reputations, and greater difficulty in securing financing, insurance, and community cooperation on future projects" (Herz et al., 2007).

Damage to the company's reputation and potential project cancellations can add up to billions of dollars. In his book, "*Just Business*," John Ruggie, the architect of the UN Global Compact, cited a Goldman Sachs study of 190 projects operated by multinational oil companies. Ruggie described an important finding of this confidential report, to which he had access: "Nontechnical risks accounted for nearly half of all risk factors faced by the oil majors, with 'stakeholder related risk' constituting the single largest category of nontechnical risk" (Korngold, 2014). Ruggie also reported that one particular company "may have accrued $6.5 billion in such costs over a two-year period, amounting to a double-digit percentage of its annual profits."

Ruggie commented on the staff time devoted to managing conflicts within communities. "If these conflicts are left unattended, they may escalate, which can lead to property damage and injury, or worse, to community members and company employees" (Ruggie, 2013).

Companies that are effective in addressing human rights issues do so with a keen understanding of the value to their brand; the credibility they will garner among customers, employees, and investors; and the expectations of regulatory groups. Additionally, as you will see in this chapter, many of the most effective business initiatives seek to drive systemic and inclusive change through coalitions and partnerships with NGOs.

Stakeholders Expect Businesses to Adhere to Human Rights Principles

Key stakeholders recognize that success in achieving human rights requires the full engagement of businesses. Following World War II, the United Nations put forward the Universal Declaration of Human Rights (UDHR), a formal charter for human rights (Universal Declaration, undated). The UDHR represented the international community's commitment to never allow atrocities like those of World War II to happen again. Eleanor Roosevelt was recognized as the driving force for the Declaration's adoption by the UN General Assembly on December 10, 1948. The UDHR addresses the state's duty to protect against human rights abuses by third parties, including *business enterprises*, through regulation, policymaking, investigation, and enforcement.

Historically, a major impetus for improved worker conditions and safety has come from international quasi-governmental bodies, such as the International Labour Organization (ILO). The ILO was founded in 1919 following World War I of "promoting social justice and internationally recognized human and labour rights, pursuing its founding mission that social justice is essential to universal and lasting peace" (ILO "Mission", undated). The ILO seeks to promote rights at work, encourage decent employment, and strengthen dialogue on work-related issues (Ibid.).

In 1998, the ILO adopted the Declaration on Fundamental Principles and Rights at Work. Amended in 2022, the Declaration is an "expression of commitment by governments, employers' and workers' organizations to uphold basic human values - values that are vital to our social and economic lives. It affirms the obligations and commitments that are inherent in membership of the ILO, namely: freedom of association and the effective recognition of the right to collective bargaining; the elimination of all forms of forced or compulsory labour; the effective abolition of child labour; the elimination of discrimination in respect of employment and occupation; and a safe and healthy working environment" (ILO "Declaration", 2022a).

Launched in 2000, the United Nations Global Compact (UNGC) provides a framework for development and implementation of responsible and sustainable business practices (United Nations Global Compact, undated). The UNGC refers to itself as the world's largest corporate sustainability initiative. Its strategy is "to provide a principle-based framework, best practices, resources, and networking events that have revolutionized how companies do business responsibly and keep commitments to society. By catalyzing action, partnerships and collaboration, we make transforming the world possible – and achievable – for organizations large and small, anywhere around the globe" (United Nations Global Compact, undated). There are over 21,000 organizational members of the UNGC from 162 countries.

In 2005, UN Secretary-General Kofi Annan appointed Professor John Ruggie as the special representative of the Secretary-General on human rights and transnational corporations and other business enterprises to further define the human rights responsibilities of business. Following six years of multi-stakeholder discussions, the United Nations Human Rights Council (UNHRC) unanimously endorsed the *United Nations Guiding Principles on Business and Human Rights: Implementing the United Nations "Protect, Respect, and Remedy" Framework*, on June 16, 2011 (United Nations Human Rights, 2011b).

The Guiding Principles are intended to provide operational clarity for the principles of the Global Compact, requiring companies to ensure that they are not engaged in human rights abuses (United Nations Global Compact 2011a). The Guiding Principles encompass three axioms applying to all states and businesses: "the state duty to *protect* against human rights abuses by third parties, including business; the corporate responsibility to *respect* human rights; and greater access by victims to effective *remedy*, both judicial and non-judicial" (Ibid.).

By 2021, adherence to human rights principles became a regulatory matter. "The [2021] Securities and Exchange Commission (SEC) disclosure rule broadly requires that certain companies submit a filing that describes their efforts to conduct a reasonable country-of-origin inquiry for necessary conflict minerals used in their products" (GAO 2022).

In addition to facing regulatory accountability with regard to human rights, companies also incur legal risks. Top fashion brands face legal challenges over garment workers' rights in Asia (Kelly, 2021).

While this chapter features specific approaches that some companies are taking to eliminate human rights abuses, other corporate actors have created and continue to perpetuate such threats. Only with such an understanding can we move forward together to find solutions. The purpose of this book is to provide examples of effective practices, with the hope of rallying more in the corporate sector to think creatively and collaboratively about ameliorating these issues.

Businesses that manage vast human and financial capital across nations have the power to implement the golden rule throughout the world: That which is hateful to you *don't* do unto others. Companies are learning that it is not only humane to follow this doctrine, but it is also more profitable in a world where customers, employees, members of communities, and investors will no longer tolerate child sex trafficking in the hotels where they sleep, deaths in factories where their clothing is sewn, or tech companies that are complicit with authoritarian governments. Corporations are recognizing the value to stakeholders when they practice respect, dignity, safety, and a fair wage, equitably, and inclusively, for employees and customers worldwide.

Companies Seek to Address Supply Chain Violations of Worker Safety and Security

Labor conditions and the treatment of workers present the modern global corporation with a serious human rights challenge and responsibility. For just over a decade, highly publicized, tragic, and avoidable deaths of garment workers have brought greater public scrutiny of the condition of workers producing goods for the developed world. Some companies are taking steps to address the humanitarian issues for their workers and within their supply chains.

Companies are motivated out of a desire to protect their brands, manage risk, and satisfy employees, customers, and investors. Furthermore, as described by BSR: "With tangible civil liability and monetary fines on the horizon, as well as basic business responsibility, the importance of examining and managing potential human rights risks has never been greater, both for companies' management teams and their investors" (Williams & Frame, 2022). BSR is a sustainable business network and consultancy that provides more than 300 member companies with insight, advice, and collaborative initiatives to help them see a changing world more clearly, create long-term value, and scale impact.

Investors too are beginning to understand their role in ensuring that companies address these vital human rights issues, including in their supply chains. As explained by BSR,

> Investors, like companies, have a responsibility to undertake enhanced due diligence in their investment decisions and stewardship of companies in conflict-affected areas. The consequence of not doing so can not only increase legal and financial risk but exacerbate human suffering and exploitation. (Ibid.)

Some companies are leading the way in addressing human rights issues for workers by engaging with NGOs and quasi-governmental partners. The case studies in this chapter describe some of these initiatives.

Businesses Combat Human Trafficking to End Forced Labor and Sexual Exploitation

Businesses are playing an important role in the fight against global trafficking, with some companies taking the lead. To these companies, combatting trafficking is a moral issue and an imperative, raising employee morale, engendering good will with customers, protecting the brand, and attracting socially responsible investors.

Forced labor is any work that is imposed on a person against their will through the use of coercion, fraud, or force, according to the International Labor Organization (ILO) Forced Labor Convention, 1930. There must be both a lack of free and informed consent and coercion for a job to be considered forced labor (ILO "Slavery", 2022b).

A turning point for human trafficking came with the adoption of The Protocol to Prevent, Suppress and Punish Trafficking in Persons, Especially Women and Children (the "Trafficking Protocol"), (United Nations General Assembly, 2001) by the General Assembly resolution of the United Nations in 2000 (UNODC, undated). The Trafficking Protocol became effective on December 25, 2003 (United Nations General Assembly, 2001). For the first time, it provided a legally binding instrument on trafficking with an agreed-upon definition. The Trafficking Protocol defined human trafficking to include forced labor, sexual exploitation, and the removal of human organs:

"Trafficking in persons" shall mean the recruitment, transportation, transfer, harbouring or receipt of persons, by means of the threat or use of force or other forms of coercion, of abduction, of fraud, of deception, of the abuse of power or of a position of vulnerability or of the giving or receiving of payments or benefits to achieve the consent of a person having control over another person, for the purpose of exploitation. Exploitation shall include, at a minimum, the exploitation of the prostitution of others or other forms of sexual exploitation, forced labour or services, slavery or practices similar to slavery, servitude or the removal of organs.

Additionally, based on the Trafficking Protocol, trafficking includes activity that occurs across country borders and within countries; it victimizes men, as well as women and children; and is perpetrated by individuals as well as by organized crime. One of the Trafficking Protocol's purposes is to facilitate international cooperation in investigating and prosecuting trafficking. Another is to protect and assist human trafficking's victims with full respect for their rights as established in the Universal Declaration of Human Rights

(United Nations "Universal Declaration", undated). According to the United Nations Office on Drugs and Crime, 154 countries ratified the Trafficking Protocol.

Through the adoption of the Sustainable Development Goals (SDGs) by all member states of the UN in 2015, the global community has committed to ending modern slavery universally by 2030 and among children by 2025 (SDG8). Progress on forced labor is threatened, however, by the COVID-19 pandemic, armed conflicts, and climate change. These conditions are disrupting employment and education, thereby increasing extreme poverty, forced and unsafe migration, and a rise in gender-based violence. This makes already vulnerable people even more at risk for forced labor; this includes people who are poor and socially excluded, workers in the informal economy, migrant workers, and people subject to discrimination.

Currently, there are over 27.6 million people experiencing forced labor at any point in time, including over 3.3 million children, according to the International Labor Organization (ILO), Walk Free, and the International Organization for Migration (IOM). Most cases of forced labor (86 percent) are in the private sector, in all industries, from services (excluding domestic work), to manufacturing, construction, agriculture, and domestic work (United Nations General Assembly, 2001). Human trafficking occurs not only in countries with poor governance, but also in all 50 of the United States—victimizing men, women, and children in cities, suburbs, and rural communities (Polaris Project, 2023).

Moreover, around 6.3 million people are in situations of forced commercial sexual exploitation on any given day. "Gender is a key determining factor: nearly four out of every five people trapped in these situations are girls or women," according to the ILO (ILO "Slavery", 2022b).

"It is shocking that the situation of modern slavery is not improving. Nothing can justify the persistence of this fundamental abuse of human rights," said ILO Director-General, Guy Ryder.

We know what needs to be done. Effective national policies and regulation are fundamental. But governments cannot do this alone. International standards provide a sound basis, and an all-hands-on-deck approach is needed. Trade unions, employers' organization, civil society, and ordinary people all have critical roles to play. (Ibid.)

Carlson Was the First US Company to Sign a Code to Protect Children from Trafficking

Governments alone have not been able to combat human trafficking. Businesses have an opportunity and a responsibility to address this vital challenge in partnership with NGOs and governments. Carlson, which at the time was a global hospitality and travel company, was the first United States-based global hospitality company to sign the travel industry's international "Code of Conduct for the Protection of Children from Sexual Exploitation in Travel and Tourism" (the Code) in 2004. The Code, having a mission to prevent the sexual exploitation of children, was developed by ECPAT (End Child Prostitution and Trafficking). The Code is a multi-stakeholder initiative providing awareness, tools, and support to the tourism industry to prevent the sexual exploitation of children.

By 2013, over 40 companies, tour operators, travel agencies, tourism associations, and tourism unions endorsed the Code, committing themselves to implement the measures shown below. The number of tourists impacted by the Code was estimated to reach over 30 million per year, travelling to destinations in over 16 countries worldwide. As of 2023, 401 companies in 245 countries have endorsed the CODE (The Code "Members", undated).

The Code commits endorsers to establish a corporate ethics policy against commercial sexual exploitation of children; train personnel in the country of origin and travel destinations; introduce clauses in contracts with suppliers, stating a common repudiation of sexual exploitation of children; provide information to travelers through catalogues, brochures, inflight films, ticket-slips, and websites; provide information to local "key persons" at destinations; and report annually.

Lori Cohen, Chief Executive Officer of ECPAT USA, says it is no longer difficult to build company engagement. "Public perception and good will are paramount to business, especially in the hospitality and travel industry. A company seeks to protect the integrity of its brand and its premises, so that employees and customers feel that the properties are safe places" (Cohen, 2022). Cohen reports that the American Hotel and Lodging Association (AHLA) is a strong advocate for ECPAT. "Through vigilance, training and commitment to prioritizing the prevention of human trafficking, the hotel industry will continue to play an instrumental role in ending the scourge of this modern-day form of slavery," says *Chip Rogers, AHLA President & CEO.* (American Hotel & Lodging Association, 2023).

In addition to interfacing with private sector parties, ECPAT-USA also provides youth and community education, and conducts advocacy work. Advocacy focuses on the need for trauma-informed care, foster youth and child sex trafficking, and criminal justice reform and trafficking of victims of color. (ECPAT-USA, 2022)

The story of how and why Carlson came to be the first US-based company to sign the Code is illuminating. In 2004, Marilyn Carlson Nelson, then chairman and chief executive officer of Carlson, was approached by US Ambassador John R. Miller to sign the Code. At the time, Ambassador Miller was leading the State Department's efforts to combat sex trafficking under President Bush.

Nelson and the company already had a history of protecting children at risk from abuse and exploitation. In 1999, Her Majesty Queen Silvia of Sweden had invited Carlson to join her and several corporations in establishing The World Childhood Foundation, an NGO whose very mission is to "defend the rights of the child and to promote better living conditions for vulnerable and exploited children at risk all over the world" (Korngold, 2014).

When Ambassador Miller asked Nelson to sign the Code, she was personally inclined to say yes, but she wanted to review the decision with her executive team. Discussions were complicated by concerns over potential legal exposure and public relations—the very hindrances that had kept other US companies from signing the Code. Nonetheless, the Carlson team agreed to proceed simply because they felt it was the right thing to do. Nelson reported the decision to sign the Code to Ambassador Miller. (Ibid.)

Signing the Code would involve a tremendous investment on Carlson's part. With hundreds of thousands of employees at 1300 hotels in operation and under development, and a global footprint spanning 160 countries under many brands, the training demands and logistics were massive. At that time, Carlson encompassed Radisson, Park Plaza, Park Inn by Radisson, and Country Inns & Suites. Additionally, Carlson added a clause in its supplier contracts that it would not work with companies involved in child trafficking.

Carlson's executive team embarked on the decision of signing the Code with some trepidation. They did not anticipate the response they would receive from employees and customers. "To our surprise," said Deborah Cundy, who was then vice president, Office of the Chairman at Carlson, "things caught on fire with this issue! Employees were thrilled. Customers were thrilled. All our fears were washed away!" (Ibid.)

Stating the business case for signing the Code of Conduct, Cundy said, "To begin with, child trafficking is illegal criminal activity. We don't want that in our hotels. It endangers our employees and our guests. Also, there's just this sense of righteous indignation. There were lots of reasons not to do this, but none of them more compelling than the case to do it. We're really proud of it. We didn't do it to win accolades. But I can't tell you how many people get in touch with me to praise our leadership. Employees feel proud... so thrilled... such expressions of gratitude."

Elaborating on her decision to sign the Code, Nelson explained further that "it's one more indication of moral authority. In today's world, particularly the millennials want to feel comfortable that they're working in an organization that lives its credo and its mission. That means that if you talk about an inclusive and respectful environment, then it's totally consistent to want to protect and stand for human rights."

Moreover, Nelson emphasized that trafficking is illegal regardless of sovereignty. "Businesses around the world are recognizing that corruption undermines business and trade. Taking a stand against corrupt practices supports the rule of law and court system." Nelson pointed out that human trafficking is often conducted by organized crime. "I don't think that any hospitality company is eager to have this take place in its establishment." She added that the "safety and security of our employees and guests is important." Like Cundy, Nelson noted how much pride the company's position has engendered among employees, as well as good will among customers, partners, and suppliers.

Nelson pointed out that "most companies are identifying a range of risk, particularly brand risk. I think that it's impossible to control all variables when you have a global collection of hotels, but to at least have established a policy and procedure to protect against illegal activities like this is an important element of protection from brand risk" (Ibid.).

By 2013, Hilton, Wyndham, and Delta Airlines signed the Code. Hilton signed the Code a year or so after a highly publicized sex prostitution ring scandal at one of their franchise hotels in Beijing (Ibid.). Wyndham was introduced to ECPAT and the Code via the Interfaith Center on Corporate Responsibility, Christian Brothers Investment Services, Mercy Investment Services, and a few additional socially responsible investment companies; this underscores the importance of investors as drivers.

Wyndman signed the ECPAT Code in 2011 under pressure following a child sex trafficking scandal at a Wyndham-franchised hotel. This demonstrates the power of the media and the concerns of businesses regarding investors, customers, and employees.

These companies did the right thing; they also benefitted their businesses by protecting and building their brands, reducing risks, elevating employee morale, and attracting socially responsible investors.

Companies Join Together to Combat Human Trafficking

While ECPAT addresses child trafficking in particular, other corporate initiatives seek solutions to the human trafficking of adults as well as children. In 2012, nine global companies launched the Global Business Coalition Against Human Trafficking (GBCAT) to fight human trafficking in company operations and supply chains. GBCAT's founding members included Carlson, The Coca-Cola Company, Delta Air Lines, ExxonMobil, LexisNexis, Manpower-Group, Microsoft, NXP, and Travelport (Korngold, 2014). At that time, 21 million people worldwide were victims of forced labor, bonded labor, child labor, and sexual servitude, according to the ILO (Ibid.). GBCAT's initial mission was to mobilize the power, resources, and thought leadership of the business community to end human trafficking, including all forms of forced labor and sex trafficking.

GBCAT's mission reflected the values of the founding companies. Eliminating trafficking is a moral mandate for businesses. Companies that are leading the way with GBCAT also recognize the value of their involvement in strengthening employee morale, enhancing their brand and reputation, and appealing to customers and investors, in addition to addressing legal and regulatory expectations.

At the GBCAT launch, President Barack Obama praised the coalition for its commitment to fight trafficking: "The good news is more and more responsible companies are holding themselves to higher standards. And today, I want to salute the new commitments that are being made. That includes the new Global Business Coalition Against Trafficking—companies that are sending a message: Human trafficking is not a business model, it is a crime, and we are going to stop it" (Ibid.).

At the time of its founding, GBCAT's core programs were "designed to assist companies in training and education for employees, vendors, and sub-contractors; awareness programs to combat sex trafficking, notably in travel and tourism; identifying and preventing forced labor in supply chains and operations; and the transfer of best practices," explained Robert Rigby-Hall, co-chair of GBCAT at its founding (Ibid.). "Those of us who formed GBCAT are passionate about stopping all forms of human trafficking," he said. "We see ourselves as advocates in our industries to engage other companies in GBCAT."

In 2017, BSR became GBCAT's Secretariat to grow the organization to achieve its greater potential. *BSR collaborations* bring together more than 400 companies, spanning multiple sectors and geographies, "to strengthen company performance, improve markets and industries, and contribute to systemic change for a more just and sustainable world" (GBCAT "Who", 2018b). GBCAT is one of 56 collaborations that BSR has formed and led to date.

GBCAT has evolved since its founding. Its current mission is "to harness the power of business across sectors to prevent and reduce human trafficking, and support survivors." It describes itself as a "coalition of businesses committed to combating human trafficking in company operations and supply chains." GBCAT's work focuses on survivor empowerment and employment, corporate supplier capability building, and resources and guidance for employers to navigate anti-slavery tools, training, and organizations (GBCAT "About", 2018a).

GBCAT's members include Carlson, The Coca-Cola Company, Google, Marriott, and Boost Engagement. "GBCAT is about getting your own house and supply chain in order and having a leadership voice in the corporate sector beyond compliance to identify and prevent trafficking, while also advocating for strong public policy to protect vulnerable people," says Sara Enright, Director of Sustainability Collaborations at BSR.

In 2019, Tech Against Trafficking (TAT), a separate anti-trafficking initiative selected BSR to serve as its Secretariat. TAT is a coalition of "companies collaborating with global experts to help eradicate human trafficking using technology" (Tech Against Trafficking webpage, 2020). Its mission is to "work with civil society, law enforcement, academia, technologists, and survivors to advance and scale the use of technology to prevent, disrupt, and reduce human trafficking and increase and expand survivors' access to resources." BSR explains further on its website.

> Through their expertise, capacity for innovation, and global reach, technology companies can play a major role in preventing and disrupting human trafficking and in empowering survivors. Digital information and communication technologies offer opportunities for a step change in tackling this crime. Technological solutions to date include mobile apps that help identify victims of sex trafficking; satellite imagery that tracks down fishing vessels carrying victims of forced labor; and web scraping tools that aggregate child abuse images to help law enforcement track down children in need of help. But there are many more tools out there in need of support. Tech Against Trafficking hopes to accelerate the development, scale, and resulting impact of these tools.

TAT's flagship initiative is the Accelerator Program, launched in 2019. The Accelerator identifies promising uses of technology to combat trafficking. By drawing on the expertise and resources of member companies, the Accelerator promotes and scales these anti-trafficking technologies to assist victims, law enforcement, business, and civil society. The Accelerator also offers network access, mentorship, training, and education to participating organizations (Tech Against Trafficking "How", 2020a).

TAT has supported the important work of three anti-trafficking organizations in the past two years, (Takisalp, 2022) according to Lale Tekişalp, Manager, Technology and Human Rights at BSR. Working with the Counter-Trafficking Data Collective (CTDC), managed by the UN's International Organization for Migration, TAT organized an effort by Amazon, AT&T, BT, Microsoft, and Salesforce.org to enhance and scale a privacy-preserving data platform for anti-trafficking (Counter Trafficking Data Collaborative, undated). The new tech makes it possible for CTDC to share more data and to conduct more effective research, while protecting the privacy and civil liberties of victims and survivors (Do & Darnton, 2020). Microsoft highlighted the solution on its website (Edge et al., 2020).

Additionally, TAT supported the Lantern Project (Lantern Project website, 2022) and Unseen UK (Unseen UK webpage 2021) to optimize their data infrastructure, identify patterns, and generate insights that improve operational efficiency, and enable the organizations to provide more effective services to reduce human trafficking (Tekisalp et al., 2022). TAT also published an interactive map of technology tools being used across the world to fight human trafficking (Tech Against Trafficking "Map", 2020b).

In its Tech Against Trafficking Summit in 2022, BSR presented tech enabled anti-trafficking solutions, engaging an audience of companies, NGOs, and government officials (BSR, 2022).

> The summit brought together over 160 leaders from the anti-trafficking field, including businesses, survivors and activists, governments, investors, and civil society, to expand opportunities for collaboration and accelerate the impact of innovative technology solutions addressing human trafficking.

"What is new in the anti-trafficking movement is the focus on 'rights holders,' people who have been victims and survivors of trafficking," explained Sara Enright, Director of Sustainability Collaborations, including GBCAT. "There is a shift to engage rights holders not just as voices for victims but also as advisors, employees, and people in positions of power" (Enright, 2022). Changes will involve power-sharing by companies that have organized and funded anti-trafficking initiatives—working alongside rights holders as change agents and decision makers. The Survivor Leadership Fund is an example of an initiative "to *uplift and support survivor-led organizations by providing unrestricted grants*" (Freedom Fund, undated).

GBCAT and TAT will be merged into one collaborative initiative in 2023. Enright will continue to be an Advisor. She oversees BSR's portfolio of collaborative initiatives and advises companies on the advancement of inclusive business models (BSR 2023).

The role of business is essential in the fight against trafficking. Some companies are leading the way in partnership with NGOs. To these companies, combatting trafficking is a moral imperative, that also elevates employee morale, engenders good will with customers, protects the brand, attracts socially responsible investors, and aligns with legal and regulatory expectations.

RISE Brings Together the Apparel Industry's Women's Empowerment Programs

Forced labor is linked to another fundamental problem: the lack of women's empowerment in social, political, and environmental spheres make them particularly vulnerable in the workplace. Many female employees in global supply chains experience high levels of harassment and violence, both in the workplace and in their personal relationships (BSR/HERproject, 2023). "This violence, which can be economic, emotional, physical, or sexual, deprives women of their basic human rights and compromises their well-being," according to BSR (Ibid.). Furthermore, women have been disproportionately impacted by the economic and social consequences of COVID-19.

Not only are these toxic conditions bad for women, but evidence shows that when the well-being of workers suffers, businesses and economies are negatively impacted. "Violence against women is bad for business, and there is a high cost to inaction," states BSR (Ibid.). Some of the consequences for companies resulting from harassment and violence against women include employee absenteeism, distraction, and tardiness; increases in employee turnover; declines in productivity and employee morale; and harm to brand perception and reputation (Deloitte 2019; EVERFI, 2023).

BSR established the HERproject in 2007 to improve conditions for women in the workplace by using interventions to advance health, financial inclusion, and gender equality. Convening global brands and their suppliers, as well as local NGOs, the HERproject has been effective in more than 1000 workplaces across 17 countries, increasing the well-being, confidence, and economic potential of well over a million women (BSR/HERproject, 2023).

Building on this initiative, BSR has joined forces with the CARE International, Gap Inc.'s P.A.C.E. Program, and ILO-IFC Better Work to increase its impact in serving women (Empower@Work webpage, undated). Together, these four major women's empowerment programs formed RISE in 2021. BSR serves as its Secretariat. In 2023, RISE will become its own free-standing NGO to accelerate and expand gender equity and women's empowerment across global supply chains, through the delivery of proven trainings and services. RISE will initially focus on apparel and footwear, and eventually expand to tech, agriculture, and other consumer packaged good companies (CPGs).

The newly established NGO will be well positioned to achieve important progress. According to The World Bank, women's employment can be a central driver of inclusive growth, advancing development goals such as health, education, and food security, while addressing climate change, gender-based violence, forced displacement, conflict and fragility (World Bank, undated). Given the scope of its work, RISE could fit in any chapter in this book, but it seems that human rights is particularly well aligned.

"Fundamental to our success will be our work with local NGO partners. While some standards might be global, it is essential that implementation be contextualized according to needs of particular communities," explains Christine Svarer, Executive Director of RISE (Sawyer, 2022).

Participating companies and suppliers will benefit by strengthening company performance, improving operational efficiency within facilities, helping to foster a healthier workforce with higher retention and lower absenteeism, enhancing company reputation, and providing data and reports for companies to comply with governmental regulations.

Company Challenges: Cybersecurity, Privacy on the Internet, and Protecting Freedom of Expression

Cybersecurity attacks, misleading content, loss of privacy on the Internet, and constraints on freedom of expression bring broad social and economic costs. These questions invoke fundamental human rights issues and questions about unwanted intrusions on highly personal matters. This is also important to businesses, on a basic level of compliance with regulations and avoidance of liability for privacy breaches. Moreover, companies can suffer significant damage to their reputations and brands by knowingly or even accidentally compromising or misusing the data of customers and others. Smart companies have been working to mitigate the threat of loss of data privacy.

"Cybersecurity risks to the financial system have grown in recent years, in part because the cyber threat landscape is worsening; in particular, state-sponsored cyberattacks targeting financial institutions are becoming more frequent, sophisticated, and destructive," according to the Carnegie Endowment for International Peace (Carnegie Endowment for International Peace, 2023). For individual consumers, common cyber-related crimes include identity theft, frauds, and scams (FDIC, 2022). Breaches involve invasions of personal health information, stolen or compromised credentials, and ransomware attacks.

Cyberattacks affect every sector, including businesses, nonprofits, and governments. Furthermore, IBM warns that "it's not if a data breach will happen, but when. Usually more than once" (IBM, 2022). Moreover, McKinsey warns that "cyberattacks are proliferating, causing trillions of dollars of damage every year" (McKinsey, 2022). PWC cautions that "companies must implement robust data governance and give consumers more control over how their personal information is used…Companies must put cybersecurity and privacy at the forefront of business strategy to win customers' hearts – and earn their trust" (PWC, 2017).

"The coming year will begin to clarify how new U.S. laws and regulations outlined in 2022 might strengthen corporate and infrastructure resilience," reports The Wall Street Journal (Rundle, 2022). For companies, cybersecurity represents both threats and opportunities. McKinsey suggests that "The cybersecurity industry has a chance to step up and seize the opportunity. $2 trillion market opportunity for cybersecurity technology and service providers" (McKinsey, 2022).

Additionally, the pandemic has revealed the tremendous harm caused by false and misleading information. "Misinformation and disinformation have contributed to reduced trust in medical professionals and public health responders, increased belief in false medical cures, politicized public health countermeasures aimed at curbing transmission of the disease, and increased loss of life," according to the Johns Hopkins Bloomberg School of Public Health Center for Health Security (Bruns et al., 2021).

The Internet can be a dangerous platform to spread hate and incite violence. "Online platforms are not neutral…their algorithms can fuel hateful and misleading content and *exacerbate real world harms*," says Amnesty International, in reference to "seismic events – from the Covid-19 disinformation to the Facebook Papers and the ongoing *information warfare* in the context of the Ukraine crisis" (Prettner, 2022).

Social media can contribute to deadly violence. The House Select Committee to Investigate the January 6th Attack on the UN Capitol "found evidence that tech platforms – especially Twitter – failed to heed their employees' warnings about violent rhetoric on their platforms and bent their rules to avoid penalizing conservatives...out of fear of reprisals" (Zakrewski et al., 2023). Committee staffers wrote in emails:

> The sum of this is that alt-tech, fringe, and mainstream platforms were exploited in tandem by right-wing activists to bring American democracy to the brink of ruin. These platforms enabled the mobilization of extremists on smaller sites and whipped up conservative grievance on larger, more mainstream ones. (Ibid.)

As with many other issues, vulnerable people suffer disproportionately. Women, and gay and bisexual men and women, are at particular risk in terms of nonconsensual pornography. So are people from diverse racial and ethnic backgrounds and disability status (Citron, 2022). "Over the course of my career, I've witnessed the entrenchment of the notion that the bodies of women and minorities are not their own," says Danielle Keats Citron, author of *The Fight for Privacy: Protecting Dignity, Identify, and Love in the Digital Age* (Ibid.). These threats "deny humans their rights to full freedom of expression, equal opportunity, and personal identity, and, as such, intimate privacy should be considered a civil and human right under law" (Powell & Dent, 2023).

Furthermore, Citron cautions that "vulnerable groups are often 'canaries in the coalmine' for digital threats that could extend to the larger population" (Ibid.). In the blog post, "Data is the New Gold, But May Threaten Democracy and Dignity," published in the Council of Foreign Relations, it is noted that "few safeguards protect our private data in today's information economy" (Ibid.). This poses threats to personal safety as well as national security. "Deepfakes, increasing realistic, faked audio and video recordings, could alter the outcomes of an election." Although Citron recommends a legal framework to defend intimate privacy, she also recognizes that "moral suasion from the public can incentivize companies to protect this information in the meantime" (Ibid.).

Dunstan Allison-Hope explains the imperative for companies to collaborate with each other, as well as nonprofits and governments to address these threats. Allison-Hope is Vice President of BSR and the author of *Protecting Human Rights in the Digital Age*. He leads BSR's work at the intersection of technology and human rights (Allison-Hope, 2011). "There are some matters that companies must address on their own. But many of the challenges are system-wide, so we encourage companies to be part of coalitions to drive progress." notes Allison-Hope, who advises Google, Meta, Salesforce, and other major tech companies. He mentions in particular the Partnership on AI, that brings together diverse voices from across the AI community to create resources for advancing positive outcomes for people and society (Partnership on AI webpage, 2023); Ranking Digital Rights, that advances corporate accountability for human rights in the digital age (Ranking Digital Rights, undated); the Digital Trust and Safety Partnership, promoting a safer and more trustworthy internet (Digital Trust and Safety Partnership, 2021); and the Global Internet Forum for Counter-Terrorism (GIFCT) (GIFCT, undated).

It is in their best interests for companies to advance the important human rights of privacy on the Internet and free expression. These principles are fundamental in protecting their customers, serving core business values, enhancing company reputations, and promoting the company's competitive position in the marketplace. Free and accurate expression and privacy on the Internet are important ingredients to the stable society that business requires to effectively operate.

The UN Guiding Principles Provide a Human Rights Framework for Companies

Human trafficking, women's empowerment, and freedom of expression and privacy on the internet are just a few human rights issues where corporations have opportunities and responsibilities. The UN Guiding Principles on Business and Human Rights provide the framework for companies to assess and iteratively improve their practices (Allison-Hope et al., 2022; United National Human Rights, 2011b).

> There are certain key features that distinguish a human rights-based approach: reviewing and addressing impacts against all human rights; prioritizing risks to people based on severity—i.e., scope (the number of people impacted), scale (how grave the impact), and remediability (whether the impact can be made good); and paying particular attention to the rights of individuals from vulnerable groups or populations. (Allison-Hope et al., 2022)

The Golden Rule Is Good for Business and Society

As employers of tens of millions of people worldwide, purchasers at the top of massive supply chains, and owners of vast global property and agribusinesses, global corporations affect the rights of many people who live on this planet. Laws and the commitment to enforcement vary from one country to another. Multinational corporations, however, are in a powerful position to respect and protect human rights throughout the world. The voices of customers, employees, and investors matter. Companies can grow their value while improving the human condition.

References

Allison-Hope, D. (2011). Protecting human rights in the digital age. BSR, Feb. https://www.bsr.org/reports/BSR_Protecting_Human_Rights_in_the_Digital_Age.pdf. Accessed 31 Jan 2023.

Allison-Hope, D., Darnton, H., Andersen, L., & Khan, A. (2022). Human rights everywhere all at once. BSR, 08 Sep. https://www.bsr.org/en/blog/human-rights-everywhere-all-at-once. Accessed 31 Jan 2023.

American Hotel and Lodging Association. (2023). No room for trafficking. https://redesign-americanhotelandlodgingassociation.pantheonsite.io/noroomfortrafficking. Accessed 31 Jan 2023.

Bouie, J. (2023). Opinion, New York Times, 14 Jan. https://messaging-custom-newsletters.nytimes.com/template/oakv2?campaign_id=129&emc=edit_jbo_20230114&instance_id=82765&nl=jamelle-bouie&productCode=JBO&regi_id=46898255&segment_id=122561&te=1&uri=nyt%3A%2F%2Fnewsletter%2F04d955b4-fa29-5178-9ede-698325200a9e&user_id=b2ce85b95e6d3b2ecbff6f23cebcfdce. Accessed 31 Jan 2023.

Bruns, R., Hosangadi, D., Trotochaud, M., & Kirk Sell, T. (2021). COVID-19 vaccine misinformation and disinformation costs an estimated $50 to $300 million each day. Johns Hopkins, Bloomberg School of Public Health, Center for Health Security, 20 Oct. https://www.centerforhealthsecurity.org/our-work/pubs_archive/pubs-pdfs/2021/20211020-misinformation-disinformation-cost.pdf. Accessed 31 Jan 2023.

BSR. (2023). Collaboration: high-impact collective action to address global challenges. https://www.bsr.org/en/collaboration/. Accessed 31 Jan 2023.

BSR. (2022). Tech against trafficking summit. https://www.bsr.org/en/events/tech-against-trafficking-summit. Accessed 31 Jan 2023.

BSR/HERproject. (2023). HER respect. https://herproject.org/programs/herrespect. Accessed 31 Jan 2023.

Carnegie Endowment for International Peace. (2023). Timeline of cyber incidents involving financial institutions. https://carnegieendowment.org/specialprojects/protectingfinancialstability/timeline. Accessed 31 Jan 2023.

Citron, D. K. (2022). *The fight for privacy: Protecting dignity, identity, and love in the digital age*. W.W. Norton

Cohen, L. (2022). Interview with Alice Korngold. 12 Oct.

Counter Trafficking Data Collaborative. (undated). Global data hub on human trafficking. https://www.ctdatacollaborative.org/. Accessed 31 Jan 2023.

Deloitte. (2019). The economic costs of sexual harassment in the workplace, Mar. https://www2.deloitte.com/content/dam/Deloitte/au/Documents/Economics/deloitte-au-economic-costs-sexual-harassment-workplace-240320.pdf. Accessed 31 Jan 2023.

Digital Trust and Safety Partnership Webpage. (2021). https://dtspartnership.org/. Accessed 31 Jan 2023.

Do, M., & Darnton, H. (2020). Accelerating toward data insights. BSR, 20 Feb. https://www.bsr.org/en/blog/tech-against-trafficking-successfully-concludes-accelerator. Accessed 31 Jan 2023.

ECPAT-USA. (2022). Legislative advocacy. https://www.ecpatusa.org/legislative-advocacy. Accessed 31 Jan 2023.

Edge, D., Yang, W., Cook, H., Galez-Davis, C., Darnton, H., Lytvynets, K., & White, C. (2020). Design of a privacy-preserving data platform for collaboration against human trafficking. Microsoft Research, May. https://www.microsoft.com/en-us/research/publication/design-of-a-privacy-preserving-data-platform-for-collaboration-against-human-trafficking/. Accessed 31 Jan 2023.

Empower@work webpage. (undated). https://www.empoweratwork.org/. Accessed 31 Jan 2023.

Enright, S. (2022). Interview with Alice Korngold. 23 Dec.

EVERFI. (2023). How does sexual harassment affect the workplace? https://everfi.com/blog/workplace-training/the-effects-of-sexual-harassment-in-the-workplace/. Accessed 31 Jan 2023.

Federal Deposit Insurance Corporation. (2022). Cybersecurity, 22 Aug. https://www.fdic.gov/resources/consumers/consumer-assistance-topics/cybersecurity.html. Accessed 31 Jan 2023.

Freedom Fund. (undated). Survivor Leadership Fund. https://freedomfund.org/programs/community-building/survivor-leadership-fund/. Accessed 31 Jan 2023.

GBCAT. (2018a). About ("About"). https://www.gbcat.org/overview-history. Accessed 31 Jan 2023.

GBCAT. (2018b). Who we are ("Who"). https://www.gbcat.org/who-we-are-1. Accessed 31 Jan 2023.

Global Internet Forum to Counter Terrorism (GIFCT). (undated). https://gifct.org/governance/#civil-society. Accessed 31 Jan 2023.

Government Accountability Office (GAO). (2022). Conflict minerals: Overall peace and security in eastern Democratic Republic of the Congo has not improved since 2014. GAO-22-105411, 14 Sep. https://www.gao.gov/products/gao-22-105411#:~:text=These%20minerals%20include%20tin%2C%20tungsten,the%20source%20of%20their%20minerals. Accessed 31 Jan 2023.

Greig, J. (2022). Governments intentionally shut down Internet 182 times in 34 countries in 2021: report. The Record, 28 Apr. https://therecord.media/governments-intentionally-shut-down-internet-182-times-across-34-countries-in-2021-report/. Accessed 31 Jan 2023.

Gunther, M. (2013). What's the cost of cheap clothing? Greenbiz.com, 25 Feb. https://www.greenbiz.com/article/whats-cost-cheap-clothing. Accessed 31 Jan 2023.

Hasnat, S., & Schmall, E. (2021). Dozens die as another factory fire strikes Bangladesh. New York Times, 09 Jul. https://www.nytimes.com/2021/07/09/world/asia/bangladesh-factory-fire.html. Accessed 31 Jan 2023.

Herz, S., La Vina, A., & Sohn, J. (2007). Development without conflict: The business case for community consent. World Resources Institute, May. http://pdf.wri.org/development_without_conflict_fpic.pdf. Accessed 31 Jan 2023.

IBM. (2022). Cost of a data breach 2022. https://www.ibm.com/reports/data-breach. Accessed 31 Jan 2023.

International Labour Organization (ILO). (2022a). Declaration on Fundamental Principles and Rights at Work ("Declaration"). https://www.ilo.org/declaration/thedeclaration/lang--en/index.htm. Accessed 31 Jan 2023.

International Labour Organization (ILO). (2022b). Global estimates of modern slavery: forced labour and forced marriage ("Slavery"), Sep. https://www.ilo.org/wcmsp5/groups/public/---ed_norm/---ipec/documents/publication/wcms_854733.pdf. Accessed 31 Jan 2023.

International Labour Organization (ILO). (undated). Mission and impact of the ILO ("Mission"). https://www.ilo.org/global/about-the-ilo/mission-and-objectives/lang--en/index.htm. Accessed 31 Jan 2023.

International Labour Organization (ILO). (undated). The Rana Plaza accident and its aftermath. https://www.ilo.org/global/topics/geip/WCMS_614394/lang--en/index.htm. Accessed 31 Jan 2023.

Keep It On. (2022). The return of digital authoritarianism: Internet shutdowns in 2021. https://www.accessnow.org/cms/assets/uploads/2022/05/2021-KIO-Report-May-24-2022.pdf. Accessed 31 Jan 2023.

Kelly, A. (2021). Top fashion brands face legal challenge over garment workers' rights in Asia. Guardian, 09 Jul. https://www.theguardian.com/global-development/2021/jul/09/top-fashion-brands-face-legal-challenge-over-garment-workers-rights-in-asia. Accessed 31 Jan 2023.

Korngold, A. (2014). *A Better World, Inc.: How companies profit by solving global problems where governments cannot.* Palgrave Macmillan.

Lantern Project Website. (2022). https://thelantern.net/. Accessed 31 Jan 2023.

McKinsey. (2022). New survey reveals $2 trillion market opportunity for cyber-security technology and service providers, 27 Oct. https://www.mckinsey.com/capabilities/risk-and-resilience/our-insights/cybersecurity/new-survey-reveals-2-trillion-dollar-market-opportunity-for-cybersecurity-technology-and-service-pro viders. Accessed 31 Jan 2023.

Partnership on AI Webpage. (2023). https://partnershiponai.org/. Accessed 31 Jan 2023.

Polaris Project. (2023). Human trafficking. https://polarisproject.org/human-traffi cking/. Accessed 31 Jan 2023.

Powell, C., & Dent, A. (2023). Data is the new gold, but may threaten democracy and dignity. Council on Foreign Relations, 05 Jan. https://www.cfr.org/blog/data-new-gold-may-threaten-democracy-and-dignity-0. Accessed 31 Jan 2023.

Prettner, C. (2022). Putting the brakes on big tech's uncontrolled power. Amnesty International, 25 Apr. https://www.amnesty.org/en/latest/campaigns/2022/04/putting-the-brakes-on-big-techs-uncontrolled-power/. Accessed 31 Jan 2023.

PWC. (2017). Consumer intelligence series: protect.me. https://www.pwc.com/us/en/advisory-services/publications/consumer-intelligence-series/protect-me/cis-pro tect-me-findings.pdf. Accessed 31 Jan 2023.

Ranking Digital Rights Webpage. (undated). https://rankingdigitalrights.org/. Accessed 31 Jan 2023.

Ruggie, J. G. (2013). *Just business.* W.W. Norton.

Rundle, J. (2022). Hackers had a banner year in 2022. U.S. regulators aim to slow them down in 2023. Wall Street Journal, 30 Dec. https://www.wsj.com/story/hackers-had-a-banner-year-in-2022-us-regulators-aim-to-slow-them-down-in-2023-9d973fc8. Accessed 31 Jan 2023.

Sawyer, C. (2022). Interview with Alice Korngold. 05 Dec.

Sengupta, S. (2013). Letting our guard down with web privacy. New York Times, 30 Mar. https://www.nytimes.com/2013/03/31/technology/web-privacy-and-how-consumers-let-down-their-guard.html. Accessed 31 Mar 2023.

Stevenson, B. (2015). *Just mercy: a story of justice and redemption.* One World/Random House.

Tech Against Trafficking. (2020a). How we work ("How"). https://techagainsttraffic king.org/how-we-work/. Accessed 23 Jan 2023.

Tech Against Trafficking. (2020b). Interactive map ("Map"). https://techagainsttraf ficking.org/interactive-map/. Accessed 23 Jan 2023.

Tech Against Trafficking Webpage. (2020). https://techagainsttrafficking.org/. Accessed 23 Jan 2023.

Tekisalp, L. (2022). Interview with Alice Korngold. 23 Nov.

Tekisalp, L., Darnton, H., Hannegan, T., & Formisano, C. (2022). Harnessing the power of data to combat human trafficking. BSR, 17 May. https://www.bsr.org/en/blog/harnessing-the-power-of-data-to-combat-human-trafficking. Accessed 31 Jan 2023.

The Code. (undateda). About ("About"). https://thecode.org/about/. Accessed 31 Jan 2023.

The Code. (undatedb). Our members "Members". https://thecode.org/ourmembers/. Accessed 31 Jan 2023.

United Nations. (undated). The Universal Declaration of Human Rights "Universal Declaration". https://www.un.org/en/about-us/universal-declaration-of-human-rights. Accessed 31 Jan 2023.

United Nations, Global Compact. (2011a). The UN protect, respect and remedy framework for business and human rights: relationship to UN global compact commitments, 01 Jul. https://www.business-humanrights.org/en/latest-news/pdf-the-un-guiding-principles-on-business-and-human-rights-relationship-to-un-global-compact-commitments/. Accessed 31 Jan 2023.

United Nations, Human Rights. (2011b). Guiding Principles on Business and Human Rights. https://www.ohchr.org/sites/default/files/documents/publications/guidingprinciplesbusinesshr_en.pdf. Accessed 31 Jan 2023.

United Nations, General Assembly. (2001). Protocol to Prevent, Suppress and Punish Trafficking in Persons, Especially Women and Children. https://www.unodc.org/documents/treaties/Special/2000_Protocol_to_Prevent_2C_Suppress_and_Punish_Trafficking_in_Persons.pdf. Accessed 31 Jan 2023.

United Nations, Global Compact. (undated). Mission. https://www.unglobalcompact.org/what-is-gc/mission. Accessed 31 Jan 2023.

United Nations, Office on Drugs and Crime ("UNODC"). (undated). https://www.unodc.org/unodc/en/human-trafficking/human-trafficking.html. Accessed 31 Jan 2023.

Unseen UK Webpage. (2021). https://www.unseenuk.org/. Accessed 31 Jan 2023.

Williams, S., & Frame, K. (2022). Conflict and modern slavery: The investment perspective. BSR, 02 Sep. https://www.bsr.org/en/blog/conflict-and-modern-slavery-the-investment-perspective. Accessed 31 Jan 2023.

World Bank. (undated). The World Bank in gender. https://www.worldbank.org/en/topic/gender/overview. Accessed 31 Jan 2023.

Zaki, J. (2019). Making empathy central to your company culture. Harvard Business Review, 30 May. https://hbr.org/2019/05/making-empathy-central-to-your-company-culture. Accessed 31 Jan 2023.

Zakrewski, C., Lima, C., & Harwell, D. (2023). What the Jan. 6 probe found out about social media, but didn't report. Washington Post, 17 Jan. https://www.washingtonpost.com/technology/2023/01/17/jan6-committee-report-social-media/. Accessed 31 Jan 2023.

7

Corporate Governance for an Inclusive, Sustainable, and Prosperous Future

Fight for the things that you care about, but do it in a way that will lead others to join you.

–Hon. Ruth Bader Ginsburg (2015)

DEFEATING POVERTY, MITIGATING THE PACE OF GLOBAL WARMING AND THE destruction of the natural environment, and advancing education, health, and human rights are ambitious goals. National governments do not have global authority and resources to offer sufficient solutions, nor has the international community achieved binding and actionable agreements to address global problems. NGOs are often effective in addressing problems, but their capacity to achieve scope and scale is limited. As shown in this book, echoing the original edition, only multinational corporations have the vast resources, global footprint, and market incentives to find innovative solutions to the world's greatest challenges. Furthermore, businesses that are leading the way are demonstrating that innovative solutions to social, economic, and environmental challenges can be profitable.

Promoting inclusion and sustainability is the path forward for companies to build a more prosperous world that grows their own profits as well. Inclusion, because large swaths of humanity are left out of the current economic system—BIPOC individuals, women, migrants and asylum seekers, LGBTQ+ individuals, people with disabilities, and people who were formerly incarcerated, among others. By squandering human capital, companies and society are pushing a multitude of people out of the equation—people who could contribute to and participate in vibrant economies. Sustainability, because there is no future for people or planet unless greenhouse gas emissions are halved by 2030—and dropped to net-zero by 2050.

There are three critical factors for companies to be successful: First, ensuring effective board governance that puts inclusion and sustainability at the center of the company's vision and strategy; second, engaging with stakeholders, including employees, customers, investors, and communities, in an iterative conversation on global problem-solving; and third, collaborating with other companies, NGOs, and governments to drive toward an inclusive, sustainable, and prosperous future. This chapter will highlight lessons from the cases presented in the book, and underscore the vital role of corporate boards.

Boards Have the Responsibility and the Authority to Shape the Global Agenda

Companies have the capacity and self-interest to advance progress in addressing climate change and vital social concerns. It is the boards of directors, however, that have the ultimate responsibility and authority to guide and shape corporations to grow their value. To do so, boards must drive the global agenda for an inclusive, sustainable, and prosperous future.

To fulfill their responsibilities to shareholders and stakeholders, boards must be comprised of qualified individuals. Given the challenges and opportunities facing businesses today, an effective board must be constituted with people who have the diversity of experience, expertise, and backgrounds to envision the company's greater potential in the global marketplace and to ensure that the company has the leadership and culture to achieve success. Additionally, boards must focus their attention on what matters most, including the social, economic, and environmental factors that are critical to grow value.

Boards Are Becoming Better Qualified to Lead

Boards are better qualified today than ever before, and the trajectory is promising. Compare board composition in 2022, to board composition in 2014, just after the original edition of this book was published. The Spencer

Stuart Board Index, reporting on S&P 500 public companies, provides useful data that is presented below (Spencer Stuart, 2014; Spencer Stuart, 2022).

Even though the very topics addressed in this book were already of grave importance in 2014, as described in the original edition, board members often came from homogeneous and privileged backgrounds, with little diversity in terms of gender, age, race and ethnicity. Most rose to business leadership positions in the late twentieth century; they had limited familiarity with climate change, cybersecurity, geopolitical conflicts, and other pressing issues that plague the world today.

In the past decade, however, companies have become more intentional about building highly qualified boards comprised of directors from more diverse backgrounds. Among *new* directors added to boards in 2022, 46% are women, 46% are from diverse racial and ethnic backgrounds, and 18% are under the age of 50 (Ibid.). They are recruited for their expertise in the most relevant global issues.

Board directors interviewed for this book point out priority areas of expertise for which people are being sought. April Miller Boise stresses that "in addition to traditional CEO and CFO experience that boards often seek out, more and more when recruiting directors, boards are looking for critical skills in areas like ESG, technology, digital, and cybersecurity." Boise is a Board Director at Trane, and Executive Vice President and Chief Legal Counsel at Intel. (Boise, 2023)

With regard to board competencies, Michael Cherkasky describes cybersecurity and supply chain challenges facing companies and their boards. "Boards always focused on financial risks. Today, they must also look at operational risks; these are compliance issues." Cherkasky is Co-Founder and a Director of Exiger, a company that provides end-to-end supply chain visibility, and risk management and compliance solutions (Cherkasky 2023).

Furthermore, a sophisticated understanding of technology threats and opportunities is essential. "We're about to go through another tech evolution like in the 1990s and early 2000s. Through a combination of blockchain tech and artificial intelligence." explains JoAnn Holmes, Digital Assets & Intellectual Property Attorney, Web3 Advisor, and Outside General Counsel. "There are important implications for boards. These technologies are going to be disruptive" (Holmes 2023).

More turnover, driven by term limits and retirement age requirements, will provide opportunities to further refresh board composition and ensure board independence. Boise advises that "there is often a concern by institutional investors that when directors are on boards for too many years, they can become less independent of management. Independence from management is important to evaluate enterprise risk and provide oversight" (Boise 2023).

Although overall board composition is changing, there is room for growth in the leadership ranks on boards and in C-suite positions. Very few board chairs and company CEOs are women or people from diverse racial and ethnic backgrounds. Among the S&P 500 companies, twenty-four women serve as independent board chairs, and 48 as leading/presiding board chairs. More promising is that 164 women serve as nominating/governance committee chairs. Only thirty-four women serve as CEOs of S&P 500 companies.

Within the S&P 500, there only forty-five independent board chairs, 50 leading/presiding board chairs, and 90 nominating/governance committee chairs who are members of underrepresented racial groups (According to another study, only six Black people serve as CEOs of Fortune 500 companies.) (Jeong et al., 2022) (Table 7.1).

Importantly, boards are adding new directors who are under 50 years of age. "Younger directors may not only enhance a board's generational diversity, but can help companies chart a path forward in an increasingly complex and technology-dependent business environment," says MSCI (Sommer, 2023), which provides ESG and climate products.

Not only are companies strengthening board composition, but they are also providing more training resources to their directors. In 2014, only 39% of boards offered new board member orientations; only 20% provided access to third party education programs; and only 64% of boards made visits to the company's on-site facilities and operations. Today, there is a plethora of board training programs at universities, such as Harvard, Stanford, Wharton, and IMD; law firms; and independent private and public organizations that specialize in board governance. Paul Polman, the former CEO of Unilever, and co-author of Net Positive, stresses the importance of rigorous board training and education, and visits to company sites around the world (Polman, 2022; Polman & Winston, 2021).

Companies seeking to grow value in the coming decade will need to be highly strategic in constituting their boards and elevating the right people to leadership; focusing boards on the critical challenges and opportunities; and ensuring that boards are well trained in terms of the most critical issues, board governance, and the company itself.

Table 7.1 Board membership data—2014, 2022

Board Membership Data—2014, 2022	2014	2022
Size	10.8	10.8
Independent directors	84%	86%
Average age (years)	63.1	63.1
Average tenure (years)	8.4	7.8
Specify term limits	3%	7% (range from 10 to 20 years)
Mandatory retirement	30% (set at 75 years)	70% (53% set it at 75 years or older)
Independent board chair	28%	36%
Diversity		
Women	19%	32%
Two or more women on board	68%	98% (81% have 3 or more)
50 years or younger	No available data	6%
Diverse racial and ethnic	15% (Top 200)	22% (S&P 500)
Board members of non-US origins	8% (Top 200)	15% (S&P 500)
Number of independent board members added	371	395
NEW board members		
Women	30%	46%
Diverse racial and ethnic	12%	46%
50 years or younger	No available data	18%
First time directors (on public company boards)	39%	34%

Source Spencer Stuart Board Indexes 2014 and 2022

Board Diversity, Equity, and Inclusion (DEI) is Critical

As shown above, boards are making some progress in including more women and people from diverse racial and ethnic backgrounds. This transition in board composition will serve companies and society well. The Corporate Governance Institute reports that "diverse boards make better decisions and result in better outcomes and profits for big companies." (Conmy, 2021). The Harvard Law School Forum on Corporate Governance indicates that "research finds correlation between board diversity and company's financial performance" (Joshi, 2020).

Additionally, boards with people from diverse backgrounds are more likely to understand a broader set of market opportunities to grow the company's value. Underscoring the relevance of DEI, the US Securities and Exchange

Commission (SEC) is expected to adopt new rules this year on human capital metrics and board diversity.

April Miller Boise says that "policy directives from Nasdaq, proxy advisory firms like ISS and Glass Lewis, and states like California and Illinois, help drive greater board diversity. Although some laws are being challenged, a number of companies are already following new guidance and rules for board diversity" (Boise 2023).

This is a critical time for boards, and the officer ranks, to become diverse with regard to gender, race and ethnicity, and age. With a broader set of perspectives, directors will be better equipped to imagine and advance the company's greater potential in the global marketplace.

The Consumer Interests of BIPOC Americans Represent a Business Opportunity

Board directors from diverse backgrounds may bring a more expansive concept of market opportunities to grow the company's value. For example, according to McKinsey, in the United States alone, companies could tap into an additional $300 billion of value annually by expanding local access to goods and services and creating offerings that are better tailored to the needs and preferences of Black households (McKinsey, 2021). This would be in addition to consumer expenditures by Black households that totaled approximately $835 billion in 2019. "Combined spending by all Black households has increased 5 percent annually over the past two decades. It has outpaced the growth rate of combined spending by White households (3 percent), driven mostly by faster population growth." (Ibid.) In addition, McKinsey's report shows that:

> Black consumers are younger, more plugged into smartphones, and more brand-aware than other groups. The median age of Black Americans is 34, a decade younger than the median for White Americans. Black consumers are highly digital: they are more likely to own a smartphone, and they use their phones 12 percent more than White Americans. They are nearly three times more likely than White Americans to expect the brands they use to align with their values and support social causes. (Ibid.)

Moreover, eliminating discrimination against BIPOC individuals would enhance the general economy, providing increased opportunities and returns for companies. Current inequities are a drag on the economy.

According to an April 2021 report from the San Francisco Federal Reserve Bank, labor market disparities are associated with significant economic losses for the U.S. economy. Specifically, the authors estimate that 2019 output would have been $2.6 trillion dollars higher if race and gender gaps in labor market opportunities and returns were eliminated. Further, they estimate that race and gender gaps cost the U.S. economy a collective $70.8 trillion (in 2019 dollars) between 1990 and 2019. (Wilson, 2022)

With greater appreciation of the economic potential of serving more diverse markets with a more diverse workforce, boards will strengthen companies as well as society.

Directors Must Bring an Understanding of Global Risks and Opportunities

Only 15% of board members are of non-US origin, and most of these directors are from the UK and Europe. This limits the depth of the board's understanding of both risks and opportunities in the global arena. Geopolitical risks are highlighted as a significant and growing threat in the World Economic Forum's, 2023 Global Risk Report (World Economic Forum, 2023). Polman shares this perspective: "Every day we see news of geopolitical tensions and inequality. These global challenges are on the radar of most companies. Governments and multilateral organizations have not been able to affect much change. So, more is expected of companies" (Polman, 2022).

Moreover, boards with additional directors of non-US origin would be better qualified to envision and advance the company's greater potential in the international marketplace. Specifically, given market opportunities in Asia and Africa, boards can help position companies to serve regions that represent the world's future workforce and consumers. Most of the world's biggest cities will be in Asia by 2025, and the world's biggest cities will be concentrated in Africa, by 2100 (Bearak et al., 2021).

Today, "the consumer class is global and increasingly Asian. Spending by the Asian middle class exceeds that in Europe and North America combined. Under current projections, Asia will represent half of the world's consumer spending by 2032" (Kharas, 2021). Markets in Africa also present opportunities.

Growing at unprecedented rates, and shaped by forces both familiar and new, dozens of African cities will join the ranks of humanity's biggest megalopolises between now and 2100. Several recent studies project that by the end of this century, Africa will be the only continent experiencing population growth.

Thirteen of the world's 20 biggest urban areas will be in Africa — up from just two today — as will more than a third of the world's population. (Ibid.)

Furthermore, according to Brookings, "Africa's population is the most youthful globally, with about 60 percent below 25 years. The time is now to turn this youth bulge into a demographic dividend to drive growth and development. Investing in the human capital of Africa's youth is fundamental." The report continues (Ordu, 2022):

Africa is on the cusp of an economic transformation. By 2050, consumer and business spending on the continent is expected to reach roughly $16.1 trillion. The coming boom offers tremendous opportunities for global businesses – especially US companies looking for new markets (Signe, 2022).

The opportunity for investment in Africa is not lost on the Chinese government that has enlarged its footprint in Africa.

Trade between China and African countries reached a historic high of $254 billion in 2021. In comparison, trade between the United States and African countries [was] just $64 billion in 2021. To truly forge new partnerships with Africa, the United States should place economic diplomacy at the core of its engagement. This approach should draw on America's unparalleled strengths in advanced technologies and private capital while streamlining the U.S. visa system to allow for more business-to-business ties between the United States and the continent. (Usman, 2022)

Women represent yet another high-growth global market. "By 2028, women will own 75% of the discretionary spend, making them the world's greatest influencers" (Nielsen, 2020). It is time for boards to build the right composition to grow their value according to worldwide demographics and opportunities.

Investors and Regulators Are Driving ESG

Environmental, Social, and Governance (ESG) is a business framework driven by investors and regulators. As described throughout this book, as well as the original edition, companies will reduce costs, mitigate risks, and grow value by finding innovative solutions to environmental (E) and social (S) problems; doing so requires effective board governance (G). Paul Polman is recognized for leading a public company to embrace a uniquely strong ESG approach. Polman comments here:

Boards need to see ESG as a value creation model. Yet some boards have an awareness gap and a skills gap; they need a deeper understanding of the long-term value for companies to invest in innovative solutions to social, economic, and environmental challenges.

There needs to be a radical change in board composition, and boards need to be educated and trained about their responsibilities with regard to ESG. These matters cannot be left to a committee; instead, the entire board needs to realize the importance of an effective ESG strategy that is based on a double materiality analysis. Then the question is how to internalize sustainability goals so that they become part of the culture.

Companies need to set targets that are science-based and sufficiently ambitious. Companies have an opportunity to drive change. (Polman, 2022)

A recent study indicates:

Our findings indicate a positive association between CCP and CFP for firms engaging in SBTs, implying a positive relation between decarbonization efforts and financial results. (...) On a practical level, we provide transparency on the effects of SBTs for managers and climate-change advocates. (Bendig et al., 2022)

The information and case studies in each of this book's chapters illustrate the benefits of an ESG orientation. The featured companies are building their corporate visions, strategies, and operations by advancing ESG. Trane Technologies, for example, by bringing efficient and sustainable climate solutions to buildings, homes, and transportation; HP, through accelerating digital equity for 150 million people by 2030; and UPS, by providing technical expertise in logistics systems to increase access to essential healthcare services, medicines, and vaccines to people in remote villages in Africa. These companies are engaged in improving environmental (E) and social (S) conditions of the world as part of a strategy to grow the company's value.

Investors are driving ESG because the framework is designed for companies to mitigate risks, while also growing value by using their unique super-powers to improve the environment and the social condition. "ESG assets may hit $53 trillion by 2025, a third of global assets under management," according to BSR (Haggebrink, 2023).

Regulators are increasingly driving ESG. The US Securities and Exchange Commission (SEC) is expected to announce final rules on climate, board composition and diversity, and cybersecurity issues. Other countries are expected to continue to enhance their disclosure requirements (Paul Weiss, 2022). Moreover, the SEC in its end of 2022 press release noted its actions in various ESG matters (SEC Release, 2022). Greenwashing—the overstatement or misrepresentation of a company's ESG activities or investment fund offerings–is increasingly receiving attention. This not only adds to potential liability of the company, but the SEC's express mention of examining actions based on the principle of fiduciary duty could mean increased director liability for ESG violations by the company (Ibid.).

It is no wonder that "nearly 40% of CEOs think their company will no longer be economically viable a decade from now, if it continues on its current path. The pattern is consistent across a range of economic sectors, including technology (41%), telecommunications (46%), healthcare (42%) and manufacturing (43%)," according to a recent report from PwC.

> Underlying these figures, we believe, is consciousness among today's leaders that we are living through extraordinary times, with five broad megatrends— climate change, technological disruption, demographic shifts, a fracturing world and social instability—reshaping the business environment. Although none of these forces is new, their scope, impact and interdependence are growing, with varied magnitude across industries and geographies. (PWC 2023)

Companies must consider the new expectations of investors and regulators in building boards and elevating leaders who are qualified to guide and shape the enterprise in this dynamic and challenging environment.

Companies Are Expected to Disclose Their Material Impacts

Beginning in the 1930s, the term "material" related to *SEC requirements that companies disclose information* in financial statements that would be most relevant to investors in making informed decisions. Beginning in the early 2000s, however, some investors thought more broadly about the concept of materiality. They considered potential investments in the context of sustainability—the company's "impacts" on the environment and society—and the implications for the viability and success of the company in light of these impacts.

For a company to disclose this information, they would need to conduct a materiality assessment to determine what impacts were most relevant to the company. For financial institutions, for example, material issues would likely include cybersecurity and protecting the privacy of customers' information, as problems in these areas could jeopardize the company's financial. For apparel manufacturers, material issues would likely include an examination of forced labor in their supply chains, as such practices could threaten the company's brand, reputation, and sourcing of legitimate labor. For energy companies, material issues would focus on the company's effect on the climate, because present and future regulations pose existential challenges to the company. These are all matters involving the impact of the company on the environment and society, and which can fundamentally diminish the value of the company.

Today, in response to investor interests, many companies are shifting to double materiality assessments. These address both *financial materiality*, related to the company's economic value creation, and *impact materiality*, relating to the company's effects on the environment and society.

Conducting materiality assessments involves a methodical stakeholder engagement process and thorough analysis. Companies seek the perspectives of employees, customers, communities, and nonprofits, as well as investors. The analysis is reflected in a materiality matrix, which can usually be found on a company's website.

Board directors whose experience is derived from twentieth century corporate matters may not be prepared for the breadth of the ESG framework. It is important for boards to be well equipped and trained to lead and to provide oversight in the context of today's ESG environment.

ESG Company Ratings Are Important to Investors and Other Stakeholders

ESG ratings matter. There is confusion, however, related to measuring ESG factors. Some estimate that there are more than a hundred ratings agencies that publish ESG company grades and scores. Causing even further turmoil, there are wide variations in a company's rank, depending on the approach of each ratings agency.

In spite of the large number of ratings organizations, there is a small group that are well regarded for their integrity and science-based methods for assessing companies' climate and social impacts. The challenge for companies is collecting, analyzing, and presenting a different, yet voluminous and complex, report for each of these important ratings. Some relief may be ahead to the extent that global ESG reporting networks consolidate.

Measurement is difficult. Especially when you are looking at non-traditional metrics. It is, however, essential to measure and evaluate where you are, where you want to be, and how to get there—in terms of the environment, society, and the business enterprise. It is all the more reason that companies require board directors and C-suite executives with diverse and highly relevant experience.

Valuable Lessons Have Emerged from Corporate Efforts to Address Global Problems

As discussed in Chapter 1, experience during the past ten years has revealed important lessons to address deeply entrenched systemic problems. These lessons are important for companies seeking to drive change. They are discussed in each chapter of the book, and they are illustrated by the case studies. One of the lessons is particularly relevant. That is importance of collaboration. One business alone cannot solve a single issue addressed in this book. With that understanding, businesses have continued to explore a variety of ways of working together with NGOs, governments, and each other.

As described in the Chapters on Human Rights, and Climate and Environment, the global NGO BSR has been playing a key role in forming, supporting, advancing, and sometimes merging or spinning off, more than 50 collaborative initiatives involving companies and other stakeholders. Aron Cramer, CEO of BSR, shares his perspective.

> The importance of collaboration has never been more important. The decisive decade demands solutions, yet the world is fragmenting in many ways – politically, culturally, economically – with technology and competing concerns inhibiting our ability to design and deliver the systemic solutions that are so urgently needed. Addressing the climate crisis in the context of already having reached several tipping points, means industry transformation, capital allocation, and taking innovation to scale, all of which require business to work together, and business-government-civil society collaboration to an unprecedented degree. (Cramer, 2023)

Based on BSR's experience with collaborative approaches, the organization and its partners continue to adapt and enhance their models to have the greatest impact for the environment, society, and business. It is important for companies to participate in joint efforts to address issues that are most relevant to the enterprise.

Nonprofit Board Service Provides Valuable Experience for Business People

Given the scope, impact, and interconnectedness of global challenges, some business people appreciate the opportunity for cross-sector learning and engagement by serving on nonprofit boards. In quarterly discussions with business and NGO leaders, convened by Alice Korngold, they share ideas about approaches to advance DEI, become effective board members, and address vital issues such as climate change, human rights, and access to healthcare and education. Themes of particular interest include:

- The value of nonprofit board service to gain a deeper understanding of issues that are as relevant to their companies as they are to society—issues like food security, global migration, and economic development.
- The imperative for nonprofit boards to become diverse, equitable, and inclusive in order to understand the extent to which racial equity and justice are fundamental to achieve nonprofit missions, as well as the Sustainable Development Goals SDGs) (Korngold, 2022).

"My work on nonprofit boards informs my work in the business sector as well as my academic engagements. Each experience relates to the other," explains Luciana Aquino-Hagedorn. As an attorney, investor, and asset manager, her contributions are a mix of legal, governance, and policy. Aquino-Hagedorn serves on two global NGOs: Landesa, an organization that promotes stronger rights for land, and at the International Center for Research on Women (ICRW), where she serves as Vice Chair. She is the General Counsel of NCX, a US forest carbon developer and on the board of Qarlboro Nature Capital AB, a natural capital investment company and asset manager. She is a lecturer at Boston University School of Law and a Senior Fellow at Columbia University's Center on Sustainable Investment. "For me, nonprofit board service is essential. It helps me understand how nonprofits address issues, and that helps inform how for-profits can advance progress." Aquino-Hagedorn also appreciates learning from observing different styles of leadership, governance, management, strategic decision-making, and finance (Aquino-Hagedorn, 2022).

Venkata Kishore is Vice President, and Global Head of Vegetable Seeds, Smallholders, and Sustainability at Bayer Crop Sciences. He also appreciates gaining cross-sector perspectives from working in business, serving on three nonprofit boards, and engaging on behalf of the nonprofits in public policy. The boards where Kishore serves are International Development Enterprises (iDE), that powers entrepreneurs to end poverty for families and communities; Hunger Free America; and the Foundation for Food and Agriculture Research. Kishore believes that given the convergence of challenges in global health, food security, climate change, and agriculture, "everyone needs to lean-in and give 150% to help advance the Sustainable Development Goals (SDGs). By being engaged in all three sectors – private, nonprofit, and government – you will see the exponential impact." In each of his various roles, he gets ideas that he can share across the sectors and connects people to help advance important work. At the same time, board service is a valuable learning experience in terms of governance (Kishore, 2023).

Increasingly, companies are providing resources and support for their executives to serve on nonprofit boards. Annual studies conducted from 2017 to 2022 show the value of nonprofit board service for business people, nonprofits, communities, and companies (Korngold, 2017–2020, 2022).

Creating an Inclusive, Sustainable, and Prosperous Future

This book shows the way for companies to achieve their greatest potential by advancing an inclusive, sustainable, and prosperous future for all. Global corporations have the vast resources, global footprint, and market incentives to make this possible. The cases in this book show that companies are the likeliest institutions to build a better world, that they are beginning to show promise of their capacity to do so, and that everyone can play a part in making this so. NGOs are vital partners—essential for their expertise, commitment to mission, credibility, and relationships with diverse, marginalized, and sometimes remote communities. Governments too have an important role. By engaging together in an iterative process, we can achieve "A Better World."

References

Aquino-Hagedorn. (2022). Interview with Alice Korngold. 07 Dec.

Bearak, M., Moriarity, D., & Ledur, J. (2021). Africa's rising cities, Washington Post, 19 Nov. https://www.washingtonpost.com/world/interactive/2021/africa-cities/?tid=usw_passupdatepg. Accessed 31 Jan 2023.

Bendig, D., Wagner, A., & Lau, K. (2022). Does it pay to be science-based green? The impact of science-based emission-reduction targets on corporate financial performance. *Journal of Industrial Ecology*. https://doi.org/10.1111/jiec.13341. Accessed 31 Jan.

Boise, A. M. (2023), Interview with Alice Korngold. 23 Jan.

Cherkasky, M. (2023). Interview with Alice Korngold. 06 Jan.

Conmy, S (2021). The proof is in—Diverse boards are good for culture and performance. Corporate Governance Institute, 17 Aug. https://www.thecorporategovernanceinstitute.com/insights/news-analysis/board-diversity-leads-to-better-profits/#:~:text=The%20research%20also%20found%20that,can%20take%20to%20encourage%20diversity. Accessed 31 Jan 2023.

Cramer, A. (2023). Email to Alice Korngold. 30 Jan.

Ginsburg, R. B. (2015). Ruth Bader Ginsburg tells young women: "Fight for things you care about." Harvard Radcliffe Institute, 06 Feb. https://www.radcliffe.harvard.edu/news-and-ideas/ruth-bader-ginsburg-tells-young-women-fight-for-the-things-you-care-about. Accessed 31 Jan.

Haggebrink, E. (2023). Upcoming regulations in ESG ratings: Three implications for business. BSR, 25 Jan. https://www.bsr.org/en/blog/upcoming-regulations-in-esg-ratings-three-implications-for-business. Accessed 31 Jan 2023.

Holmes, J. (2023). Interview with Alice Korngold. 04 Jan.

Jeong. S.-H., Mooney, A., Zhang, Y., & Quigley, T. (2022). How do investors really react to the appointment of Black CEOs? *Strategic Management Journal* https://doi.org/10.1002/smj.3454. Accessed 31 Jan.

Joshi, R. (2020). Board diversity is no longer optional. Harvard Law School Forum on Corporate Governance, 11 Oct. https://corpgov.law.harvard.edu/2020/10/11/board-diversity-no-longer-optional/. Accessed 31 Jan 2023.

Kharas, H., Fengler, W. (2021). Which will be the top 30 consumer markets of this decade? 5 Asian markets below the radar. Brookings, 31 Aug. https://www.brookings.edu/blog/future-development/2021/08/31/which-will-be-the-top-30-consumer-markets-of-this-decade-5-asian-markets-below-the-radar/. Accessed 31 Jan 2023.

Kishore, V. (2023). Interview with Alice Korngold. 3 Jan.

Korngold, A. (2022). The imperative to transform nonprofit boards to become diverse, equitable, and inclusive (and how to), Jan. https://www.alicekorngold.com/wp-content/uploads/2022/01/Diverse-Equitable-and-Inclusive-Nonprofit-Boards-Achieving-the-Vision-by-2025.pdf. Accessed 31 Jan 2023.

Korngold, A. (2017–2020, 2022). Nonprofit board leadership reports: evidence of the benefits of nonprofit board service for companies, employees, nonprofits, and communities. https://www.alicekorngold.com/studies/. Accessed 31 Jan 2023.

McKinsey. (2021). A $300 billion opportunity: serving the emerging Black American consumer, 06 Aug. https://www.mckinsey.com/featured-insights/diversity-and-inclusion/a-300-billion-dollar-opportunity-serving-the-emerging-black-american-consumer. Accessed 31 Jan 2023.

Nielsen. (2020). Wise up to women, Mar. https://www.nielsen.com/insights/2020/wise-up-to-women/. Accessed 31 Jan 2023.

Ordu, A. U. (Ed.). (2022). Foresight Africa: Top priorities for the continent in 2023. Brookings, Africa Growth Institute. https://www.brookings.edu/wp-content/uploads/2023/01/foresightafrica2023_fullreport.pdf. Accessed 31 Jan 2023.

Paul Weiss Rifkind & Wharton ("Paul Weiss"). (2022). A guide to the SEC's proposed climate disclosure requirements, Apr. https://www.paulweiss.com/media/3981948/a_guide_to_the_secs_proposed_climate_disclosure_requirements.pdf. Accessed 31 Jan 2023.

Polman, P. (2022). Interview with Alice Korngold. 23 Sep.

Polman, P., & Winston, A. (2021). *Net positive: How courageous companies thrive by giving more than they take.* Harvard Business Review Press.

PWC. (2023). Winning today's race while running tomorrow's: PWC's 26th annual global CEO survey, 16 Jan. https://www.pwc.com/ceosurvey. Accessed 31 Jan 2023.

Signe, L. (2022). The key to unlocking Africa's economic potential. Project Syndicate, 23 Sept. https://www.project-syndicate.org/commentary/regional-integration-is-the-key-to-unlocking-africa-economic-potential-by-landry-signe-2022-09. Accessed 31 Jan 2023.

Sommer, F. (2023). Building the corporate boards of the future. MSCI, 23 Jan. https://www.msci.com/www/blog-posts/building-the-corporate-boards/03610156236. Accessed 31 Jan 2023.

Spencer Stuart. (2022). Board index 2022. https://www.spencerstuart.com/-/media/2022/october/ssbi2022/highlights/2022_us_spencerstuart_board_index_highlights_final.pdf. Accessed 31 Jan 2023.

Spencer Stuart. (2014). Board index 2014. https://www.spencerstuart.com/-/media/pdf%20files/research%20and%20insight%20pdfs/ssbi2014web14nov2014.pdf%20target=. Accessed 31 Jan 2023.

United States Securities and Exchange Commission (SEC). (2022). Press release--SEC announces enforcement results for FY22, 15 Nov. https://www.sec.gov/news/press-release/2022-206. Accessed 31 Jan 2023.

Usman, Z. (2022). How America can foster an African boom. Foreign Affairs, 11 Aug. https://www.foreignaffairs.com/africa/how-america-can-foster-african-boom. Accessed 31 Jan 2023.

Wilson, V. (2022). The costs of racial and ethic labor market discrimination and solutions that can contribute to closing employment and wage gaps. Economic Policy Institute, 20 Jan. https://www.epi.org/publication/wilson-testimony-costs-of-racial-and-ethnic-labor-market-discrimination/. Accessed 31 Jan 2023.

World Economic Forum. (2023). Global risks report 2023, 11 Jan. https://www3.weforum.org/docs/WEF_Global_Risks_Report_2023.pdf. Accessed 31 Jan 2023.

Index